Alain Fayolle and Philippe Riot have managed to bring together world-class researchers who have helped shape the field of entrepreneurship and the way we perceive it today. By inviting them to critique, challenge and question our understandings, assumptions and beliefs about the field and its future, these great minds take the reader on a stimulating journey which enables them to engage with the field's past but also see the critical role they might play in its future. An inspiring read and very timely addition.

Sarah Jack, *Professor, Lancaster University, UK*

Rethinking Entrepreneurship

Entrepreneurship is a growing field of research, attracting researchers from many different disciplines including economics, sociology, psychology, and management. The concept of entrepreneurship, and research in the field, is becoming institutionalized, increasingly oriented by influential trends, theories, and methods, following the mainstream and being shaped accordingly.

The objective of this book is to move beyond mainstream approaches and assumptions which are dominating the field, and to raise questions about the nature and process of entrepreneurship research. Over twelve chapters, leading international thinkers in the field debate the impact and the consequences of institutionalization. Taking key research orientations including multidisciplinarity, international entrepreneurship, social entrepreneurship, and ethics, it takes a critical and constructive and sometimes controversial posture and encourages a reexamination of the way we look at the social and economic phenomenon of entrepreneurship.

This book is vital reading for entrepreneurship researchers and educators, advanced students, and policymakers in Entrepreneurship, Economics, Sociology, and Psychology.

Alain Fayolle is Professor of Entrepreneurship and Founding Director of the Entrepreneurship Research Centre at EM Lyon Business School, France.

Philippe Riot is Head of the Strategy, Organizations and Entrepreneurship Department at EMLYON, France.

Routledge Rethinking Entrepreneurship Research
Edited by Alain Fayolle and Philippe Riot

The current focus on entrepreneurship as a purely market-based phenomenon and an unquestionably desirable economic and profitable activity leads to undervaluing and underresearching important issues in relation to power, ideology, or phenomenology. New postures, new theoretical lenses, and new approaches are needed to study entrepreneurship as a contextualized and socially embedded phenomenon. The objective of this series therefore is to adopt a critical and constructive posture towards the theories, methods, epistemologies, assumptions, and beliefs which dominate mainstream thinking. It aims to provide a forum for scholarship which questions the prevailing assumptions and beliefs currently dominating entrepreneurship research and invites contributions from a wide range of different communities of scholars, which focus on novelty, diversity, and critique.

Rethinking Entrepreneurship
Debating research orientations
Edited by Alain Fayolle and Philippe Riot

Rethinking Entrepreneurship
Debating research orientations

Edited by Alain Fayolle
and Philippe Riot

LONDON AND NEW YORK

First published 2016
by Routledge
2 Park Square, Milton Park, Abingdon, Oxon OX14 4RN

and by Routledge
711 Third Avenue, New York, NY 10017

Routledge is an imprint of the Taylor & Francis Group, an informa business

© 2016 Alain Fayolle and Philippe Riot

The right of the editor to be identified as the author of the editorial
material, and of the authors for their individual chapters, has been
asserted in accordance with sections 77 and 78 of the Copyright, Designs
and Patents Act 1988.

All rights reserved. No part of this book may be reprinted or reproduced
or utilised in any form or by any electronic, mechanical, or other
means, now known or hereafter invented, including photocopying and
recording, or in any information storage or retrieval system, without
permission in writing from the publishers.

Trademark notice: Product or corporate names may be trademarks or
registered trademarks, and are used only for identification and explanation
without intent to infringe.

British Library Cataloguing in Publication Data
A catalogue record for this book is available from the British Library

Library of Congress Cataloging-in-Publication Data
Rethinking entrepreneurship : debating research orientations / edited by
    Alain Fayolle and Philippe Riot.
        pages cm. — (Routledge rethinking entrepreneurship research)
    Includes bibliographical references and index.
    1. Entrepreneurship.   2. Entrepreneurship—Research.   I. Fayolle,
Alain.   II. Riot, Philippe.
    HB615.R487 2016
    338′.04072—dc23
    2015016298

ISBN: 978-1-138-80253-7 (hbk)
ISBN: 978-1-315-75415-4 (ebk)

Typeset in Bembo
by Apex CoVantage, LLC

Printed and bound in the United States of America by Publishers Graphics,
LLC on sustainably sourced paper.

Contents

List of illustrations	ix
Contributors	x

1 Introduction 1

ALAIN FAYOLLE AND PHILIPPE RIOT

2 Dimly through the fog: institutional forces affecting the multidisciplinary nature of entrepreneurship 12

HOWARD E. ALDRICH

3 Moving on: affirming the entrepreneurial in entrepreneurship research 28

DANIEL HJORTH

4 The economic reification of entrepreneurship: re-engaging with the social 44

ALISTAIR R. ANDERSON

5 Social entrepreneurship: to defend society from itself 57

KARIN BERGLUND AND ANNIKA SKOGLUND

6 Is international entrepreneurship research a viable spin-off from its parent disciplines? 78

NICOLE E. COVIELLO, MARIAN V. JONES, AND
PATRICIA P. McDOUGALL-COVIN

7 Navigating the growing field of entrepreneurship inquiry: successionist and relational modes of theory development 100

DENISE FLETCHER AND PAUL SELDEN

viii *Contents*

8 **Institutionalization of the field and its impact on both the ethics and the quality of entrepreneurship research in the coming decades** 123
BENSON HONIG

9 **Legitimacy or relevance – that is the question** 137
BENGT JOHANNISSON

10 **What makes scholarly works "interesting" in entrepreneurship research? learning from the past** 147
HANS LANDSTRÖM

11 **Entrepreneurship research without passion: let's fall in love again** 171
MATTHIAS FINK, ISABELLA HATAK, RICHARD LANG, AND DANIELA MARESCH

12 **Conclusion: final thoughts and perspectives** 179
PHILIPPE RIOT AND ALAIN FAYOLLE

Index 187

Illustrations

Figure

6.1   Patterns of primary theme emergence (1989–2012)   84

Tables

6.1   The parameters of international entrepreneurship research   83
6.2   Nature of empirical studies in IE research (1989–2012)   86
6.3   Patterns of home/informing disciplines, 1989–2012 (n = 551)   87
6.4   Assessing IE relative to Hambrick and Chen's (2008) proposed elements of an admittance-seeking social movement   88
6.5   Journals with IE research in 'top 15' list based on citations   91
10.1   A general construct of what makes studies "interesting" in entrepreneurship research: challenging our assumptions   158
11.1   Empirical evidence   174

Contributors

Howard E. Aldrich is Kenan Professor of Sociology, Chair of the Sociology Department, the University of North Carolina, Chapel Hill, and Fellow, Sidney Sussex College, Cambridge University. His main research interests are entrepreneurship, entrepreneurial team formation, gender and entrepreneurship, and evolutionary theory. His 1979 book, *Organizations and Environments,* was reprinted in 2007 by Stanford University Press. His book, *Organizations Evolving* (Sage, 1999), was co-winner of the Max Weber Award from the Organizations, Occupational Work section of the American Sociological Association. His latest book, *An Evolutionary Approach to Entrepreneurship: Selected Essays,* was published by Edward Elgar in 2012. In October 2014 he received an honorary doctorate from Mid Sweden University. You can learn more about him from his homepage: http://howardaldrich.org

Alistair R. Anderson has had a lifelong interest in entrepreneurship, first as a small business owner and latterly as an academic. Indeed intellectual curiosity about entrepreneurship enabled his career shift. He is professor of entrepreneurship at Aberdeen Business School Robert Gordon University, guest professor at Sveriges Lantbruks Universitet (Swedish University of Agricultural Science) in Uppsala, and honorary professor at Lancaster University. He also holds and has held a number of other visiting and honorary entrepreneurship roles. He is editor of *Entrepreneurship and Regional Development* and serves on the editorial board of a number of other journals. His research interest centres on the "social" in entrepreneurship; networking, social capital and the like. He argues that we need to fully appreciate the context, social and spatial, of entrepreneurship if we wish to understand the phenomenon. Alistair has published a number of papers directed towards that theme.

Karin Berglund is Associate Professor and Centre Director for Stockholm School of Entrepreneurship at Stockholm University. She has focused how entrepreneurship has been manifested in different forms in contemporary society. In this work she has highlighted individuals other than the Western male hero stereotype, and has drawn attention to processes other than those resulting in the establishment of new enterprises. She uses her (mainly) ethnographic studies to contribute to critical management, organization, and entrepreneurship studies. She has published in international journals covering different topics related to entrepreneurship such as gender, education, innovation, critical pedagogy, and regional development and social/societal entrepreneurship.

Nicole E. Coviello is the Betty and Peter Sims Professor of Entrepreneurship and Professor of Marketing at Wilfrid Laurier University in Waterloo, Canada. She received her PhD in Marketing and International Business from the University of Auckland. Her research appears in the top journals in three disciplines: marketing, entrepreneurship, and international business. Examples include the *Journal of Marketing, Journal of Business Venturing*, and *Journal of International Business Studies*. She sits on a range of editorial boards across these fields and is Field Editor for both Marketing and International Entrepreneurship at *Journal of Business Venturing*. In addition to her appointment in Canada, Nicole is Visiting Research Professor at the University of Turku in Finland. She has held similar appointments at Hanken (the Swedish School of Economics and Business Administration) in Finland, and the University of Glasgow in Scotland. She was also an Erskine Visiting Fellow at the University of Canterbury in New Zealand (2011). In 2010, she received an Honorary Doctorate from the Turku School of Economics in Finland.

Alain Fayolle is a professor of entrepreneurship, the founder and director of the entrepreneurship research centre at EM Lyon Business School, France. His research interests cover a range of topics in the field of entrepreneurship. He has been (or still is) acting as an expert for different governments and international institutions (OECD, EC, UNIDO).

Alain published twenty-five books and over one hundred articles in leading international and French-speaking journals. Among his editorial positions, he is notably an Associate Editor of *JSBM* and an Editor of two leading French-speaking journals.

In 2013, Alain Fayolle got the 2013 European Entrepreneurship Education Award and has been elected officer of the Academy of Management Entrepreneurship Division (a five year commitment culminating with position as Chair of Division in 2016).

Matthias Fink is head of the Institute for Innovation Management (IFI) at the Johannes Kepler University Linz, Austria and a professor for Innovation and Entrepreneurship at the Institute for International Management Practice, ARU Cambridge, UK. Matthias holds a PhD and a postdoctoral qualification (Habilitation) from WU Vienna University of Economics and Business. He was visiting professor at several universities e.g. Universitat Autònoma de Barcelona, Spain and University of Twente, Netherlands. In research, Matthias' focus is on the role of innovation in new venture creation and xii *Contributors*

small business management. His current interests include entrepreneurship as a driver of innovation and change in regional contexts, entrepreneurial finance, and ethical issues in business research. His research has been published in journals such as *Journal of Business Venturing, Entrepreneurship Theory & Practice, British Journal of Management, Journal of Banking and Finance, Technological Forecasting and Social Change*, as well as *Regional Studies.*

Denise Fletcher completed her PhD degree in 1997 at The Nottingham Trent University, UK. At this time, she was a lecturer in European Business at Nottingham Trent (1990–2004) becoming a Principal Lecturer in Entrepreneurship in 1998 and Director of Entrepreneurship Research in Centre for Growing Businesses in 2004. From 2006, she moved to a Senior Lecturer role at University of Sheffield, becoming a Reader in Entrepreneurship and Family Business in February 2011. Between 2008 and 2011, she also ran a small business with her partner. Since April 2011, Denise Fletcher has been Professor of Entrepreneurship and Innovation at the University of Luxembourg. She is Academic Director of the Management Group within the Centre for Regional Economics and Management and study director for the Masters in Entrepreneurship and Innovation programme at the University of Luxembourg. Her principle research interests include; entrepreneurship (opportunity emergence, relational perspectives, business start-up, "copreneurship", internationalization, and organizational change of small firms) and family business (family discourses, family business in the television media, growth, organizational culture, family heritage, succession planning, and strategic renewal of family firms). Dr Fletcher has published widely in the small business and entrepreneurship journals and she is editor of a monograph entitled: *Understanding the Small Family Business*, London: Routledge.

Isabella Hatak is an Associate Professor at the IFI at the Johannes Kepler University Linz and the Institute for Small Business Management and Entrepreneurship at the WU Vienna University of Economics and Business. She holds a PhD and a postdoctoral qualification (Habilitation) from the WU Vienna University of Economics and Business and an MSc in coaching and organizational development. Isabella studied international business relations at the Charles University in Prague (Czech Republic) and the HES School of Business in Amsterdam (Netherlands). Isabella is a visiting fellow to the Institute for International Management Practice at ARU Cambridge. Furthermore, she is an academically certified systemic coach, human resources developer and organizational consultant. Her interdisciplinary work was published in journals such as *Journal of Business Ethics, Family Business Review, Journal of Managerial Psychology*, and *Technological Forecasting and Social Change.*

Daniel Hjorth is professor of entrepreneurship and organization at the Department of Management, Politics and Philosophy, Copenhagen Business School, where he also is the Academic Director of the across CBS Entrepreneurship Business in Society Platform. Hjorth is the editor of the four "Movements in Entrepreneurship" books for Edward Elgar Publ. (together with Prof. Chris Steyaert), initiating a European School of Entrepreneurship Research. He has also contributed to the opening up of Organisational Entrepreneurship (2012) as research field, and recently co-edited the Oxford University Press *Handbook on Process Philosophy and Organization Studies* (2014). Hjorth is Senior Editor of Organization Studies (Journal, SAGE) and member of the editorial boards of e.g. Organization (SAGE), Entrepreneurship and Regional Development (Taylor and Francis), and International Small Business Journal (SAGE).

Benson Honig (PhD Stanford University) is the Teresa Cascioli Chair in Entrepreneurial Leadership, DeGroote School of Business, McMaster University. Studying entrepreneurship worldwide, his research includes over 60 books and articles on business planning, nascent entrepreneurship, transnational entrepreneurship, social entrepreneurship, social capital, scholarly ethics, and entrepreneurship in environments of transition. He is currently chair of the Academy of Management's Ethics Education Committee, and a blogger on the ethicist. Honig is co- winner of the Grief award for highest five year impact article in entrepreneurship in 2009, as well as the most cited paper for *JBV,* 2003–2009. He is a former editor of *ET&P* and serves on eight editorial boards, including *JBV SEJ, AMLE,* and *JMS.*

Bengt Johannisson is a senior professor of Entrepreneurship at Linnaeus University. In 1998–2007 he was the editor-in-chief of Entrepreneurship and Regional Development and he himself has published widely on entrepreneurship, personal networking, family business, as well as on local and regional development. His current research interests are process and practice theories and enactive methodology as applied to different arenas for entrepreneurship. In Sweden Bengt Johannisson has initiated several inter-university networks on research and postgraduate studies in entrepreneurship and for fifteen years he was a co-director of the European Doctoral Programme in Entrepreneurship and Small Business Management. Bengt Johannisson is the first Scandinavian Winner of the Global Award for Entrepreneurship Research (2008) and in 2015 he received the European Entrepreneurship Education Award.

Marian V. Jones is Professor of International Business and Entrepreneurship at the Adam Smith Business School, University of Glasgow, Scotland. Her research concerns the international growth and development of new and small firms. Her theoretical contributions reflect temporal and spatial aspects of internationalization, and draw on knowledge, capabilities and cognitive reasoning theories. With co-authors, notably Nicole Coviello, she has advanced understanding of International Entrepreneurship through theory blending conceptual work, systematic review, and ontological classification. Her work is published in journals such as *Journal of International Business Studies* and *Journal of Business Venturing.* She has served as an advisor to academic standards committees and as expert at United Nations xiv *Contributors*

Conference on Trade and Development and United Nations Industrial Development Organization policymaking conferences.

Hans Landström attained his PhD in Industrial Management at Lund Institute of Technology in Sweden. He holds the Chair in Entrepreneurship at Lund University and he is visiting professor at Vienna University of Economics and Business Administration in Austria. He is co-founder of two research centers at Lund University: Sten K. Johnson Centre for Entrepreneurship (SKJCE) and Center for Innovation, Research and Competence in the Learning Economy (CIRCLE). His research interests include entrepreneurial finance, informal and institutional venture capital, entrepreneurial learning and teaching, and the history of entrepreneurship research. He has published in journals such as *Research Policy, Journal of Business Venturing, Entrepreneurship Theory and Practice, Small Business Economics, Entrepreneurship and Regional Development*, and *Journal of Small Business Management.*

Richard Lang is a Marie Curie Research Fellow at the School of Social Policy at University of Birmingham, England and an Assistant Professor at the IFI at Johannes Kepler University in Linz, Austria. Since January 2014, he holds an APART-fellowship of the Austrian Academy of Sciences. He conducted his PhD studies at WU Vienna and KU Leuven in Belgium and was a William Plowden Research Fellow at the University of Birmingham. Richard's research interests include social innovation, social capital and networks, social and community entrepreneurship, cooperative and community-led housing, civil society governance, as well as urban and regional development. He has published several contributions to international conferences and peer-reviewed journals, such as *Voluntas, Technological Forecasting and Social Change, European Planning Studies, and International Small Business Journal*, as well as the recently co-authored book on community-based entrepreneurship and rural development in the Regional Studies' 'Regions and Cities' Series published by Routledge (2012).

Patricia P. McDougall-Covin is the William L. Haeberle Professor of Entrepreneurship and Director of the Institute for International Business at Indiana University's Kelley School of Business. She helped pioneer the growing field of International Entrepreneurship. She and her co-author were presented the *JIBS* 2004 Decade Award for their article on the early internationalization of new ventures. She has co-edited four books and published numerous articles which appear in a variety of academic and professional journals and books. Her business cases appear in more than twenty-five books, and her research has also been presented in the business press, including *Inc.* magazine, *USA Today*, and *The Wall Street Journal*. She is an Academy of International Business Fellow, 21st Century Entrepreneurship Research Fellow, former Chair of the Academy of Management's Entrepreneurship Division, and former Vice President-Programs of the Academy of International Business. She received her PhD in strategy from the University of South Carolina.

Daniela Maresch is an Assistant Professor at the IFI at the Johannes Kepler University Linz, Austria. She studied International Business at WU Vienna University of Economics and Business (Austria) and at EMLYON Business School (France). Daniela holds a PhD from WU Vienna and WWU Münster (Germany). Daniela gained practical experience in financial reporting working for a major Austrian utility. Additionally, she completed an LL.M. (WU) in Business Law. Before joining the IFI team in March 2014, Daniela worked in corporate law for a renowned Viennese law firm. Daniela has published in the area of auditing and financial reporting and will now employ her interdisciplinary expertise in research into topics at the intersection of innovation, finance, and business law. Currently her research focus is on the role of trust in bank lending, the social impact of disruptive technologies such as additive manufacturing and the protection of intellectual property rights in business angel investments. Her latest publication will appear in the *Journal of Financial Research*.

Philippe Riot began his career as a professor of Philosophy. He worked for several years with Michel Foucault, when he was involved in the research linked to the preparation of several of Foucault's books. He joined EMLYON Business School in 1995 where he became a fulltime professor of Strategy and Organization. He is presently the Head of the "Strategy, Organizations and Entrepreneurship" Department of EMLYON. He is a member of the OCE (Organization, Careers, and new Elites) research center of EMLYON and a co-founder of the College of Professors of EMLYON. He has published book chapters and articles and is a reviewer for "Society and Business Review" and has led several studies, most of them focusing on the development of small and medium enterprises, on behalf of the French Ministry of Industry and Research.

Paul Selden completed his PhD degree in 2008 at The Nottingham Trent University, UK. The focus on his doctoral thesis was a cognitive constructivist approach to the temporality of creative entrepreneurial decision-making processes. Since then he has continued to pursue an interest in the entrepreneurial experience of time into the areas of practical narrative, the relational causality of entrepreneurial action-context relationships, the creation of entrepreneurial opportunities, the nature of context, entrepreneurship as an artificial science, entrepreneurship as a complex emergent system, as well as entrepreneurship theory development and modes of explanation.

Annika Skoglund is Associate Senior Lecturer at Uppsala University. She is currently involved in two research projects, one on green activism within a criticized utility company and one about social entrepreneurship at the Hungarian IT company Prezi. She uses these and other empirical settings to develop theory for critical management and organization studies. She has also published cross-disciplinary research in the journals *Renewable Energy, Children's Geographies,* and *Resilience: International Policies, Practices and Discourses.*

1 Introduction

Alain Fayolle and Philippe Riot

Rethinking Entrepreneurship: Debating Research Orientations is the title of the first, foundational, book of a series entitled *Routledge Rethinking Entrepreneurship Research*.

Entrepreneurship has been seen for years as a young and emerging field of studies. It was often described *"with terms such as 'developing', 'emerging' and 'promising'"* (Rehn et al., 2013). The field of entrepreneurship was emerging not yet established.

Since 2000 and the publication of the Shane and Venkataraman article, the scientific status of the field has been changing. Entrepreneurship is now described as a very fast growing field which is getting a better scientific and social recognition. To give just an example, from 2000 to 2010, the growth of the entrepreneurship division of the Academy of Management has been over 230%. This division is one of the biggest of the association, with over 3,000 members in 2014. There are more and more articles published in entrepreneurship journals and, more importantly, there is a growth of the penetration rate of entrepreneurship research in top-tier management journals, such as *Administrative Science Quarterly, Management Science, Academy of Management Review, Academy of Management Journal, Strategic Management Journal*, and *Journal of Management*.

In 2010, Shane and Venkataraman's article, "The Promise of Entrepreneurship as a Field of Research", won the Academy of Management Review Decade Award. This article got over 2,500 citations and has been influential for some reasons (Shane, 2012). It offers a process-based conceptualization of discussion of entrepreneurship as a distinctive domain of research with its own questions and theories. It also opens new research avenues at the nexus of individuals and opportunities. Since the beginning of the third millennium, we see in the academic literature an ongoing theoretical conversation on the discovery versus the creation of entrepreneurial opportunities. A more nuanced view of entrepreneurship is also developing in the field, giving some importance to cognition, intuition, emotion, failure, learning, and expertise. There is also a shared view that entrepreneurship research is becoming more theory-driven (Wiklund et al., 2011). Finally, researchers have identified specific mechanisms and theories of entrepreneurial action: effectuation, causation, bricolage, improvisation (Fisher, 2012).

In other words, entrepreneurship is now quite established as a field even if entrepreneurship remains a complex and multidimensional research object. We can still observe a lot of epistemological and theoretical debates within the field. While, in 2000, Shane and Venkataraman, the two winners of the Academy of Management Review Decade Award, appeared to share the same line of thoughts, since that date their research avenues seem to be divergent. As Shane (2012), 10 years later, is analyzing the impact of the *"Promise of entrepreneurship as field of research"* and offering new perspectives to go further, Venkataraman is exploring a new avenue considering with Sarasvathy that entrepreneurship is a science of the artificial (Venkataraman et al., 2012). Moreover, as it has been emphasized recently by influential scholars, entrepreneurship is a context-based phenomenon (Welter, 2011; Zahra & Wright, 2011), and this adds to the complexity of the field. The context can be seen and studied in different ways and dimensions: spatial, industry, market, temporal, social, and institutional (Zahra & Wright, 2011). Obviously, there are big issues and challenges for entrepreneurship scholars in designing and doing research aiming at getting a better understanding of the importance and the role of context in its different dimensions.

But, there are other important issues and research perspectives to be considered. To just open some doors, Zahra & Wright (2011) consider with others that entrepreneurship research has to be relevant and emphasize the need for entrepreneurship research to be useful. They talk about the *"raison d'être de l'entrepreneuriat"*, which is its usefulness. It seems also really important that entrepreneurship research throws some light on the dark side of entrepreneurs and the hidden face of entrepreneurship, as has been done by, among others, Jones & Spicer (2010), Anderson et al. (2009), and Fayolle (2011). Finally, taking as a starting point the existence of a huge gap between what our textbooks in entrepreneurship say and what entrepreneurs really do, and following the line of research from Sarasvathy (2001) and Baker & Nelson (2005), based on fine observations of the activities of entrepreneurs, entrepreneurship research should be more often focused on the behavior of real-life entrepreneurs, paying some attention to the dilemma and the problems they face and the way they deal with them. The question here is how can we develop such innovative and 'out-of-the-box' research while the field is becoming increasingly institutionalized and *"thereby beset by an increasing number of assumptions, even myths"* (Rehn et al., 2013). Assumptions and myths concern both the focus (i.e. the main research objects/topics) and the ways (theories, methods) we should use to study entrepreneurship as a social and economic phenomenon. The institutionalization of a field of studies is certainly a positive thing for a research community, but is it a good thing for all the research stakeholders and for the whole society? Does it allow researchers to think about alternatives, new paths, and original ways in studying the phenomena? The institutionalization process and the foundations it contributes to build *"can also be a hindrance, blinding the field to alternatives and new paths"* (Rehn et al., 2013). More fundamentally, the institutional conditions and professional norms (for example, incremental gap-spotting research in entrepreneurship) can lead, by paraphrasing[1] Alvesson and Sandberg (2013), entrepreneurship studies to lose its way and weaken the desire within the scholarship community for more imaginative and innovative research. An interesting way to counterbalance the negative effects of the institutionalizing process of a field of studies is to challenge the main beliefs and assumptions and to encourage critical approaches and perspectives on entrepreneurship. Some initiatives have been done, mainly in Europe. Research workshops and conferences have been organized focusing on critical studies. Books, articles in journals, and special issues have also been published. Our book series and this book are exactly positioned on this stream of thoughts.

More precisely, the objective of this book is a first attempt to challenge the main research streams, theories, methods, epistemologies, assumptions, and beliefs dominating the field of entrepreneurship. By doing so, we are raising questions and issues about the institutionalizing process of entrepreneurship research. The book comes from a workshop that we (the editors of the book) organized at EMLYON Business School in June 2013 as a pre-conference of the 2013 BCERC. The title of our workshop was: *"Institutionalization of Entrepreneurship: Hopes and Pitfalls for Entrepreneurship Research"*. The keynote speakers (the contributors of the book) were asked to adopt a critical and constructive posture towards the questions raised and the issues covered and move the frontiers between thinking and acting, academic and practice worlds, and between disciplines looking at entrepreneurship as a social and economic phenomenon. Before introducing the different chapters of the book and the key logic behind its content, we would like to highlight, just as examples, some recent and original pieces of research in line with what the book series and the book aim to achieve.

Rethinking entrepreneurship research by going "out of the box"

This section is a call for thinking and designing entrepreneurship research "out of the box". By doing so, the four contributions proposed here show the importance of the multidisciplinary dimension of entrepreneurship, the use of the historical perspective, the power of analogy and metaphor, and the need for more qualitative methods. These contributions, which have to be seen as some inspiring examples, come from a recent Handbook of Research on Entrepreneurship (Fayolle, 2014).

William Gartner has been interested for a long time in studying the organizing process leading to the creation of a new organization. The contribution he is bringing to our collective thinking on the future of entrepreneurship research is around organizing. He is developing ideas and thoughts about entrepreneurship as a field of research.[2] For him, entrepreneurship can be conceptualized as organizing emergence. By "organizing emergence", William Gartner suggests "a commonality in phenomena (both theorized and studied) that involve situations where something develops from one state to another

4 Alain Fayolle and Philippe Riot

and that within that development there is a process in which the phenomena become more 'organized' ". Entrepreneurship as "organizing emergence" can be studied and theorized from a wide range of disciplines. These disciplines, such as sociology, psychology, philosophy, and so on, can bring value to the concept of entrepreneurship, but the opposite is true, entrepreneurship can add value to the disciplines which study the phenomena. Thinking in this stream, William Gartner offers interesting thoughts to look at the ways disciplines are informed by and informing entrepreneurship. The other main idea explored by William Gartner is that of community. Is there a need of a unique entrepreneurship scholar community? Would it be realistic? William Gartner is inviting us, as entrepreneurship scholars, to think about a set of questions in relation to this issue of community. In his conclusion, he "wishes that all entrepreneurship scholars consider how they can both speak to the expertise in their narrow community while offering ways to connect to the broader network of entrepreneurship scholars overall". It is here probably the greatest challenge entrepreneurship will need to deal with.

Thinking entrepreneurship research "out of the box" is also based on a good understanding of the history of entrepreneurship research, and Hans Landström is becoming a specialized scholar on the topic. In his contribution, he applies an historical perspective to the field of entrepreneurship.[3] History matters and entrepreneurship as a field has a long history, so the main aim of the author is to help us in getting a better understanding of the roots and the foundations of entrepreneurship research. We fully agree with Hans Landström when he states that "[e]ntrepreneurship is a complex, heterogeneous and multi-level phenomenon, and there is a need to use knowledge from many different research fields in order to understand it". Consequently, entrepreneurship has attracted a lot of scholars from many different fields, which creates a potential for the importation of concepts and theories from many other fields of research. Hans Landström develops what he calls "early entrepreneurial thinking" focusing first on the seminal contribution of Joseph Schumpeter and then inviting us in a discussion about three eras of the evolution of entrepreneurship in relation to three core disciplines: economics, social sciences, and management studies. He also claimed the importance of the multidisciplinary dimension of entrepreneurship highlighting the need and the challenge for entrepreneurship scholars to engage in the future in more systematic theory-driven research.

Bengt Johannisson is offering the third "out of the box" view. He has always been a creative and original entrepreneurship scholar. He develops, in his contribution, innovative ideas mobilizing the concept of entrepreneuring.[4] To him, this notion seems well appropriated to qualify a phenomenon, entrepreneurship, that is generically associated with movement and process (Steyaert, 2007). Bengt Johannisson sees "entrepreneurship as a collective phenomenon, as creative organizing – of thoughts, actions and people in projects which accumulate for the individual into an existential endeavour, as an approach to and way of life". His main goal here is to offer "conceptual ideas of entrepreneurship as a

Introduction 5

phenomenon that is made comprehensive through encounters between theory, art and practice". In this way, he shows first that entrepreneuring can be understood as a process of becoming, and children are natural-born entrepreneurs because they live in a world of becoming where experiencing new things and learning from mistakes and failures are essential components of their lives. Based on this analogy and empirical material, a strong argumentation is developed by Bengt Johannisson, highlighting the interrelationships among theory, art, and practice, three modes which capture entrepreneurship as a phenomenon.

Good and useful entrepreneurship research is not exclusively quantitative and positivist. It is why entrepreneurship scholars should use and develop more intensively qualitative research. Helle Neergaard, in her contribution to the collective discussion of doing entrepreneurship research "out of the box", maps the landscape of qualitative methods in entrepreneurship, with a particular focus on Europe in order to provide qualitative researchers with some recommendations for how to handle the publication game.[5] It will take as a starting point review articles from different countries: France, Germany, the UK, and Scandinavia. It will then analyze the trends and identify the major themes and approaches used in qualitative entrepreneurship research in four journals from 2004 to the present, picking up where a former review covering the period from 1995 till 2003 left off. It will provide an overview of the challenges that scholars using qualitative methods meet and discuss the new land we need to explore. The findings show that the challenge for qualitative researchers remains the same; there has been no change in the number of articles reporting the use of qualitative methods in recent years, although an increase in the use of combinations of qualitative and quantitative research can be seen.

Rethinking entrepreneurship research by challenging and debating

Challenging and debating around the hopes and pitfalls of the institutionalizing process of entrepreneurship research were the key words of the foundational research workshop in 2013 and of our collective journey in this research-driven book. To bring challenging views, we asked five influential scholars (Howard Aldrich, Benson Honig, Nicole Coviello, Hans Landström, and Alistair Anderson) to develop their thoughts based on a topic we proposed them. To discuss, debate, and enrich (we hope) these intellectual developments, we asked five other well-known scholars (Daniel Hjorth, Bengt Johannisson, Denise Fletcher, Matthias Fink, and Karen Berglund) to react on the papers and add their own ideas. We introduce in the rest of this section each chapter in this volume.

In Chapter 2, "*Dimly through the Fog: Institutional Forces Affecting the Multidisciplinary Nature of Entrepreneurship*", Howard Aldrich briefly presents the forces (social networking mechanisms, increase of publication opportunities, training and mentoring of scholars, role of major foundations, individual scholarship recognition, globalization) that have collectively created the institutional

6 Alain Fayolle and Philippe Riot

infrastructure underlying the field of entrepreneurship and addresses two main interrelated questions in his essay. The former relates to the contribution from various social science disciplines (anthropology, economics, history, psychology, and sociology) to the field of entrepreneurship. The latter is centred on the identification of the institutional obstacles to creating a truly multidisciplinary field.

Echoing Gartner (1988), Howard Aldrich sees the contribution from anthropology in the study of what entrepreneurs actually do. The main obstacle here comes from the resource-intensive nature of mainly observational and longitudinal methods. Looking at economics, he underlines the powerful lenses of the transaction cost economics perspective, useful to explain how entrepreneurs seek to minimize transaction and governance costs with the aim to use resources in the most efficient way. The theory is relevant but some difficulties remain when it is applied to the field of entrepreneurship. There are disagreements among researchers around the operationalization and measurement of the key constructs. Moreover, very few dynamic analyses are conducted to understand how organizations adapt to their evolving environments. From Howard Aldrich, history matters in the sense that the historical perspective is increasing attention to context and contingency and highlights the importance of time and space. The organizations, and particularly the youngest ones, are social entities, which strongly relate, in a dialogic way, with their socio-historical environments. History can help to understand how the past affects the present. But, there are actually tensions in relation to the divergence between two types of research approaches: narrative/interpretive historical approaches and the deductive/structural approaches. Psychology is actually bringing an interesting contribution to entrepreneurship, and Howard Aldrich has identified two promising streams of research, the role of emotions/affects in decision-making and cognitive shortcuts (heuristics) in human decisions and behaviors. The latter benefits from the "heuristics and biases" research programme created by Tversky and Kahneman (1981). One obstacle in entrepreneurship psychology research is how to take into consideration and analyze the complex contingencies entrepreneurs face in their context. Finally, sociology contributes to entrepreneurship, mainly through life course and embeddedness studies. Entrepreneurs generally start their new businesses after previous experiences in different jobs and companies. They often used knowledge and competences gained and contacts made in these previous experiences. From a complementary point of view, entrepreneurs are embedded in social networks due to the cooperative nature of most entrepreneurial action. As with anthropology, the main barrier comes from the nature of sociological entrepreneurship research, which is time- and money-consuming.

In his conclusion, Aldrich offers a perspective for the future of entrepreneurship research, claiming that: "*My own prescription for an integrated and synthetic approach to entrepreneurship research lies with evolutionary theory, but that part of the story is not yet ready to be told*".

Daniel Hjorth, in Chapter 3, "*Moving on: Affirming the Entrepreneurial in Entrepreneurship Research*", discusses the Aldrich chapter. For him, "Enacting entrepreneurship (research) out of the box", the title of our 2013 EMLYON Business School's workshop, could be understood and practiced, using process thinking (process philosophy), as a matter of intensity, desire, creation, and emergence. Evoking Howard Aldrich's multidisciplinary approach, he makes a claim that entrepreneurship studies could benefit (more) from an interdisciplinary perspective. Interdisciplinary studies are not so much about objects of study that belong to several disciplines but rather objects, and therefore research issues, that belong to no one in particular. Process thinking is Hjorth's main suggestion for moving entrepreneurship study into a capacity to grasp emergence, the creation of the new, organization-in-creation, and organization becoming. In his chapter, Daniel Hjorth develops five aspects as central to this process thinking: temporality, wholeness, openness and the open self, force, and potentiality. In relation to this way of thinking about and moving entrepreneurship studies, he argues that there is a need to affirm the entrepreneurial dimension in entrepreneurship research. By doing this, he is referring to the positioning of a European School of Entrepreneurship Research, focusing on creativity and contextual approaches and using as research methods or ways to study entrepreneurship, imagination, invention, and narratives or storytelling. Daniel Hjorth is definitely, in this chapter, opening new boxes for entrepreneurship research.

In Chapter 4, *"The Economic Reification of Entrepreneurship, Re-Engaging with the Social"*, Alistair Anderson shows that throughout history entrepreneurship has been associated with specific economic roles. The problem is that this functionalist and reductionist view does not permit us to take into account the fine grain of context and temporality that characterize entrepreneurship. In this 'economistic' black box, in which positivistic approaches dominate, little place is given to non-mechanistic behavior, human being, human meaning, and human action. Alistair Anderson underlines the problems, gaps and paradoxes in the economistic view, opening the door and paving the path towards a more socialized conception of entrepreneurship. For him, the social lens enables us to get a better understanding of how and why people are motivated to become entrepreneurial and act as entrepreneurs in a wide range of situations and contexts.

Responding to Anderson's chapter, Karin Berglund and Annika Skoglund in Chapter 5, *"Social Entrepreneurship: To Defend Society from Itself"*, argue that entrepreneurship has probably reached a state in its development where it must be defended, to become more ingrained in the everyday life of the social citizen. For them, entrepreneurship can be seen as a solution to various social problems and can serve as protection against present insecurities and uncertain futures. They state themselves that the broader aim of their chapter is to open up for a rethinking of entrepreneurship through discussing the effects of the transformation from 'regular' (neo-classical approach) entrepreneurship to the proliferation and dissemination of new forms of entrepreneurship. To achieve this, they describe and analyze three forms of entrepreneurship that have been implemented in Sweden and relate to, as social entrepreneurs, ex-criminals, students, and ethnic minorities.

8 *Alain Fayolle and Philippe Riot*

In Chapter 6, "*Is International Entrepreneurship Research a Viable Spin-Off from Its Parent Disciplines?*", Nicole Coviello, Marian Jones, and Patricia McDougall-Covin argue that the new academic fields are advanced through the process of differentiation, mobilization, and legitimacy building. They suggest that some of the signals used to establish a field include the adoption of a 'name' for the field, members refer to it as such and efforts are made to develop community studies. As observed by the authors themselves, research on international entrepreneurship (IE) seems to have followed such a pattern, beginning with early efforts to position itself at the interface of entrepreneurship and international business. The main aim of the chapter, starting with a discussion about origins and evolution of IE, is to bring a response to the question: Is IE research a viable spin-off of its parents' disciplines ? In other words, is IE a field ? To achieve this, Coviello, Jones, and McDougall-Covin extend previous works and update an ontological review of IE. They then assess how IE has emerged (as a field of research) using the criteria of differentiation, mobilization, and legitimacy building.

Denise Fletcher and Paul Selden, in Chapter 7, "*Navigating the Growing Field of Entrepreneurship Inquiry: Successionist and Relational Modes of Theory Development*", respond to Coviello, Jones, and McDougall-Covin by questioning the complexity and the fragmentation of entrepreneurship and offering a perspective to address a main challenge in the field of research. Looking at the growing multi-disciplinary field of entrepreneurship, they identify an opportunity, the possibility to combine multiple perspectives in new and innovative ways, and a challenge, navigating the complex landscape of entrepreneurship research output in relation to its fragmentation, heterogeneity and 'multi-disciplinary jigsaw'. This challenge is clearly an obstacle to the exploitation of theory development opportunities in the field. To address the challenge of field navigation, Fletcher and Selden propose to group and compare entrepreneurship perspectives in terms of modes of theory development. A mode of theory development is defined by the authors as the "holistic characterization of a type of theory development process that encompasses a range of apparently divergent research perspectives". Based on this line of thoughts, theory development processes are characterized by the temporal organization of causal relationships between units of theory building in two modes: successionist (intertemporal) and relational (interdependent).

In Chapter 8, "*Institutionalization of the Field and Its Impact on Both the Ethics and the Quality of Entrepreneurship Research in the Coming Decades*", Benson Honig is going to present a somewhat novel explanation for the global diffusion of the entrepreneurship 'myth'. He refers to it as a myth, at the risk of being castigated by his entrepreneurial scholarly colleagues, because, in reality, there are so very few who truly achieve the 'star status' of the Richard Bransons, Larry Ellisons, Steve Jobses, and Bill Gateses of the world, the aspirations of so many entrepreneurial entrants (none of whom, it should be noted, completed a university degree or had formal entrepreneurship training). Reflecting on the rapid growth and the institutionalization of entrepreneurship, Honig discusses some issues in relation to education, research, and ethics in the field. He offers notably a set of recommendations to the main entrepreneurship journals aimed at limiting non-ethical behaviours in a period where the pressure to get published on the entrepreneurship scholar's shoulders is becoming higher and higher.

Bengt Johannisson in Chapter 9, "*Legitimacy or Relevance – That Is the Question*", is commenting on Benson Honig's chapter. Johannisson examines mainly in his chapter one aspect of the contribution from Honig. In his view, Honig, elaborating upon what measures should be taken in order to construct a more solid scientific foundation for entrepreneurship studies, through his concern for increased legitimacy at best provides another box that remains closed. Johannisson fully agrees with Benson Honig when he thinks that the community of established entrepreneurship scholars has a responsibility towards future generations of researchers. But he disagrees with his image of entrepreneurship doctoral students as docile victims of both established institutional orders and the egocentricity of senior faculty members. For Johannisson the primary responsibility of established entrepreneurship scholars is rather, on the one hand, to increase the self-confidence of doctoral students and, on the other hand, to expect them to take their own responsibility for becoming academic professionals.

In Chapter 10, "*What Makes Scholars 'Interesting' in Entrepreneurship Research – Learning from the Past*", Hans Landström briefly describes the evolution of entrepreneurship as a field of research and explains the background, to his view, of what is interesting in such research. He then discusses some contributions that have challenged his own assumptions about entrepreneurship and that he regards as interesting. These contributions are placed in three categories: interesting subjects, interesting methodologies, and interesting theories and concepts. Finally, Landström develops some reflections on "interesting" as a concept and a discussion on what makes entrepreneurship research interesting. The discussion turns around a set of key aspects looking at interesting research: time dependency, context dependency, and the balance between novelty and continuity. The discussion also emphasizes the similarities and the differences between interesting, important, and relevant. In his conclusion, Hans Landstrom gives some recommendations to PhD students in entrepreneurship, notably in terms of helping them to make their own voices in the field.

Matthias Fink, Isabella Hatak, Richard Lang, and Daniela Maresch, in Chapter 11, "*Entrepreneurship Research without Passion – Let's Fall in Love Again*", respond to Hans Landström's chapter by first agreeing with his conclusion that entrepreneurship is perceived as interesting if it breaks new ground by challenging existing subjects, methodologies, and concepts/theories. However, they take "one step back and argue that entrepreneurship researchers will only engage in challenging state of the art, and thus produce interesting research, if they change their attitudes towards formulating their own research agenda". Most entrepreneurship researchers design their research agenda by targeting the future "hot topics" in the field in somewhat of a logic of 'publish and perish'. From Fink and his colleagues, this kind of practice may lead to high

10   *Alain Fayolle and Philippe Riot*

levels of frustration. Based on an empirical survey, among entrepreneurship researchers, they show that even the researchers themselves do not find their research interesting. In the line of such results, they argue that a prerequisite for interesting research are researchers who are passionate and fascinated by the topics they investigate rather than by their publication lists, h-indices, and career positions. To a certain extent, this chapter gets back to the essence of research and the main qualities researchers might own.

In Chapter 12, *"Conclusion: Final Thoughts and Perspectives"*, Philippe Riot and Alain Fayolle try to ponder the lessons from the contributions presented here as well as outline some research perspectives for the coming years. The questions they started with and the way they are being raised today may be regrouped under three main themes: 1) the capacity for entrepreneurship research to renew itself; 2) the relationships between entrepreneurship research and the non-academic stakeholders of entrepreneurship; 3) the evolution of research practices with regard to the two aforementioned points.

Conclusion

Rethinking the future of entrepreneurship research by challenging and debating research orientations is not only an intellectual exercise. It seems to us that it is also and above all a necessity to get to the field of research more legitimacy at both academic and policy levels. In the different chapters of the book, throughout their contributions, a group of well-known entrepreneurship scholars engage in such discussion by identifying the hopes and pitfalls for entrepreneurship of the increasing institutionalization of the field. Almost all share the view that entrepreneurship research must go out of the box and offer their own recommendations to do so. It is quite impossible to synthesize their rich thoughts in a simple and consensual argument, but if we had to extract a unique implication from their contributions, we would probably conclude that one prerequisite to advancing entrepreneurship research out of the box would be to differently educate, advise, train, supervise, coach, and mentor our PhD students and young researchers in the field. Improving their understanding of what an interesting research means, a scientific inquiry and process, the diversity of need from research stakeholders is one way to follow. A complementary way and probably the most important would be to help them have fun, pleasure, and be passionate in designing and doing useful research in entrepreneurship.

Notes

1 The title of the Alvesson and Sandberg's article (2013) is "Has Management Studies Lost Its Way? Ideas for More Imaginative and Innovative Research".
2 Gartner, W. (2014). Organizing entrepreneurship (research). In A. Fayolle (ed.), *Handbook of Research on Entrepreneurship* (pp. 13–22). Cheltenham, UK: Edward Elgar Publishing.
3 Landström, H. (2014). A history of entrepreneurship research. In A. Fayolle (ed.), *Handbook of Research on Entrepreneurship* (pp. 23–62). Cheltenham: Edward Elgar Publishing.
4 Johannisson, B. (2014). Entrepreneurship: Theory, art and/or practice. In A. Fayolle (ed.), *Handbook of Research on Entrepreneurship* (pp. 63–85). Cheltenham: Edward Elgar Publishing.

5 Neergaard, H. (2014). The landscape of qualitative methods in entrepreneurship: A European perspective. In A. Fayolle (ed.), *Handbook of Research on Entrepreneurship* (pp. 86–105). Cheltenham: Edward Elgar Publishing.

References

Alvesson, M. & Sandberg, J. (2013). Has management studies lost its way? Ideas for more imaginative and innovative research. *Journal of Management Studies*, 50(1): 128–152.

Anderson, A. R., Drakopoulou Dodd, S., & Jack, S. L. (2009). Aggressors; winners; victims and outsiders: European schools' social construction of the entrepreneur. *International Small Business Journal*, 27(1): 126–136.

Baker, T. & Nelson, R. E. (2005). Creating something from nothing: Resource construction through entrepreneurial bricolage. *Administrative Science Quarterly*, 50(3): 329–366.

Baumol, W. (1990). Entrepreneurship: Productive, unproductive and destructive. *Journal of Political Economy*, 98(5): 893–921.

Fayolle, A. (2011). Necessity entrepreneurship and job insecurity: The hidden face of entrepreneurship. *International Journal of E-Entrepreneurship and Innovation*, 2(3): 1–10.

Fayolle, A. (2014). *Handbook of Research on Entrepreneurship*. Cheltenham, UK: Edward Elgar Publishing.

Fisher, G. (2012). Effectuation, causation and bricolage: A behavioral comparison of emerging theories in entrepreneurship research. *Entrepreneurship Theory & Practice*, 36(5): 1019–1051.

Gartner, W. (2014). Organizing entrepreneurship (research). In A. Fayolle (ed.), *Handbook of Research on Entrepreneurship* (pp. 13–22). Cheltenham: Edward Elgar Publishing.

Johannisson, B. (2014). Entrepreneurship: theory, art and/or practice. In A. Fayolle (ed.), *Handbook of Research on Entrepreneurship*. (pp. 63–85). Cheltenham: Edward Elgar Publishing.

Jones, C. & Spicer, A. (2010). *Unmasking the Entrepreneur*. Cheltenham: Edward Elgar.

Landström, H. (2014). A history of entrepreneurship research. In A. Fayolle (ed.), *Handbook of Research on Entrepreneurship* (pp. 23–62). Cheltenham: Edward Elgar Publishing.

Neergaard, H. (2014). The landscape of qualitative methods in entrepreneurship: A European perspective. In A. Fayolle (ed.), *Handbook of Research on Entrepreneurship* (pp. 86–105). Cheltenham: Edward Elgar Publishing.

Rehn, A., Brännback, M., Carsrud, A., & Lindahl, M. (2013). Challenging the myths of entrepreneurship? *Entrepreneurship and Regional Development*, 25(7–8): 543–551.

Sarasvathy, S. (2001). Causation and effectuation: A theoretical shift from economic inevitability to entrepreneurial contingency. *Academy of Management Review*, 28(2): 243–263.

Shane, S. (2012). Reflections on the 2010 AMR decade award: delivering on the promise of entrepreneurship as a field of research. *Academy of Management Review*, 37(1): 10–20.

Shane, S. & Venkataraman, S. (2000). The promise of entrepreneurship as a field of research. *Academy of Management Review*, 25(1): 217–226.

Venkataraman, S., Sarasvathy, S., Dew, N., & Forster, W. R. (2012). Reflections on the 2010 AMR decade award: Whither the promise? Moving forward with entrepreneurship as a science of the artificial. *Academy of Management Review*, 37(11): 21–33.

Welter, F. (2011). Contextualizing entrepreneurship – conceptual challenges and ways forward. *Entrepreneurship Theory & Practice*, 35(1): 165–184.

Wiklund, J., Davidsson, P., Audretsch, D. B., & Karlsson, C. (2011). The future of entrepreneurship research. *Entrepreneurship Theory & Practice*, 35(1): 1–9.

Zahra, S. A. & Wright, M. (2011). Entrepreneurship's next act. *Academy of Management Perspectives*, 25(4): 67–83.

2 Dimly through the fog

Institutional forces affecting
the multidisciplinary nature of
entrepreneurship

Howard E. Aldrich

Introduction

Entrepreneurship research, as an academic field, has grown from groups of isolated scholars to an international community of departments, institutes, and foundations. Growth has produced progressively systematic and unified knowledge, with growing numbers of knowledge producers and knowledge users sharing core concepts, principles, and research methods. Landström et al. (2012) characterized the field as increasingly formalized and anchored in a small set of intellectual bases, although the disciplinary roots of scholars generating the research are still evident. Indeed, it is not clear that there is a distinct "discipline" called entrepreneurship studies, rather than a collection of researchers studying similar phenomena from disparate disciplinary origins. What are the prospects for greater cooperation across disciplinary boundaries?

As I argued in Aldrich (2012), six forces have collectively created the institutional infrastructure underlying the field. First, social networking mechanisms have created a social structure facilitating connections between researchers. Second, publication opportunities have increased dramatically. Third, training and mentoring have moved to a collective rather than individual apprenticeship model. Fourth, major foundations and many other smaller funding sources have changed the scale and scope of entrepreneurship research. Fifth, new mechanisms have emerged that recognize and reward individual scholarship, reinforcing the identity of entrepreneurship research as a field and attracting new scholars. Sixth, globalizing forces have affected all of these trends. In my earlier essay, I noted the possible effects of American hegemony on choices of research topics and methods, and the possible loss of theoretical eclecticism. In this essay, I ask how research in this evolving field could benefit by drawing on ideas from various social science disciplines – anthropology, economics, history, psychology, and sociology – and what the institutional obstacles are to creating a truly multidisciplinary field.

The development of the entrepreneurship field has much in common with the more general process underlying the growth of scientific/intellectual movements, as described by Frickel & Gross (2005). A scientific/intellectual movement is a collective effort to pursue research programmes and projects

Dimly through the fog 13

while overcoming resistance from others in the scientific/intellectual community. Scientific/intellectual movements try to produce and distribute knowledge, go beyond existing ways of approaching problems, and defeat opposition from others by taking organized collective action. They are embedded in specific historical circumstances and may attempt to alter the boundaries of existing scientific/intellectual fields.

Three "theoretical presuppositions" are particularly relevant to the emergence of entrepreneurship as a field (Frickel & Gross, 2005). First, the popularity of an idea rests not only on the extent to which it is scientifically valid, but also on social processes that institutionalize particular ways to pursue that idea. When multiple social science disciplines are involved, we must investigate the institutional dynamics within each of those fields if we are to understand the prospects for a truly synthetic approach to entrepreneurship. Second, the ultimate shape of a scientific/intellectual movement is contingent upon the historical circumstances within which it emerges. Robust and reflective research on entrepreneurship has only been under way for a little more than two decades, and thus the history of the late 20th and early 21st centuries is most relevant to understanding the field of entrepreneurship research. Third, the wider cultural and political environment critically affects the emergence of a scientific/intellectual movement. Demands from policymakers that research on entrepreneurship be relevant to economic development and especially job creation has put additional pressure on entrepreneurship researchers.

I will examine each of the five contributing social science disciplines in turn – anthropology, economics, history, psychology, and sociology – by asking what each could potentially contribute to our understanding of entrepreneurship. For each social science field, I will focus on themes that I think are particularly relevant to research on entrepreneurship, rather than trying to cover the entire field. I will note points of internal disagreement within and between social science fields, indicating how I think they affect the potential for integration and synthesis.

Potential contribution from anthropology: an ethnographic orientation

Anthropology has much to commend it, but I want to focus on the traditional research technique used by anthropologists: ethnography or intensive on-site fieldwork. Such fieldwork-based approaches involve obtaining information directly from participants through observation, interviews, and so forth.

Anthropology and ethnography

Anthropology prizes intensive immersion in field-based research with the objective of understanding a phenomenon "on the ground" as seen through the eyes of participants. Anthropologists are particularly concerned with the meaning of activities to people participating in them. I believe Gartner (1988) captured this anthropological orientation very well in his paper that argued that "who is an entrepreneur?" was the wrong question. He urged entrepreneurship researchers to go into the field to discover what entrepreneurs actually do: "I believe that research on entrepreneurial behaviors must be based on fieldwork similar to Mintzberg's (1973) study of managerial work. Researchers must observe entrepreneurs in the process of creating organizations. This work must be described in detail and the activities systematized and classified" (1988: 63). As has been documented elsewhere (Martinez et al., 2011), with few exceptions (Stewart, 1989; Baker & Nelson, 2005), entrepreneurship researchers have not heeded Gartner's call.

Several sociologists have recently renewed the call for field-based methods in the study of organizations and, by extension, entrepreneurship. Watson (2011) strongly championed the need for ethnographic studies in the field of organizations and management, arguing that researchers need to watch what people actually do, rather than just tape recording interviews with them. He defined ethnography more broadly than most, calling it a writing style "which draws upon the writer's close observation of and involvement with people in a particular social setting and relates the words spoken and practices observed or experienced to the overall cultural framework within which they occurred" (Watson, 2011: 205). His eclectic definition thus includes not only observation but also interviews, analysis of documents, statistical analysis, and even surveys. The critical element to the method is linking people's words to their actions.

Vaughan (2009) argued that the right kind of ethnography seeks mechanism-based explanations that link multiple levels of analysis. She defined ethnography more narrowly than Watson, describing it as "research conducted by situating oneself in a social setting to observe and analyze individual interaction in order to understand some complex social process, event, activity, or outcome" (2009: 690). She argued that analytical ethnography is evidence based and aims for reliable and valid observations and explanations. Ethnographers spend considerable time in their settings because they need to see the full scope of processes, including beginning and ending points, and go into the field with no clear guidelines as to how long the process might take.

Barriers to learning from anthropology

In their review of research methods in entrepreneurship, Aldrich and Baker (1997) noted the scarcity of entrepreneurial ethnographies and concluded that the resource-intensive nature of observational methods discouraged most investigators from trying them. More recently, in their analysis of recently published articles, Martinez, Yang, and Aldrich (2011) confirmed that the situation had not changed. Few entrepreneurship researchers are trained in anthropological ethnographic methods, and many attempts to use fieldwork-like methods yield superficial results. Moreover, there also seems to be some resistance among anthropologists to the concept of studying "commercial" organizations. I experienced that when I tried to set up a multi-year series of workshops on entrepreneurship and the social sciences in my home institution. Field researchers like Alex Stewart (1989) are few and far between.

Being more receptive to an anthropological approach could mean that ethnographically oriented entrepreneurship researchers become more involved in studying entrepreneurs engaged in startup processes (Jack, 2005). Such ethnographies would enable us to document what entrepreneurs are doing, at the micro level, and allow us to link their actions to routines and social mechanisms at higher levels of analysis. For example, Kurke & Aldrich (1983) replicated Mintzberg's (1973) study of managerial work, following the same number of managers over the same interval of time as Mintzberg and confirming almost all of his findings regarding how managers use their time.

Potential contribution from economics: transaction cost economics and model building

Mainstream economists showed little interest in entrepreneurship research until recently, except in a highly abstract and formulaic way, similar to their long-term disinterest in organizational structure. Oliver Williamson (1975, 2000) labored tirelessly for decades to convince his colleagues that organizational analysis had something to say to them. Although some organizational researchers have been highly critical of this programme (Perrow, 1986), I think there are some aspects of it that might well be emulated by entrepreneurship researchers.

Economics and modelling

Economics prizes rigorous modelling and working from a small set of first principles, helping us understand how people organize to pursue the things they value. In the field of organization studies, perhaps the best-known application of economic thinking to the analysis of organizations is the transactions cost economics perspective, developed by Williamson (2000). He has worked continuously on creating a formalized, deductive scheme from which propositions may be derived. Beginning with plausible assumptions about human behaviour, Williamson and his followers crafted a strong challenge to non-economic theories. He has pushed theorists from other perspectives to consider alternative explanations for the organizational forms they observe, asking them to examine the costs and benefits of various arrangements. In his concern with "the main case" – a theory's claimed domain of applicability – he has challenged others to "sort the wheat from the chaff" and develop the "refutable implications" of their arguments (Williamson, 1994: 86). Meeting these challenges can only enhance the rigor of entrepreneurship theories.

When applied to the founding of new organizations, which is where I think the field of entrepreneurship has contributed the most to organization studies, transaction cost economics (TCE) posits that entrepreneurs face, at the extreme, two choices about how to structure their activities. Should they purchase the goods or services they need on the open market, or should they bring the production of such necessities inside their organization? They can obtain what they need by engaging in transactions with other independent actors in the market, or they can internalize the production of the needed resource, thus subjecting it to their own hierarchical control. Depending on the choices they make, new ventures can range from completely self-contained firms supplying most all of their needs internally to new ventures that are minimalist organizations (Halliday et al., 1987), drawing most of what they need through relationships with organizations and other entities. The great virtue of TCE in explaining entrepreneurial behaviour is that it posits entrepreneurs almost single-mindedly devoted to minimizing transactions and governance costs, thus substantially simplifying analytic modelling.

Given a resource-scarce environment, actors will be under pressure to find ways to economize on transactions' costs. TCE models make selection a matter of matching organizational actions to organizational goals. "Goals" are typically defined as the efficient use of resources in the competitive context of a market, a context familiar to entrepreneurship researchers. Selection processes posited by TCE turn on the consequences of human shortcomings, which are clearly spelled out. Given bounded rationality and opportunism, transactions with other actors are almost always problematic and potentially quite costly.

The TCE lens is a powerful tool with which to examine entrepreneurship because it is so transparent with regard to the assumptions it makes about social action. TCE posits actors who have rational intentions but who also face constraints on their capabilities. TCE emphasizes the serious limits to human information-processing and monitoring capabilities and takes a rather jaundiced view of human nature. Two assumptions derived from the Carnegie school tradition of March and Simon (1958) dominate TCE thinking about social behaviour: actors operate within the constraints of *bounded rationality*, and much of human behaviour is driven by *opportunism*. Most actors are intendedly rational, but they are denied textbook rationality because of human limitations. They are precluded from making optimal choices by cognitive deficiencies and peculiarities, limits on information availability, and constraints on information processing. Information search costs, in particular, lead most actors to choose satisfactory, rather than optimal, alternatives. Actors must also contend with the tendency of other actors to behave opportunistically, pursuing their own self-interest at the expense of others.

Barriers to learning from economics

With the growth of heightened public policy interest in entrepreneurship and its consequences, and the availability of research funds, economists have begun flooding into the area over the past decade or so. Economics is a notoriously insular discipline, often showing little knowledge of important and relevant prior work in other disciplines; because it values parsimony in model building, it tends to make unrealistic assumptions about humans and their capabilities. The use of TCE within entrepreneurship studies has been hampered by several problems. Theorists have had difficulty in operationalizing the concept of transaction costs *a priori*, and they have also been reluctant to conduct dynamic analyses of organizations actually adapting to their environments (Shelanski & Klein, 1995). TCE research has been troubled by a fundamental ambiguity about whether organizations are really units of analysis (Hirsch et al., 1990). Most research has been descriptive, rather than hypothesis testing, using cross-sectional designs, and has focused on very large publicly held corporations (Hesterly et al., 1990).

Transaction cost models have the potential of generating falsifiable hypotheses, to the extent that transactions' costs can be spelled out *a priori*. However, the lack of a strong research tradition, and disagreement on how to measure key constructs, inhibits TCE from accumulating a stock of reliable and valid empirical generalizations. Moreover, with its reliance on cross-sectional observations and its eagerness to attribute existing structures to the constraining effects of markets, it mostly ignores evolutionary issues. Hesterly et al. (1990) pointed out that much of TCE theorizing is implicitly functionalist. Functional thinking can be helpful in leading us to consider the benefits of a current structure, which can then direct our search for historical explanations (Dennett, 1995: 124–145). However, functionalist explanations fall short to the extent that they infer the origins of a structure by only examining its consequences, rather than the processes that brought it about.

Potential contributions from history: the significance of time and place

The historical turn in organization studies has brought with it increased attention to context, contingency, and the importance of time and place (Bucheli & Wadhwani, 2014). For entrepreneurship scholars, this comes as welcome news. But for the field of historical studies to truly inform entrepreneurship research, a number of tensions will have to be negotiated.

History and context

Organizations, as fundamental social units, have a reciprocal relationship with their socio-historical environments. Just as organizations shape and give meaning to social life, they are themselves shaped by the worlds they inhabit. Given the complexity of organizations and their environments, no two organizations have identical experiences, even in the same historical era or during the same event. A new wave of entrepreneurship research focusing on the historical dynamics within and external to organizations has highlighted these nuances (Aldrich, 2009). The key features of classical historical research involve a focus on temporality, context, and the role of events in the structuring and development of social life, carried out with sensitivity to the meaning of events and their contexts, with a generalizable framework from which hypotheses can be generated and tested.

I follow Lippmann and Aldrich (2014) in identifying four major differences between classical approaches to organizational analysis versus the narrative/interpretive approach: relative emphasis on context, the generalizability of research results, the role of events in explanations, and the value of unique phenomenon. First, with regard to context, purely structural research strives to transcend particular contexts, whereas narrative/interpretive research focuses explicitly on the variety of social, economic, political, and other contexts in which social processes unfold. As Sewell (2005: 10) noted, "historians tend to explain things not by subsuming them under a general or 'covering' law, but by relating them to their context." For example, Stinchcombe's (1965) path-breaking essay on organizational imprinting argued that the contextual conditions at the time of an organization's founding continued to exert an influence on organizational structure and outcomes across its life, as shown in the persistence of core features. Second, with regard to generalizability, classical narrative/interpretive scholars tend to resist generalizing from their findings. Many historians rejected the move towards generalizability which characterized developments in the social sciences after the mid-20th century, which moved toward a more deductive/structural model. In the eyes of historians, such cross-case applications ignored context, contingency, and case-specific details. Clearly, entrepreneurship researchers today face strong pressures to generalize from their research findings, and thus must contend with how to deal with historians' resistance.

Third, with regard to the analysis of events, a major explanatory mechanism employed in narrative/interpretive models of change is the "event," seen not as a "data point" but instead as an historical conjuncture laden with meaning that must be deconstructed. For historians, significant happenings punctuate and define social life and are the external stimuli to which actors must respond. In doing so, the course of theory often changes. Some singular events, such as the commercialization of the Internet, can give meaning to particular historical time, while others, like the worldwide economic crisis of 2008, can usher in a new historical era (Hunt & Aldrich, 1998). Historians remind us that we must be careful about glossing over or discounting singular events simply because they are unique and often unpredictable.

Finally, with regard to uniqueness, structurally oriented theorists often criticize narrative/interpretive studies for being interested in particular events, processes, or outcomes. They claim that these findings cannot be generalized easily to other times, places, cases, or context. Although this is the nature of the historical discipline, it is also due to the nature of historical/interpretive methods. Structural researchers try to use a variety of sampling and data collection techniques to capture variations in behaviours and outcomes, using methods that allow them to test causal hypotheses about regular patterns that they posit they will find in a variety of social contexts.

Barriers to learning from history

The growth of historical research on organizations seems somewhat disconnected from the trajectory of mainstream organizational scholarship. If anything, the new historical literature may well be developing on a path parallel and unconnected to more traditional, deductive research on organizations and organizational dynamics. Much of this divergence can be traced (as Lippmann and Aldrich [2014] pointed out) to the continuing tension between narrative/interpretive historical approaches and the deductive/structural approaches that came to the fore not only in organization studies but also in the other social and management sciences in the mid-20th century.

Indeed, over the past decade, several commentaries in management journals have attempted to persuade a seemingly skeptical readership about the value of the narrative/interpretive qualitative analysis of "cases." The commentators tried to assuage fears that historical scholarship poses a threat to the mainstream, as they treated case studies of the sort conducted by historically minded organizational scholars as a preliminary step to "real" theory building and testing (Eisenhardt & Graebner, 2007; Siggelkow, 2007). Though they are not identical, historical research on organizations shares with qualitative research an attention to narrative and interpretive inquiry. In this regard, the new historical research, along with other narrative/interpretive approaches such as ethnography and grounded theory, risks becoming isolated from other research on organizations

When placed in the context of the history of social sciences, the divergence between these approaches makes sense. Theories of the middle-range and the deductive/structural, data-driven approaches to theory testing that characterized mid-20th century social science attempted to closely resemble the natural sciences and had little use for highly contextualized, case-based approaches that focused on process tracing and interpretive narratives. A similar trend away from context has more recently characterized mainstream management science (Aldrich, 2009). Lippmann and Aldrich (2014) argued that these parallel but separate trajectories are working against the best interests of organizational scholars and the research on organizational dynamics that they produce.

Although many practicing historians privilege an interpretive/narrative approach over what they label "modernist" or "constructivist" approaches, Lippmann and Aldrich (2014) believe that points of complement and commonality exist. More communication between proponents of the several approaches, coupled with more attention to alternative approaches in individual research agendas, could produce more perceptive and powerful findings. Unfortunately, given the current state of affairs, this intermingling seems problematic. Too frequently, debates about the merits of what we would call "deductive/structural" versus "narrative/interpretive" historical approaches have been framed in all-or-nothing terms, and a true integration of the approaches has seemed impossible (Hall, 1992; Burke, 2004).

Potential contributions from psychology: heuristics

As it has moved increasingly to embrace new developments in neuroscience, especially with regard to emotion and cognition, psychology has created more sophisticated ways of prying open the "black box" of human personality to understand why people behave as they do. I think two lines of work are particularly promising for the study of entrepreneurship, one having to do with understanding the role of emotions/affect in decision making and the other concerning the essential reasonableness of the many cognitive shortcuts that humans make, given the situations they face. In this essay, I will address only the latter.

Psychology and heuristics

Management and organization scholars struggle with which model of human behaviour to accept. Granovetter (1985) famously once posed a distinction between models in the social sciences of humans who were either over- or undersocialized, referring to humans who were either fully compliant with the norms and expectations of their social settings or who were totally self-regarding and only compliant to the extent that it advanced their self-interest. Similarly, with regard to perception and cognition, entrepreneurship theorists confront models that depict humans as foresighted and rational thinkers versus models that view humans as myopic and typically unaware of which actions would really advance their self-interest. Similar struggle over which model is most realistic characterizes neo-institutionalism's foray into studies of entrepreneurship (Aldrich, 2010). How are we to choose an appropriate model for entrepreneurship research?

Management science's view of human psychology has been heavily influenced by the work of Tversky and Kahneman and their followers (Tversky & Kahneman, 1981; Kahneman, 2003). For many years, this group of investigators that some called the "heuristics and biases" research programme argued that people use a variety of mental shortcuts when they are faced with uncertainty, leading to suboptimal decisions, mistakes, and accidents. These mental shortcuts, also called heuristics, don't make use of all available information and sometimes lead people to use unwisely the information they do collect. Thus, for example, researchers have shown that people rely too heavily on judgments based on small samples, are overly impressed by highly visible and easily available information, and seem unable to grasp the laws of probability (Tversky & Kahneman, 1981). Were this view of human failings to prevail in entrepreneurship studies, it would be difficult to take seriously theories that treat humans as capable of opportunity recognition and strategic planning and able to ignore short-term gains in favor of long-term interests.

Over the past several decades, several new research programmes have emerged that frame human behaviour in a more positive light. The "adaptive decision programme" has offered a different view, thinking of heuristics as strategies and searching for the conditions under which various heuristics are used. In turn, building on the adaptive decision programme, Goldstein (2009), Gigerenzer and Selten (2001), and others have developed a more optimistic view of human minds, labeled the "fast and frugal" research programme. I think their view has much to offer entrepreneurship researchers interested in interdisciplinary cooperation, as it puts human behaviour in context, thus connecting with the anthropological and historical modes of thought that I reviewed earlier.

The fast and frugal research programme asks how well people do when using simple heuristics in real-world situations. Rather than the old normative models of rationality and human fallibility, the new programme identifies much of human behaviour as ecologically rational. That is, it posits that people use information which is appropriate and helpful, given what's available in their local environments. They use simple decision rules, such as "take the best," which are good enough in situations in which time and resources must be conserved. Humans are not posited as computational machines that collect, process, and weigh all available information, but rather as doing as well as they can, under the circumstances. For example, I find this view helpful in thinking about how nascent entrepreneurs will react when they construct organizations in uncertain situations when they must make do with incomplete information and inadequate resources (Aldrich & Yang, 2014).

Barriers to learning from psychology

As an increasingly laboratory-based discipline, especially in the field of cognitive neuroscience, psychology may have difficulty analyzing the complex contingencies facing entrepreneurs in context. For example, a recent compendium of conceptual models and experiments from the fast and frugal group illustrates how mathematically sophisticated and methodologically complex the field has become (Todd et al., 2012). Few entrepreneurship researchers have the training to carry out such research themselves, and just as some trends in historical analysis point toward increasing insularity, the same might be true in this area.

Potential contributions from sociology: life course and embeddedness

Sociology prizes understanding of human behaviour in its social context, particularly with regard to the embeddedness of action in social units such as groups and organizations. In that respect, it has much in common with the developments in historical analysis I described earlier. Sociology has brought a number of important themes to the study of entrepreneurship: entrepreneurship throughout the life course (Aldrich & Kim, 2007a) and the embeddedness of entrepreneurial action in social networks, particularly with regard to the importance of cooperative action (Aldrich & Kim, 2007b).

Sociology and entrepreneurship across the life course

Entrepreneurial activity is not evenly distributed across the life course, but rather usually occurs several decades after someone enters the workforce. Most entrepreneurs are in their late 30s or early 40s when they make their first founding attempt. By that point, they have accumulated enough work experience to believe that they can recognize potential business opportunities. A few have also accumulated considerable financial resources, although lack of resources does not appear to deter people. Where they have worked, however, does make a difference. Nascent entrepreneurs often capitalize on knowledge gained and contacts made in their previous jobs. However, relying on previous experiences also constrains their search for opportunities and limits the scope of the strategies they consider (Boeker, 1988; Freeman, 1983; Romanelli, 1989).

With regard to social networks, some social locations provide substantial entrepreneurial advantages to their incumbents (Aldrich & Zimmer, 1986; Thornton & Flynn, 2003). Not all members of a society are in positions where they can readily respond to organizing opportunities. Various individuals and groups are either blocked from favorable locations or lack connections that would enable them to exploit such locations. Regardless of their personal networking abilities, nascent entrepreneurs who occupy impoverished social locations may find themselves cut off from emerging opportunities and essential resources. In the search for entrepreneurial opportunities, people need access to information and other resources. Multiple diverse contacts are important, regardless of their strength (Burt, 1992). Diversity is enhanced by ties to persons of differing social locations and characteristics, along a variety of dimensions, such as sex, age, occupation, industry, and ethnicity. Such contacts increase access to a wider circle of information about potential markets, new business locations, innovations, sources of capital, and potential investors.

Sociology and the embeddedness of entrepreneurial action

Entrepreneurship was formerly often referred to as a solo endeavor, but research over the past several decades has emphasized the cooperative nature of most entrepreneurial action. About half of all efforts to found a new business involve teams of two or more people, with the rest being solo efforts (Reynolds & White, 1997; Ruef, Aldrich, & Carter, 2003). In a few knowledge-intensive industries, founding teams of four or five persons are common. For example, in the semiconductor industry, founding team size has ranged from one to seven people, with an average of three persons involved (Eisenhardt & Schoonhoven, 1990). Cooper's (1986) review of ten studies of high-technology startups showed that the median percentage of founders with two or more full-time partners was 70 percent. Teach et al. (1986) obtained similar results in their study of microcomputer software firms. In France, Mustar (1998: 221) found that solo entrepreneurs started very few of the high-tech firms in bio-technology, artificial intelligence, and information technology.

Given the small size and precarious status of fledgling organizations, few founders can afford unilateral actions. Although they must occasionally pursue strategic actions that split their opponents and prevent them from cooperating (Burt, 1992), they more often seek ways of eliciting cooperation. The rhetoric of "leadership" and "charisma" in the classical entrepreneurship literature implied a more hierarchical structure to fledgling organizations than they actually possess. In the founding process, founders' intentions interact with those of others in the situation, especially those contributing resources, such as other founders, family, friends, and potential employees. Issue framing can enable entrepreneurs to create new schemata with powerful psychological effects (Gartner, Bird, & Starr, 1992). For example, in describing leaders' relations with their followers, Czarniawska-Joerges (1989: 7) noted a leader's "capacity to offer a convincing interpretation of reality, an attractive vision of the possible future, and a prescription on how to reach that vision."

Barriers to learning from sociology

Earlier, I noted that anthropologists favored an ethnographic approach involving intensive on-site fieldwork. An anthropological approach complements the brand of analytical sociology that offers explanations of social phenomena using the actions of people involved in social mechanisms that produce outcomes and events (Hedstrom & Udehn, 2009). The approach is event oriented, rather than variable oriented, and is of necessity process oriented because it tries to explain the dynamics of social life in cause-and-effect terms. However, it is incredibly time-consuming and resource intensive, and money for large-scale social science research is in short supply these days. Researchers often save money on their research designs by using telephone interviews and short visits to field site locations. It is not clear to me that the gains from these shortcuts make up for the loss of rich and deeply detailed knowledge of the complex social processes in which entrepreneurs are embedded. Studying the extent to which entrepreneurial processes are embedded in someone's life course and within team dynamics requires a great deal of data.

Conclusions

I began by noting that growth in the field of entrepreneurship research has much in common with the more general process underlying the growth of other scientific/intellectual movements. Growth requires attention to both internal and external forces. *Internally*, researchers must build an infrastructure that creates incentives for members to focus on common problems, value the same way of researching issues, and recruit outsiders to join them. Although all share the general goal of generating and distributing knowledge, to increase their status in the prestige hierarchy of the field, researchers must go beyond existing ways of approaching problems and defeat opposition from others by

24 *Howard E. Aldrich*

taking organized collective action. In a multidisciplinary field such as entrepreneurship, this can be problematic.

Externally, while it pursues its research programmes and projects, the field must overcome resistance from others in the adjacent and potentially competing fields. In a more applied and practice-oriented field such as entrepreneurship, researchers face a dilemma. Many of their theories and methods are borrowed from existing social science disciplines, and they recruit many of their junior scholars from such disciplines. However, as PhD programmes proliferate in entrepreneurship, the field is beginning to train its own recruits. Therein lies a danger, as those recruits will be increasingly distant from the disciplinary roots which initially gave the field its claims to scientific status. The specific historical circumstances that generated research questions and research methods may be lost to subsequent generations of entrepreneurship researchers as they lose touch with the origin disciplines.

I noted that three theoretical presuppositions are particularly relevant to the emergence of entrepreneurship as a field, and perhaps now their relevance is more salient. First, an idea's popularity depends not only on the extent to which it is scientifically valid, but also on social processes that institutionalize particular ways to pursue that idea. In the case of entrepreneurship research, where multiple social science disciplines are involved, diverse institutional dynamics within each of those fields may undermine the possibility of a truly synthetic approach to entrepreneurship. Second, the ultimate shape of a scientific/intellectual movement is contingent upon the historical circumstances within which it emerges. As the diverse social and behavioural science disciplines develop at different rates, they pull and tug at the threads holding the community of entrepreneurship research together. Third, the wider cultural and political environment critically has put additional pressure on entrepreneurship researchers that is not faced by the more pure research-oriented social and behavioural science disciplines.

My own prescription for an integrated and synthetic approach to entrepreneurship research lies with evolutionary theory, but that part of the story is not yet ready to be told.

References

Aldrich, H. E. (2009). Lost in space, out of time: How and why we should study organizations comparatively. In B. King, T. Felin, & D. A. Whetten (eds.), *Studying Differences Between Organizations: Comparative Approaches to Organizational Research.* Bingley, UK: Emerald Group 26: 21–44.

Aldrich, H. E. (2010). Beam me up, Scott(ie): Institutional theorists' struggles with the emergent nature of entrepreneurship. In W. D. Sine & R. J. David (eds.), *Institutions and Entrepreneurship.* Bingley, UK: Emerald Group Publishing Let. 21: 329–364.

Aldrich, H. E. (2012). The emergence of entrepreneurship as an academic field: A personal essay on institutional entrepreneurship. *Research Policy*, 41(7): 1240–1248.

Aldrich, H. E. & Baker, T. (1997). Blinded by the cites? Has there been progress in entrepreneurship research? In D. L. Sexton & R. W. Smilor (eds.), *Entrepreneurship 2000* (pp. 377–400). Chicago: Upstart Publishing Company.

Aldrich, H. E. & Kim, P. H. (2007a). A life course perspective on occupational inheritance: Self-employed parents and their children. In M. Ruef & M. Lounsbury (eds.), *Research in the Sociology of Organizations* (pp. 33–82). Oxford: JAI Press Elsevier 25.

Aldrich, H. E. & Kim, P. H. (2007b). Small worlds, infinite possibilities. *Strategic Entrepreneurship Journal*, 1(1): 147–165.

Aldrich, H. E. & Yang, T. (2014). How do entrepreneurs know what to do? Learning and organizing in new ventures. *Journal of Evolutionary Economics*, 24(1): 59–82.

Aldrich, H. E., & Zimmer, C. (1986). Entrepreneurship through Social networks. In D. Sexton & R. Smilor (Eds.), *The Art and Science of Entrepreneurship* (pp. 3–23). New York: Ballinger.

Baker, T. & Nelson, R. E. (2005). Creating something from nothing: Resource construction through entrepreneurial bricolage. *Administrative Science Quarterly*, 50(3): 329–366.

Boeker, W. (1988). Organizational origins: Entrepreneurial and environmental imprinting at the time of founding. In G. R. Carroll (ed.), *Ecological Models of Organization*: 33–51. Cambridge, MA: Ballinger.

Bucheli, M. & Wadhwani, R. D. (eds.) (2014). *The Historical Turn in Organizational Studies*. New York: Oxford University Press.

Burt, R. S. (1992). *Structural Holes: The Social Structure of Competition*. Cambridge, MA: Harvard University Press.

Cooper, A. C. (1986). Entrepreneurship and High Technology. In D. L. Sexton, & R. W. Smilor (eds.), *The Art and Science of Entrepreneurship*, 153–168. Cambridge, MA: Ballinger.

Eisenhardt, K. M., & Schoonhoven, C. B. (1990). Organizational growth: linking founding team, strategy, environment, and growth among U.S. semiconductor ventures, 1978–1988. *Administrative Science Quarterly*, 35(3): 504–529.

Freeman, J. H. (1983). Entrepreneurs as organizational products: Semiconductor firms and venture capital firms. In G. D. Libecap (ed.), *Advances in the Study of Entrepreneurship, Innovation, and Economic Growth*, Vol. 1: 33–52. Greenwich, CT: JAI Press.

Frickel, S. & Gross, N. (2005). A general theory of scientific/intellectual movements. *American Sociological Review*, 70(2): 204–232.

Gartner, W. B. (1988). Who is an entrepreneur? is the wrong question. *American Journal of Small Business*, 12(4): 11–32.

Gartner, W. B., Bird, B., & Starr, J. (1992). Act as if: Differentiating entrepreneurial from organizational behavior. *Entrepreneurship: Theory and Practice*, 16(3): 13–32.

Gigerenzer, G. & Selten, R. (eds.) (2001). *Bounded Rationality: The Adaptive Toolbox*. Cambridge, MA: MIT Press.

Goldstein, D. G. (2009). Heuristics. In P. Hedstrom & P. Bierman (eds.), *The Oxford Handbook of Analytical Sociology* (pp. 140–167). New York: Oxford University Press.

Granovetter, M. (1985). Economic Action and Social Structure: The Problem of Embeddedness. *American Journal of Sociology*, 91: 481–510.

Halliday, T., Powell, M. J., & Granfors, M. W. (1987). Minimalist organizations: Vital events in state bar associations, 1870–1930. *American Sociological Review*, 52(4): 456–471.

Hedstrom, P. & Udehn, L. (2009). Analytical sociology and theories of the middle range. In P. Hedstrom & P. Bierman (eds.), *The Oxford Handbook of Analytical Sociology* (pp. 25–47). New York: Oxford University Press.

Hirsch, P. M., Friedman, R., & Koza, M. P. (1990). Collaboration or paradigm shift? caveat emptor and the risk of romance with economic models for strategy and policy research. *Organization Science*, 1(1): 87–97.

Hunt, C. S. & Aldrich, H. E. (1998). The second ecology: The creation and evolution of organizational communities as exemplified by the commercialization of the world wide

26 *Howard E. Aldrich*

web. In B. Staw & L. L. Cummings (eds.), *Research in Organizational Behavior* (p. 20). Greenwich, CT: JAI Press.

Jack, S. L. (2005). The role, use and activation of strong and weak network ties: A qualitative analysis. *Journal of Management Studies*, 42: 1233–1259.

Kahneman, D. (2003). A perspective on judgment and choice: Mapping bounded rationality. *American Psychologist*, 58(9): 697–720.

Kurke, L. & Aldrich, H. E. (1983). Mintzberg was right! A replication and extension of the nature of managerial work. *Management Science*, 29(8): 975–984.

Landström, H., Harirchi, G., & Åström, F. (2012). Entrepreneurship: Exploring the knowledge base. *Research Policy*, 41(7): 1154–1181.

Lippmann, S. & Aldrich, H. E. (2014). History and Evolutionary Theory. In M. Bucheli & R. D. Wadhwani (eds.), *The Historical Turn in Organizational Studies*. New York: Oxford University Press.

March, J. G., & Simon, H. A. (1958). *Organizations*. New York: Wiley.

Martinez, M. A., Yang, T., & Aldrich, H. (2011). Entrepreneurship as an evolutionary process: Research progress and challenges. *Entrepreneurship Research Journal*, 1(1).

Mintzberg, H. (1973). *The Nature of Managerial Work*. New York: Harper & Row.

Mustar, P. (1998). Partnerships, configurations, and dynamics in the creation and development of SMEs by researchers. *Industry and Higher Education*, 12(4): 217–221.

Perrow, C. (1986). Economic theories of organization. *Theory and Society*, 15: 11–45.

Reynolds, P. D., & White, S. B. (1997). *The Entrepreneurial Process: Economic Growth, Men, Women, and Minorities*. Westport, CN: Quorum Books.

Romanelli, E. (1989). Organization birth and population variety: A community perspective on origins. In B. M. Staw & L. L. Cummings (eds.), *Research in Organizational Behavior*, 11: 211–246. Greenwich, CT: JAI Press.

Ruef, M., Aldrich, H. E., & Carter, N. M. (2003). The structure of founding teams: Homophily, strong ties, and isolation among U.S. entrepreneurs. *American Sociological Review*, 68(2): 195–222.

Sewell, W. H., Jr. (2005). *Logics of History: Social Theory and Social Transformation*. Chicago: University of Chicago Press.

Shelanski, H. A., & Klein, P. G. (1995). Empirical research in transaction cost economics: A review and assessment. *The Journal of Law, Economics, and Organization*, 11(2): 335–361.

Stewart, A. (1989). *Team Entrepreneurship*. Newbury Park, CA: Sage Publications.

Stinchcombe, A. L. (1965). Social structure and organization. In J. G. March (ed.), *Handbook of Organizations* (pp. 142–193). Chicago: Rand McNally.

Teach, R. D., Tarpley, F. A., & Schwartz, R. G. (1986). Software venture teams. In R. Ronstadt (ed.), *Frontiers of Entrepreneurship Research* (pp. 546–562). Wellesley, MA: Babson College.

Thornton, P. H., & Flynn, K. (2003). Entrepreneurship, networks and geographies. In Z. J. Acs, & D. B. Audretsch (eds.), *Handbook of Entrepreneurship Research: An Interdisciplinary Survey and Introduction*. Lancaster, UK: Kluwer.

Todd, P. M., Gigerenzer, G., & Group, A. R. (eds.) (2012). *Ecological Rationality: Intelligence in the World*. New York: Oxford University Press.

Tversky, A. & Kahneman, D. (1981). The framing of decisions and the psychology of choice. *Science*, 211(4481): 453–458.

Vaughan, D. (2009). Analytic ethnography. In P. Hedstrom and P. Bierman (eds.), *Analytical Sociology* (pp. 688–711). New York: Oxford University Press.

Watson, T. J. (2011). Ethnography, reality, and truth: The vital need for studies of how things work in organizations and management. *Journal of Management Studies*, 48(1): 202–217.

Williamson, O. E. (1975). *Markets and Hierarchies: Analysis and Antitrust Implications*. New York: Free Press.

Williamson, O. E. (1994). Transaction costs economics and organization theory. In N. Smelser & R. Swedberg (eds.), *The Handbook of Economic Sociology* (pp. 77–107). Princeton, NJ: Princeton University Press.

Williamson, O. E. (2000). The new institutional economics: Taking stock, looking ahead. *Journal of Economic Literature*, 38(3): 595–613.

3 Moving on

Affirming the entrepreneurial in entrepreneurship research

Daniel Hjorth

Originally presented at the conference on "Enacting Entrepreneurship Out of the Box", Lyon, EMLYON Business School, 4 June 2013.

Looking at the movements: on the *inter*disciplinary nature of entrepreneurship

As an opening, that is, as an attempt to increase the connecting capacity of this paper, I would like to describe what it is meant to perform. It is meant to perform a movement as such: a movement of the reader, and a movement of entrepreneurship studies. So soon after the year of Kierkegaard's 200th anniversary (5 May 2013), it seems appropriate for someone coming from the Copenhagen Business School and its Department of Management, Politics, and Philosophy (the business school's largest department) to attempt for the paper this Kierkegaardian style. – "I look only at the movements," was Kierkegaard's credo that prophesied what would come in philosophy and social sciences in the centuries to follow. Not only did he intensify the kind of philosophy we later came to label existentialism – where we might locate Dostoevsky, Sartre, and to some extent also Heidegger – but he also pointed ahead to challenges we today associate with process philosophy (Helin et al., 2014).

It is process thinking that assists us in an attempt to explain these movements I write into the aim of this paper: to move readers and entrepreneurship studies. As we shall see, affirming is a method for getting things to move. The aim is part of the response-nature of this text. Howard Aldrich has already moved me to this response and his text has already moved entrepreneurship studies. This text's capacity to move you as reader is a question of whether it can intensify your experience of what it discusses. This is also part of its capacity to move entrepreneurship studies, for it picks up the emphasis on movement from Aldrich's text like an arrow that has been shot, and it places it on the bow again and shoots it off into the context of a continued discussion of what entrepreneurship studies can (not so much should) become.[1] This will affirm the unfinalizable nature of learning to know entrepreneurship. If we affirm this movement – like in this volume and the conference that spurred it – entrepreneurship studies will be 'withdrawn into an all-encompassing relation with what it will be' (as Massumi [2002: 7] describes this), absorbed in occupying its field of potential, i.e. it will become (if ever so) slightly different. Bergson talks about another image of an arrow shot through the air. In mid-air, its becoming-different is intensified. And as it hits its target, it is qualitatively different, changed by the passing event. It is an arrow having-been-shot, an arrow having-hit-its-target. This is different from both 'an arrow-to-be-shot' and an 'arrow-in-mid-air.' Discussing, live, at a conference is a certain kind of becoming. Responding, in writing, is another. The former deals with mid-air arrows, whereas the latter picks them up from having-been-shot.'[2]

The point with the multidisciplinary (one of the arrows Aldrich's text shoots), for me, is found in the *inter*disciplinary potential that it enables. And this is how I pick up that arrow from Aldrich. Where he ends his shot, in the ground of evolutionary theory, I pick it up and suggest that evolution can also be understood as happening through *in*volution (Deleuze and Guattari, 1987: 238) – through intensive movement. That is, whatever develops becomes different not by responding to forces in the environment (evolves; which new institutionalism has focused on), but by affirming its own power (or *conatus*) to differentiate (involves). Intensive movement is an immanent affirmation of a process at the limit of what it can do. Self-affirming, if you like, is what process philosophers call 'life', Spinoza calls conatus, and Nietzsche will to power (Spindler, 2009): "The self-production of being in becoming" (Massumi, 2011: 84). This is an interdisciplinary movement, where the in-betweens – notably also the entrees of entrepreneurship research (Steyaert, 2000) – are the continuous sources of 'spaces for play' (Hjorth, 2005) where forces that make entrepreneurship (studies) processes move. Opening such spaces and releasing the forces of entrepreneurship studies can itself be described as a case of organizational emergence or 'organization-in-creation' as Katz and Gartner (1988) wrote. This makes it clear that they shot, as visionaries, an arrow into the land of interdisciplinary entrepreneurship studies.

Thinking about the study of emerging organizations, they provide another, in the context of this paper, generative lead, as they wonder: "The process of organizational emergence may be analogous to the types of interactions that take place at the atomic and subatomic levels in physics" (p. 437). They are on to kinetics, movement, what we later affirmed in the so-called Movements books series (Steyaert & Hjorth, 2003, 2006; Hjorth & Steyaert, 2004, 2009). Any boundary or surface is itself an effect of what its holding-together elementary constituents let pass, capture, or block. Any boundary is a regulated regime of movement. What we experience as the surface of a stone is itself a *relational* effect of hardness. It is relative to the nature of the movements that come to pass. The stability of an object emerges from the *interrelations* of intense movements on a subatomic level. An alpha radiation consists of particles and those are therefore relatively large and therefore stop at almost any surface. A beta radiation consists of electrons which therefore interact fairly quickly and thus also stops at most surfaces. A gamma ray is high-intense energy and it will not stop at the surface of your skin, at the surface of a piece of wood, or a brick. It will, however, get reduced quite quickly after entering lead, due to the density of that material. But

30   *Daniel Hjorth*

it will not recognize what we experience as the hard surface of a piece of lead as a hard surface at all. It will experience it (if gamma rays could experience anything) as thick fog. Thick fog will eventually take the energy out of a flashlight's light. And so, at 20 meters distance, you can no longer see the boat's lantern as the fog dims it. The interdisciplinary is a foggy space depending on how you move and with what energy as 'light.' The key to seeing 'beyond 20 meters' is of course to move, but to do so you have to embrace the fog as immanent to the dawn of even the brightest day, and you have to affirm movement. We are still at the dawn of interdisciplinary entrepreneurship studies, so let's move further.

Aldrich is thus correct? This is how we proceed – 'dimly through the fog.' Or is it? Well, the fog is an interdisciplinary matter and a stronger reason to move: the other strand is relationally constituting the space for play. At the same time it is the inter- that makes it foggy, for 'the other' challenges my spontaneity and limits the range of my light. Yet again, to the extent that my curiosity about the other (recognizing the other's otherness) is accompanied by a generosity, an opening up and sharing knowledge, our light's range is extended, as the fog grows thinner. Our energy – our curiosity's intensity, the passion of our generosity – determines what we will recognize as surfaces and thus our interactive capacity with other disciplines. The more intensely/passionately we move, the less surfaces we will recognize as hard or limits to our knowledge-creation and the more our foggy landscape is extended. But also, the more intensely/passionately we move, the stronger our light grows and the easier it gets to navigate.

So, interdisciplinary studies are not so much about objects of study that belong to several disciplines, but rather objects – and therefore research problems – that belong to no one in particular. The way we articulate our problems will either make our questions stop at the surface of other disciplines, or not. I share, with Aldrich, an understanding of entrepreneurship studies as a foggy journey. In addition, I rejoice in this fogginess, as a promise that entrepreneurship will gradually become researched in a more realistic manner.[3] Entrepreneurship, thus, recognizes few surfaces due to the intensity of its nature, due to the passion by which it moves. I, for one, affirm this mid-air status, this force of movement that is immanent to the entrepreneurial. My own research is one attempt to move *with* entrepreneurship, add to its intensity, and recognize fewer surfaces as hard in the social sciences' and humanities' interdisciplinary foggy landscape.

Movement – intensity (affect)

How do we move, then, such that we as entrepreneurship scholars might affirm the intensity with which the question of entrepreneurship arises and manifests in society? It is intensive, to me, because it is a question of creation. As Schumpeter put it: "The entrepreneurial performance involves, on the one hand, the ability to perceive new opportunities that cannot be proved at the moment at which actions have to be taken, and, on the other hand, will power adequate

Moving on 31

to break down the resistance that the social environment offers to change" (1947: 157). Imagination, creativity, and power to affect are thus central to how the modern conceptualization of entrepreneurship is inaugurated. This first generation of entrepreneurship studies generates responses in the second generation, where Gartner, Bird, and Starr (1992) pick up Schumpeter's arrow and shoot it on by thinking what 'cannot be proven' as producing an 'acting as if' behaviour (already an interdisciplinary idea emerging from a reading of the neo-Kantian philosopher Vaihinger's [1952] piece "The Philosophy of 'As If' ", originally published the same year as Schumpeter's "The Theory of Economic Development" and Frederick Winslow Taylor's "The Principles of Scientific Management" – 1911). Moving entrepreneurship studies is a question of how we think entrepreneurship and how entrepreneurship is studied. If we want to affirm the intensive nature of the entrepreneurship question as a question of creation, my best proposal today is to think it processually. That is, think it *with* process thinking, process philosophy.

Before we proceed to these two elaborations, on process thinking and on entrepreneurial creation, let me exemplify the intensity with which the question of entrepreneurship has already been articulated in the proto-interdisciplinary landscape of our research:

1 "Though the phrase 'getting a new thing done' may be adequately comprehensive, it covers a great many different activities which, as the observer stresses one more than another or as his (sic!) material displays one more than another, may, locally, temporally, or generally lend different colours to entrepreneurship" (Schumpeter, 1947, The Creative Response in Economic History) => suggesting entrepreneurship is centred on the problem of the new, but also that it is graspable from a diverse set of perspectives and empirical materials.

2 "People who study entrepreneurship exhibit a certain sort of madness in their passion for the subject. This zest for the substance of entrepreneurship is what makes the field so attractive to many of us who are refugees from other, more boring fields" (Aldrich, 1992: 191) => suggesting that the study of entrepreneurship is a practice that moves you, that generates affect, or at least makes up a less boring field of study.

3 "In the existing business, it is the existing that is the main obstacle to entrepreneurship" (Drucker, 1985: 188) => suggesting entrepreneurship is what it does, that is, becoming is the mode of thinking and acting that sets us on the course of studying entrepreneurship.

4 ". . . because researchers have not observed emerging organizations and new organizations early on, they have not recognized most entrepreneurial activity" (Katz and Gartner, 1988: 437; Gartner, 1988) => suggesting that emergence and the interdisciplinary 'fog' in-between studies of entrepreneurship and organizations holds a potential for new knowledge of entrepreneurship. On this issue, see also Aldrich and Yang (forthcoming).

32   Daniel Hjorth

How do we identify and study the new, the creation of affect, the becoming or emergence? As I said above, process philosophy or process thinking is my best suggestion for moving entrepreneurship studies into a capacity to grasp emergence, the creation of the new, organization-in-creation, organization becoming. There are, however, alternatives and Aldrich exemplifies one such with his development of evolutionary theory in organization and entrepreneurship studies. Gartner has developed an argument for narrative approaches and a 'science of imagination' (2007) as another important way to move in the interdisciplinary study of entrepreneurship. Yet again, Sarasvathy's 'science of the artificial' (2003) is another opening towards the interdisciplinary, foggy landscape. The process of creation is one theme that cuts across these examples and it seems to me that the more we affirm creation as central to entrepreneurship, the more we intensify the urge to venture into the interdisciplinary.

Before we turn to a short elaboration of how to think creation processually, a short clarification is needed. For if you think that I – by turning to creation and process – thereby have left the mode of responding I referred to as a way to position this text, you should think again. I am still in this response to Aldrich, still moving from having been moved by his text. More precisely, the following lines of thinking are the movements that were initiated by reading Aldrich's text. I use them to affirm a movement of entrepreneurship studies into a greater capacity for grasping emergence, becoming, and creation, i.e. the interdisciplinary landscape Katz and Gartner pointed out in 1988 and which has shaped the way I research entrepreneurship Hjorth, 2005). Again to Aldrich's text:

1 "Indeed, it is not clear that there is a distinct 'discipline' called entrepreneurship studies . . ." (p. 1): Looking at the movements, there is, and affirming movement is one way to find the distinctiveness of entrepreneurship studies: it is the study of the creation–process making the new value organizationally achieve being.

2 When Aldrich seeks to describe how the institutional infrastructure underlying the field has been created, he focuses on six forces (p. 1). I agree that the study of becomings needs to focus on the forces that drive how the new happens. Force is a central concept when we want to understand creation, the politics of organizational creativity, and entrepreneurial becomings. Process philosophy centres on force (Spinoza, Nietzsche, Foucault, and Deleuze all have force as central concept in their thinking) in order to conceptualize the relational dynamics of life (Deleuze, 1988a, 2006; Spindler, 2009).

3 Attention to history, as suggested by Aldrich (p. 9), and the subsequent emphasis of the importance of time and place, I agree is central (Popp & Holt, 2013). Time and timing in particular are key elements of process thinking (Tsoukas & Chia, 2002; Chia & Holt, 2009), as is the creation of space as a result from movement and a condition for moving (Hernes, 2004). The politics of creation of organizations is thereby introduced as

a central area for understanding entrepreneurship. Remember Drucker's note: in the existing business, it is the existing that is the main obstacle to entrepreneurship. All entrepreneurship takes place in the context of an overwhelming amount of existing things, practices, habits, norms, perceptions, and so the remark from Drucker is more general that his reference to 'existing business' might imply. Aldrich turns to identify four differences between classical approaches to organizational analysis and a narrative/interpretive approach (without mentioning Jean-Francois Lyotard's piece that opened up this distinction in 1979), all of which are important for a researcher's capacity to grasp becoming: emphasis on context, resistance to generalizability of research results, the role of events in explanations, and the value of unique phenomena. To the extent you emphasize context, events, and the unique, generalizability will in effect become less interesting. The general is a systematization of relations to (or observations of) the studied for the purpose of maximum repeatability (which excludes the event and the unique) of the largest number of actions with the maximum uniformity of result. Nietzsche described history that doesn't burden us with the abstracted laws that transcend and colonize our present but which genealogically understand the present in its emergence as a unique event, as effective (or *wirkliche*) history (cf. Foucault's concept of 'history of the present'; 1977: 30–31, a form of Nietzschean genealogy[4]). It thus becomes evident that attempts to grasp becoming as generalized laws for identifying 'what is the case' will always make change/movement/creation, as such, slip out of the conceptual grip. We end up with a 'what' that has changed into a 'what + 1' without knowing how this happened.

Foucault points out: " 'Effective' history, however, deal with events in terms of their most unique characteristics, their most acute manifestations. An event, consequently, is not a decision, a treaty, a reign, or a battle, but the reversal of a relationship of forces, the usurpation of power, the appropriation of a vocabulary turned against those who had once used it . . . [. . .] The forces operating in history are not controlled by destiny or regulative mechanisms. . . . They do not manifest successive forms of a primordial intention . . . [. . .]" (1977: 154). And he finishes by quoting Nietzsche: ". . . the world of effective history knows only one kingdom, without providence or final cause, where there is only 'the iron hand of necessity shaking the dice-box of chance' " (p. 155).

4 When Aldrich stresses the cooperative nature of 'most' entrepreneurial action, I see the need to stress the social, the relational nature of all entrepreneurial action. I recognize this is not what Aldrich says when he emphasizes the cooperative, but this provides me with an opening to anticipate a theme in the coming elaboration of process thinking – that of the relation nature of human action. First, Schumpeter's contribution to Aldrich's note on the cooperative: "Finally, as has been often pointed out, the entrepreneurial function need not be embodied in a

34   *Daniel Hjorth*

physical person and in particular in a single physical person. Every social environment has its own ways of filling the entrepreneurial function. [Notice how this is an argument for a contextual approach to entrepreneurship. My note.] Again the entrepreneurial function may be and often is filled co-operatively" (1949: 70–71). With Massumi (2002) we then ask: "Is it possible even to conceive of an individual outside of a society? Of a society without individuals? Individuals and societies are not only empirically inseparable, they are strictly simultaneous and consubstantial" (p. 71). Relationality comes with the social. "Relationality is the potential for singular effects of qualitative change to occur in excess over or as a supplement to objective interactions. Relationality pertains to the openness of the interaction rather than to the interaction per se or to its discrete ingredients" (Massumi, 2002: 225). In addition to the ingredients of any relation, there are the ingredients' interactions and their effects. That is, their event. This is also why there cannot be general conditions for the emergence of an event – it is relationally specific and situationally unique. We have therefore argued that entrepreneurship studies need to focus on the contextual and the creative (Hjorth, Jones, & Gartner, 2008).

5   When Aldrich ties together his disciplinary influences, those that potentially could contribute to a more multidisciplinary understanding of entrepreneurship – anthropology, economics, history, psychology, and sociology – he does so by using the concepts of event and process (p. 18). His love affair with evolutionary theory (evolution itself being fundamentally collective-relational) to me also indicates, without too much eisegesis, a process-orientation. The world is in constant qualitative growth, where every move and change adds something new to the world. It snowballs, William James said (1996). It becomes new in a creative evolution, *élan vital*, as Henri Bergson named this. Again, this brings us to the challenge of thinking becoming, process, emergence, or ontogenesis.[5] This is a challenge as it is open-endedly social. It is pure sociality before it is formed by social conventions or prior research into the hungry boxes of well-rehearsed models. Becoming, emergence, is thus ontogenetically prior to any separating out of individual from society, of specific subjectivities in relation to certain objects, and any of their interactions. It is this taking-form of such interactions that is the processual study of emergence or becoming. If you do not assume these forms to already objectively exist, if you turn your attention to how form*ing* is socially achieved, how becoming receives a form of being by drawing upon what already exists (remember Drucker's point), then you open up for the need to create new concepts for this interaction-in-the-making. Interaction-in-the-making, as Massumi (2002) suggests, is just another term for relation.

We turn now to two related elaborations: one on process thinking, and one on creativity. Both are appearing in coming publications, in various forms.

Moving on 35

Notably, the elaboration on process thinking appears in the Oxford University Press *Handbook of Process Philosophy and Organization Studies* (2014) that I edited together with Jenny Helin, Tor Hernes, and Robin Holt. The elaboration on entrepreneurial creation, conducted in closer dialogue with entrepreneurship studies, is part of a more long-term project of developing a process theory of entrepreneurship, or entrepreneuring. These are examples of how the responses above can be extended beyond the conversational mode that characterize the text so far. From here, I try to continue two central lines that were initiated by Aldrich and emphasized in my reading: process thinking and entrepreneurial creativity (processually thought).

Process thinking[6]

Working with process philosophers and process philosophy over several years (since around 2000), we[7] have arrived at a way to think process that makes use of five aspects as central to this thinking: Temporality; Wholeness; Openness and the Open Self; Force; and Potentiality. We describe those *as aspects*, following Wittgenstein, since they do not supplant one another, but can persist together, forming a relational whole that dynamically varies. If these aspects are part of how we think, we will do a much better work thinking processually, grasping process. In contemporary organization studies, which is the primary interdisciplinary relation for this chapter (in Aldrich, as well as in Katz and Gartner as mentioned above), we find these aspects present throughout discussions of process philosophy/thinking (e.g. Nayak & Chia, 2011).

Temporality

The importance of time cannot be exaggerated. The passing of time, flow, represents the perishability of the world from within which its multiple potentiality for creating new forms emerges. Process philosophers such as Bergson, Heidegger, Whitehead, and Mead all engage intensely with time. According to Bergson, clock time, left to itself constitutes a flattening and deadening of primordial, lived, or qualitative time – what he called duration. Duration is the time of becoming, of creation or actualization. Deleuze says it is 'inseparable from the movement of its actualization' (1988b: 42–43; Bergson, 1911/2002) When we see the becomings, things in our world become less 'thingly' as the process by which they become and perish gets evident. Time as duration intensifies life as movement, and simultaneously makes it clearer how we all, as actors in the stream of time, make use of clock time (and its artefacts – schedules, calendars) to establish an identity. "Process thinking invites us to treat past and future as open slates upon which the processual narrative is inscribed. The challenge remains to study life in an on-going, provisionally open present in which a provisional closure of past and future is assumed as a way to move ahead in a moving world" (Helin et al., 2014: xx).

36   *Daniel Hjorth*

Wholeness

Similar to the tradition of Hermeneutic thinking in philosophy, process thinking seeks knowledge of how the one emerges from the multiple. Illustrating this thinking in the case of trying to understand colour, Massumi puts it like this: "What is there besides the objective ingredients of color? Is it an affront to objectivism to say that there is, in addition to the ingredients, their interaction and its effect?" (2002: 221). How the colour blue appears to us as blue is a question of the event through which the interactions between its ingredients happen. This event makes blue happen as a whole, but always unique and never fully repeated. Wholeness, to move on to a more classical example for social science scholars, means we cannot think away society and focus on the individual, nor think away the individual and focus on society. In Massumi's words again: "Is it possible even to conceive of an individual outside of society? Of a society without individuals? Individuals and societies are not only empirically inseparable, they are strictly simultaneous and consubstantial. [. . .] In other words, they might be seen as differential emergences from a shared realm of relationality that is one with becoming – and belonging" (ibid.: 71). Relations, interactions under way, connect and make the event of the whole happen. We always experience the world in relation to our experience as a whole. It is from this constant multitude of relations between parts and the effects of their interactions – their events – from which the potential for newness constantly emerges. Change is always incipient. The entre-, the relational, the in-betweens are potentialized. We see this from the world of entrepreneurship studies as opportunity and venture creation. Nietzsche, another process thinker, always stressed that to understand what something is demands from us to ask how it has become, via what relations, and through what forces, at play in those relations. The world is open in the sense that there is an excess of relational potential, a multitude of incipient changes that could leap over into the actual world of concrete, contextualized practices.

Openness

Openness is in a processual sense a question of connectivity. Connectivity is a question of relational capacity. Relations are interactions-in-the-making. On this backdrop we can propose, again with Massumi (2002: 224), "Call the openness of an interaction to being affected by something new in a way that qualitatively changes its dynamic nature *relationality*" (emphasis in original). Openness is thus tied to the virtually real, to that which might becomes actualized in creation. Openness – as where the new is relationally made incipient – represents what emerges in interaction in excess over the interaction as such and the interacting elements. The self today is more understandable as a self-network, where you relate you're your self both as subject and as object. The openness of the self corresponds to its power to be affected (as Spinoza was keen to stress) and power to affect. This passional nature makes the self unfinalizable and the social world relationally unfinalizable too. A structure, a stable being, a fixed self would all be the result of an effort: closing, disconnecting, arresting. You will thus find a hesitation amongst process thinkers to depict the world in models and static snapshots. They are simply too far removed from life, too reduced, precise in a misplaced way. Precision, instead, has to be sought in the more realistic descriptions where life is still in language. Where accuracy comes from contextually found stories and images that carry movement and force. Nietzsche is the grand master of this aphoristic language that refuses to settle on a model, but insists on upsetting you as a reader – move you. It is when we can see the relation (an interaction in the making) as equally real as what it relates that the dynamics of becoming can be grasped. When the bee interacts with the flower, there is a bloc of becoming formed, relationally stabilized by the bee's power to be affected by the smell of nectar and the flower's power to receive pollen from the bee. This bloc of becoming is life furthering itself via a more healthy bee and a fertilized/pollinated flower. Force, which is ever only observable as effect, and central to Nietzsche's and Spinoza's thinking (clear traces of which are found in both Foucault's and Deleuze's work), is crucial to our understanding of life's 'rolling of the already more into a nextness' (Massumi, 2002: 271) or the process of becoming.

Force

Nietzsche points out that force is either reactive or active, and that active forces are those that go to the limit of their consequences. Reactive forces can separate active forces from what they can do and thus make them become reactive. It takes a genealogist to diagnose the nature of forces and their work in the social. When we insist on staying with and in life, rejecting resort to externalities such as 'structure' or 'society' (temporary stabilizations of the dynamic relations between people) as causing change, we become alert to creative forces. Forces are always related to other forces, and their strength and accomplishments are always relative. "This difference between forces qualified according to their quantity as active or reactive will be called *hierarchy*" (Deleuze, 2006: 40). To Nietzsche, the economic man ideal of adjusting to external circumstances is an example of inferior-reactive forces constituting a body. Such reactive forces are seen in utilitarian accommodations, Nietzsche points out, and he is much more interested in active-creative forces that can take the movement of action to the virtual fringe of things (Hjorth, 2014). Forces, Nietzsche teaches us, are never fully graspable if not related to will, will to power, which are either negative or affirmative. Will (to power) is the differential element of force. Entrepreneurship can thus be understood as a certain will (to power), a certain differential element of force, one that takes action to the virtual fringe of things. Force is perhaps the monarch of all processual characteristics. Foucault developed an analysis of force, especially how discipline and control are part of making people governable (Gordon, 1991), and contributed in this way to a Nietzschean attention to the dominated and dominant forces. Potential is

38 *Daniel Hjorth*

a curious melange of time and force, a 'felt moreness to ongoing experience,' as Massumi (2002: 141) puts it.

Potentiality

Spinoza understood a body as a dynamic composition of movements and rest. Spinoza called a body's capacity to enter into movement and rest its power to affect and be affected. Potential describes the indeterminate variation of things under way. What is an idea to one is an opportunity to another. Potentiality can also describe the virtual powers of becoming that characterize all life: we are always already acting from a belonging in the world, rather than acting on the world. There are thus always multiple becomings virtually present at any actual point in time. Bergson is careful to note that there is little difference between the real and the possible: the former is already in the latter. Creation is therefore not precisely understood as realization of the possible, but rather actualization of the virtual: one of the multiple variations of the actual is actualized. The virtual is real, but lacks actuality, and happens in creation through which it is differentiated by establishing a contextual-relational presence in an ongoing world, where forces and will to power already are at work. Also thinking is always already belonging to a life that Bergson (1911/2002: 27) calls "a current passing" through which all organisms move and flow (cf. Thrift, 2008; Massumi, 2002, and the references to ontogenesis). Separating thinking from life – the classical Cartesian move – prevents us from grasping it processually.

Affirming the entrepreneurial in entrepreneurship research

What we elsewhere have referred to as a European School of Entrepreneurship Research (ESER; Hjorth, Jones, & Gartner, 2008; Special Issue in *Entrepreneurship & Regional Development*, 25[1–2]) is identified by placing creativity and contextual approaches at the centre of entrepreneurship. Suggesting, in addition, that entrepreneurship research itself would benefit from contextual and creative ways is of course not necessarily relevant. The idea of the need for entrepreneurship research to itself become entrepreneurial is proposed in our Movements book series (2003, 2004, 2006, and 2009, for Edward Elgar Publishers) and by Johannisson (2004) and affirmed by Steyaert (2011). Steyaert also points out – while discussing Johannisson's proposal to develop enactive research strategies – that all research methods are already enactive. This refers to what we said above: in process thinking we are made aware of our belongingness in the world, that we – also our thinking and reflection – are always already participating in the world. When we research, theorize and write, we always affect the world (if ever so little) and change it (ibid.; Law & Urry, 2004; Massumi, 2002; Thrift, 2008). When we acknowledge that praxis and poiesis are wrapped up in the fields of practices we study, it is not far-fetched to argue that entrepreneurship researchers that affirm creativity as part of research process will also better grasp entrepreneurship as a creative process. 'How', as in process research, is the default question, and not so much the 'what.' If we understand the world as made, and recognize that our descriptions of that world and the world we want to make affects how it is made, looking at decisions, structures, institutions only and as if they were independent from our descriptions/theories would distance ourselves from the world. Affirming the creative and the performative nature of theory, we would instead look at deciding, structuring, institutionalizing and at the same time recognize how theories thereof are part of the field of practices and affect it. "[I]f the everyday enactments of practice come first, then we cannot identify a world accessible to mental representations beyond the practices that enact it. Theories do not represent but form practices themselves" (Beyes & Steyaert, 2011: 8). Theories and theorizing are means we use to get along and move the world (Thrift, 2008), and they add to and change the world (Massumi, 2002).

There is thus a point with describing (as I did in the opening of this essay) processual approaches as representing a more realistic line of research. Understanding one's part of what is researched, and how this is affected and changed by researching it and writing on it (as an act of participation) is to affirm the contextual nature of entrepreneurship and entrepreneurship research, and to acknowledge one's part of it rather than to imagine a place outside, untouched by the world and its languages.

There are indeed research approaches, methods, and analytical strategies in entrepreneurship studies that affirm the creative nature of both research and entrepreneurship. Steyaert (2011) refers to in(ter)vention in entrepreneurship research. Under this label we can include some of the narrative approaches (Gartner, 2007; Hjorth, 2007), humanities-influenced approaches (Hjorth & Steyaert, 2006), as well as performative ones (Beyes & Steyaert, 2011). We could see Sarasvathy & Dew's (2005) as well as Gartner's (2007; and Gartner et al., 1992) emphases on imagination and storytelling (see also Aldrich & Fiol, 1994; Lounsbury & Glynn, 2001) as ways to affirm the creative and performative in entrepreneurship and entrepreneurship studies:

"Generally speaking it could be argued that before there are products, there is human imagination; and before there is a market, there are human aspirations. Successful entrepreneurs have long been creating firms, industries and even economies by matching up the offspring of human imagination with human aspirations" (Sarasvathy & Dew, 2005: 387).

"Emerging organizations are elaborate fictions of proposed possible future states of existence" (Gartner et al., 1992: 17).

The world is imagined and narrated, represented in convincing fabulations, and this is also how it moves on, how it is made in a constant bundle/wrap of praxis and poiesis. In process language, Gartner refers to 'fictions of the virtually real,' the multiple potential becoming. For entrepreneurship to actualize the virtually real – i.e. the idea of the new, the invention – a form of fabulation, a narratively performed imagination, is crucial. Hirschman called something that appears similar to this *The Hiding Hand*: ". . . since we necessarily

40   *Daniel Hjorth*

underestimate our creativity it is desirable that we underestimate to a roughly similar extent the difficulties of the tasks we face, so as to be tricked by these two offsetting underestimates into undertaking tasks which we can, but otherwise would not dare, tackle" (1967: 13). We recognize this also from Gartner et al.'s (1992) 'acting as if' concept: "Entrepreneurs talk and act 'as if' equivocal events were non-equivocal" (ibid.: 17). Gartner et al. are here proposing that we understand entrepreneurship as 'the process of emergence' (p. 13), as the process of organization-in-creation, and we can read it as anticipating a more organization-oriented entrepreneurship research. It is, however, more of a Weickian (and therefore also pragmatism-based) relational constructionism (Hosking, 1995; Hosking and Hjorth, 2004) than a processual approach presented. Nevertheless it points us to the fruitful crossing of organization and entrepreneurship studies, and one that affirms the creative in entrepreneurship practices, more precisely studied in research that itself is entrepreneurial. 'Acting as if' is described as: "Entrepreneurs suggest (act 'as if') to different individuals [. . .] that certain outcomes [. . .] will occur from the organizing process. Entrepreneurs, therefore, both seek out, as well as develop, motivations that will enable organizations to emerge" (Gartner et al., 1992: 25). Our attempts to understand how this happens are helped by turning to imagination and narration more generally: "Our current methodologies do not let us explore very much of the 'reality' of emergence. For example, we need to legitimate the use of oral histories as a way of gathering information on the nature of entrepreneurial activities" (ibid.: 27).

Entrepreneurial emergence of organization-creation happens wrapped with fictions, virtualities, as a bundle in which this becoming is actualized. "There is no literature without fabulation," Deleuze points out (1988b: 3), and entrepreneurship too, as a creative practice, is performed both as praxis and poiesis. One way to affirm the creative and entrepreneurial in entrepreneurship research would thus be to think processually: this pulls us in the direction of asking 'how' rather than 'what' and makes it necessary to see how the world is made performatively. Existing practices, institutions, roles, positions perform too as they suggest what should pass as normal and neutral. Describing the world differently is a practice that affects how it becomes and potentially changes its ways. Process thinking will thus open up to new questions not too often asked in entrepreneurship research: how is desire to create (or aspiration in Sarasvathy and Dew's terms) producing images and subjectivities? "Desire itself is power, a power to become and produce images" (Colebrook, 2002: 94). How are subjectifications – stabilizing someone as 'entrepreneur' – working to order the field of practices: "Subjectification as a process is personal or collective individuation . . . [. . .] . . . Take Foucault himself: you weren't aware of him as a person exactly. [. . .] It was a set of intensities" (Deleuze, 1995: 115). A story of a possible future can be intensified in narratives, attracting investments and support. Institutions will perform their work, offering legitimizing forces to the extent that the entrepreneurial process pays homage to what the institution makes normal/necessary. Performing a certain subject-position, answering to the call from institutionalized expectations, might then quickly pull the process into a field of practices where the entrepreneurial gets lost. Socially coded desires – interests – are gluttonously seeking to enroll more into what is already up and running.

Enacting entrepreneurship (research) out of the box could thus be understood and practiced, using process thinking, as a question of intensity, desire, creation, and fabulation. Such a creation process can be understood as an emergence of organization, as organization-creation, which precisely operates in the foggy in-betweens where lots of institutionalized boundaries can appear as impossible to cross or break through. Similarly, doing entrepreneurial entrepreneurship research, so I have suggested in this response to Aldrich essay, should follow practice in this sense and itself dwell in the foggy interdisciplinarity of research. Our desire to know, the intensity of our images, will then help us move and see further. Processually speaking, there is no realistic promise of an end to the fog. The price of not seeing all clearly – surely what has made scholars opt for simplifying models and isolated causes – is to me by far outweighed by progressing via a more precise (i.e. attentive to the praxis–poiesis bundle that constitutes the field of practices) knowledge of entrepreneurship. This process will always build new boxes. However, to the extent that this process is moved by an interdisciplinary conversation, such boxes will also be deconstructed and left behind in the desire to follow/study how the world entrepreneurially becomes new.

Notes

1 The image is Nietzsche's and is used by Deleuze (1995: 118).
2 I sent an earlier version of this to Howard before the conference at Lyon.
3 In the Movements books, Steyaert and I continuously called for this: more entrepreneurial entrepreneurship studies, i.e. more realistic.
4 Effective history puts everything in historical motion, affirms movement, studies the genealogy of emergent and perishing truths and subject-positions and – as a history of the present – the present forces that organize cultural and institutional practices that are part of combats for truth (cf. Foucault, 1977: 154–157).
5 Following being in its genesis demands a corresponding genesis of thought, in parallel with what you try to understand (Thrift, 2008).
6 This draws upon the introduction to the *Hanbook on Process Philosophy and Organization Studies* (2014), Oxford University Press.
7 This is developed together with Robin Holt, Tor Hernes, and Jenny Helin during our work as editors for the *Handbook on Process Philosophy and Organization Studies* (Oxford University Press, 2014).

References

Aldrich, H. E. (1992). Methods in our madness? Trends in entrepreneurship research. In D. L. Sexton & J. D. Kasarda (eds.), *The State of the Art of Entrepreneurship* (pp. 191–213). Boston, MA: PWS-Kent Publishing Company.

Aldrich, H. E. & Fiol, C. M. (1994). Fools rush in? The institutional context of industry creation. *Academy of Management Review*, 19(4): 645–670.

42   Daniel Hjorth

Aldrich, H. E. & Yang, T. (Forthcoming). How do entrepreneurs know what to do? Learning and organizing in new ventures. *Journal of Evolutionary Economics*.

Bergson, H. (1911/2002). Perception of change. In K. Ansell Pearson & J. Mullarkey (eds.), *Selected Writings*. New York: Continuum.

Beyes, T. & Steyaert, C. (2011). Spacing organization: Non-representational theory and performing organizational space. *Organization*, 19(1): 45–61.

Chia, R. & Holt, R. (2009). *Strategy without Design – the Silent Efficacy of Indirect Action*. Cambridge: Cambridge University Press.

Colebrook, C. (2002). *Deleuze*. London: Routledge.

Deleuze, G. & Guattari, F. (1987). A Thousand Plateaus – Capitalism and Schizophrenia, London: The Athlone Press.

Deleuze, G. (1988a). *Spinoza: Practical Philosophy* [Trans. Robert Hurley]. San Francisco: City Lights Books.

Deleuze, G. (1988b). *Bergsonism*. New York: Zone Books.

Deleuze, G. (1995). *Negotiations*. New York: Columbia University Press.

Deleuze, G. (2006). *Nietzsche and Philosophy*. New York: Columbia University Press.

Drucker, P. F. (1985). *Innovation and Entrepreneurship*. New York: Harper & Row.

Foucault, M. (1977). *Language, Counter-Memory, Practice*, edited and with introduction by Donald F. Bouchard. Ithaca, NY: Cornell University Press.

Gartner, W. B. (1988). Who is an entrepreneur? is the wrong question. *American Journal of Small Business*, 12(4): 11–32.

Gartner, W. B. (2007). Entrepreneurial narrative and a science of the imagination. *Journal of Business Venturing*, 22(5): 613–627.

Gartner, W. B., Bird, B. J., & Starr, J. A. (1992). Acting as if: Differentiating entrepreneurial from organizational behaviour. *Entrepreneurship, Theory & Practice*, Spring: 13–31.

Gordon, C. (1991). Governmental rationality: An introduction. In G. Burchell, C. Gordon, and P. Miller (eds.), *The Foucault Effect: Studies in Governmentality* (pp. 1–51). Chicago: University of Chicago Press.

Helin, J., Hernes, T., Hjorth, D., & Holt, R. (2014). Process is how process does. In J. Helin, T. Hernes, D. Hjorth, & R. Holt (eds.). *Handbook of Process Philosophy and Organization Studies*. Oxford: Oxford University Press.

Hernes, T. (2004): *The Spatial Construction of Organization*. Amsterdam, Philadelphia: John Benjamins.

Hirschman, A. O. (1967). The principle of the hiding hand. *National Affairs*, Winter (6): 10–23.

Hjorth, D. (2004). Towards genealogical storytelling in entrepreneurship. In D. Hjorth and C. Steyaert (eds.), *Narrative and Discursive Approaches in Entrepreneurship* (pp. 210–232). Cheltenham: Edward Elgar.

Hjorth, D. (2005). Organizational Entrepreneurship – with de Certeau on creating heterotopias (or spaces for play). *Journal of Management Inquiry*, 14(4): 386–398.

Hjorth, D. (2007). Narrating the entrepreneurial event: Learning from Shakespeare's Iago. *Journal of Business Venturing*, 22(5): 712–732.

Hjorth, D. (2014). Entrepreneuring and organization-creation. In R. Sternberg and G. Krauss (eds.), *Handbook of Research on Entrepreneurship and Creativity*. Cheltenham: Edward Elgar.

Hjorth, D., Jones, C., & Gartner, W. B. (2008). Introduction for recreating/recontextualising entrepreneurship. *Scandinavian Journal of Management*, 24(2): 81–84.

Hjorth, D. & Steyaert, C. (eds.) (2004). *Narrative and Discursive Approaches in Entrepreneurship*. Cheltenham: Edward Elgar.

Hjorth, D. & Steyaert, C. (2006). American psycho/European schizo: Stories of managerial elites in a hundred images. In P. Gagliardi & B. Czarniawska (eds.), *Management Education and Humanities* (pp. 67–97). Cheltenham: Edward Elgar.

Hjorth, D. & Steyaert, C. (2009). *The Politics and Aesthetics of Entrepreneurship*. Cheltenham: Edward Elgar.

Hosking, D. M. (1995). Constructing power: Entitative and relational approaches. In D. M. Hosking, H. P. Dachler, & K. J. Gergen (eds.), *Management and Organization: Relational Alternatives to Individualism* (pp. 51–71). Aldershot, UK: Avebury.

Hosking, D. M. & Hjorth, D. (2004). Relational constructionism and entrepreneurship: Some key notes. In D. Hjorth and C. Steyaert (eds.), *Narrative and Discursive Approaches in Entrepreneurship* (pp. 255–268). Cheltenham: Edward Elgar.

James, W. (1996). *Essays in Radical Empiricism*. Lincoln: University of Nebraska Press.

Johannisson, Bengt (2004). *Between Arm's Length Research and Policy Practices – Interactive Approaches in Entrepreneurship Studies*. Tromsö, Norway. Paper presented at the 13th Nordic Conference on Small Business Research.

Katz, J. A. & Gartner, W. B. (1988). Properties of emerging organizations. *Academy of Management Review*, 13(3): 429–442.

Law, J. & Urry, J. (2004). Enacting the social. *Economy and Society*, 33(3): 390–410.

Lounsbury, M. & Glynn, M. A. (2001). Cultural Entrepreneurship: stories, legitimacy, and the acquisition of resources. *Strategic Management Journal*, 22(6–7): 545–564.

Lyotard, J-F. (1979/1984). *The Postmodern Condition: A Report on Knowledge*. Manchester: Manchester University Press.

Massumi, B. (2002). *Parables for the Virtual – Movement, Affect, Sensation*. Durham, NC: Duke University Press.

Massumi, B (2011). *Semblance and Event: Activist Philosophy and the Occurent Arts*. Cambridge, MA: MIT Press.

Nayak, A. & Chia, R. (2011). Thinking becoming and emergence: Process philosophy and organization theory. In H. Tsoukas & R. Chia (eds.), *Philosophy and Organization Theory* (pp. 281–309). Bingley: Emerald Group.

Popp, A. & Holt, R. (2013). The presence of entrepreneurial opportunity. *Business History*, 55(1): 9–18.

Sarasvathy, S. D. (2003). Entrepreneurship as a science of the artificial. *Journal of Economic Psychology*, 24: 203–220.

Sarasvathy, S. D. & Dew, N. (2005). Entrepreneurial logics for a technology of foolishness. *Scandinavian Journal of Management*, 21: 385–406.

Schumpeter, J. A. (1947). The creative response in economic history. *Journal of Economic History*, Nov: 149–159.

Schumpeter, J. A. (1949). *Economic Theory and Entrepreneurial History – Change and the Entrepreneur: Postulates and Patterns for Entrepreneurial History*. Cambridge, MA: Harvard University Press.

Spindler, F. (2009). *Spinoza: multitud, affect, kraft* [Multitude, Affect, Force]. Munkedal, Sweden: Glönta Produktion.

Steyaert, C. (2000). *Entre-concepts: Conceiving Entrepreneurship*. Paper presented at the XIV RENT Conference, Prague.

Steyaert, C. (2011). Entrepreneurship as in(ter)vention: Reconsidering the conceptual politics of method in entrepreneurship studies. *Entrepreneurship and Regional Development*, 23(1/2): 77–88.

Steyaert, C. & Hjorth, D. (2003). *New Movements in Entrepreneurship*. Cheltenham: Edward Elgar.

Steyaert, C. & Hjorth, D. (2006). *Entrepreneurship as Social Change*. Cheltenham: Edward Elgar.

Thrift, N. (2008). *Non-Representational Theory: Space, Politics, Affect*. London: Routledge.

Tsoukas, H. & Chia, R. (2002). On organizational becoming: Rethinking organizational change. *Organization Science*, 13(5): 567–582.

Vaihinger, H. (1952). *The Philosophy of 'As If': A System of the Theoretical, Practical and Religious Fictions of Mankind*. London: Routledge & Kegan Paul (original work published 1911).

4 The economic reification of entrepreneurship

Re-engaging with the social

Alistair R. Anderson

> Economics, in speaking of entrepreneurs, has in view not men, but a definite function.
>
> (Mises, 1966: 246)

Introduction

Growth and development at personal, firm, and national levels are all, quite properly, attributed to entrepreneurship. However, the importance of these entrepreneurial outcomes has shaped how we perceive entrepreneurs and the entrepreneurial concept. The significance of these positive outcomes seems to imply that entrepreneurship is primarily an economic function. In consequence throughout history, the words 'entrepreneur', 'entrepreneurial', and 'entrepreneurship' have been associated with specific economic roles and phenomena (Hébert & Link, 1989). Van Praag and Versloot (2007) go so far as to claim that almost without exception, academic studies on entrepreneurship are motivated by the economic benefits of entrepreneurship. In short, our perceptions of entrepreneurship have become functionalist. Economics has won the battle for theoretical hegemony in academia and society as a whole and such dominance becomes stronger every year (Ferraro et al., 2005). At the very least, as Minniti and Lévesque (2008) claim, many aspects of entrepreneurship and its implications have been studied taking the lens of neoclassical economics.

The problem is that this functionalist lens is narrow. Its necessary reductionism doesn't permit us to see enough of, or to take into account, the fine grain of context and circumstance, nor of the non-mechanistic behaviour, the sentient and the emotional entrepreneurial practices that characterize entrepreneurship. This is surprising, because entrepreneurship is always about novelty and newness, doing things differently and creating change. The qualities of context and idiosyncratic human behaviour are the very qualities that may provide this very novelty that makes things entrepreneurial. By confining entrepreneurship in an economic paradigm, our understanding is at risk of a procrustean trimming, a reductionism that offers poor explanatory justice. It also fails to give due explanatory weight to how entrepreneurship emerges from social and economic interactions (Anderson et al., 2012). Consequently, I want to argue that the economists' focus on outcomes means that economic "explanation" has overwhelmed "understanding" (Anderson, 2015). The economistic dominance of inquiries about *what* causes entrepreneurship are explanations of enterprise that have served us well in explaining aspects such as innovation. But they serve us poorly in understanding *how* such processes emerge.

Entrepreneurship has been put in this "economistic" black box and it does not fit very well. Too many important explanatory aspects have to be left outside the box, such that these socialized leftovers are seen as ancillary rather than at the core of the phenomenon. As Steyaert and Hjorth (2007) explain, entrepreneurship is currently reified as an economic occurrence. The problem identified here is that although we know entrepreneurship as a concept is socially constructed, it is economically construed. Yet entrepreneurship is not just socially constructed, it is also socially enacted. To understand entrepreneurship, we need to begin with process, rather than try to read back, trying to explain from outcomes. We should not try to seek an elusive, impossible universality, but should examine how context uniquely shapes practice.

The economic reification of entrepreneurship

The evidence for pervasion of the economistic perception of entrepreneurship is strong. Ireland et al. (2005) showed how a survey of published entrepreneurship research in the *Academy of Management Journal* demonstrated that many papers are in some form grounded in the classic work of scholars such as Knight, Schumpeter, and Kirzner. McDonald et al. (2014), surveying 29 years of entrepreneurship publications in the top journals, found that positivistic approaches continued to dominate the literature. Johansson (2004) analyzed economics textbooks used for entrepreneurship PhD courses and found that entrepreneurship was largely absent. He points out that what is not written could be at least as telling as what is written. Indeed not much has changed since Stanworth and Curran (1976) noted that the consistent overall theoretical perspective which unites both the dominant and minor themes in current theorizing concerning growth in the small firm is a highly positivist one. The underlying paradigm for theoretical development is an idealized version of that used in the natural sciences, what Bygrave and Hofer (1991) called physics envy. The small firm is seen as a behaving entity whose elements are related in quantifiable, systematic, and highly predictable ways and the object of theory construction is the generation of law-like propositions concerning the growth process. Karp (2006) attributes this, in part, to systems thinking and attempts to apply the method of natural science to human action. For him, most approaches to entrepreneurship are rationalistic. He is concerned that entrepreneurship may not be understood merely as an economic but also as a social activity constrained by time and place.

As Hjorth puts it, economics has become a common denominator to be employed in all theorizing processes (2004). Granovetter (1992) refers to this as economics imperialism. For Hirshleifer (1985), economics has become a

46 *Alistair R. Anderson*

universal grammar of entrepreneurship. Indeed, Keynes (1936) pointed out that the ideas of economists, both right and wrong, are more powerful than commonly understood.

Interestingly, there is also evidence of economistic thinking in the language of entrepreneurship, of how we talk about enterprise. Language is important because as Chell (2000) shows, language guides our sense of social reality, by framing, filtering, and creation to transform the subjective into a more tangible reality. Words are not passive vessels of meaning, but active forms of meaning creation. Clark and Dear (1984: 84) explain, "language is used to construct or reconstruct social reality." As Austin (1962) puts it, we do things with words, we engage in a performance with words. Words are performative (Downing, 2005). We talk of opportunities, and describe how they must be seized and exploited. Moreover such opportunistic behaviour is geared to produce competitive advantage, to win some battle by bettering our competitors. Competition itself, an economic rallying cry and leitmotif of enterprise, projects fighting for ascendency, implying only one winner and many losers. It ignores the cooperation (Street & Cameron, 2007) and the socialized networks that characterize entrepreneurship (Anderson et al., 2010). We describe the entrepreneurial process as creative destruction with as much emphasis on destroying rather than as creating. We ignore how most innovation results from collaborative knowledge (Harbi et al., 2009). We describe markets as functional, but they are as much arenas of social exchange, where there is a mutual dependency between buyers and sellers. Relationship marketing is far from an oxymoron in entrepreneurship practice (Zontanos & Anderson, 2004). These images drawn out from language are hardly benign, or very accurate. They draw a picture of ruthless exploitation of resources and competitors, a Hobbesian landscape of one against all and a zero sum game. They overlook the emancipatory empowerment evoked by enterprise. They don't seem to capture the social embeddedness of the entrepreneurial process, or the collaborations that characterize small business (Jack et al., 2008). They seem to ignore community (Johannisson, 1990) and what society values in enterprise (Anderson & Warren, 2011; Korsgaard & Anderson, 2011). Social entrepreneurship, where social welfare and well-being are both process and outcome, is deemed some sort of hybrid of business and society (Diochon & Anderson, 2009, 2011). Worst of all in this image building is the seeming feckless consumption, even destruction, of our limited natural resources (Dean & McMullen, 2007).

Sarasvathy (2010) is also very critical of the vocabulary of economics, similarly proposing that it imposes severe limitations on how we can understand entrepreneurship. Amongst others, she offers the vivid example of success or failure as a 0–1 variable. Here we can see my earlier argument about economics obsession with outcomes rather than process highlighted. She points out, with lots of examples, that "success" is most often a combination of many small failures. To that we might add that the very notion of success is highly subjective experience. For some, what I deem a failure, by say profit level, may be celebrated as a success because they have achieved an ambition to be

Economic reification of entrepreneurship 47

independent (Anderson & Ullah, 2014). It seems then that the language of economics imposes meanings that do not, and cannot reflect, the nuances and variety of what it means to be entrepreneurial. By focusing on what can be measured, we may lose sight of what actually occurs.

These words, these images, have impact. Studies of young peoples' attitudes towards the appeal of entrepreneurship (Drakopoulou Dodd et al., 2013a; Anderson et al., 2009) asked for metaphors to describe their understanding of entrepreneurship. No social metaphors were offered, but economic or natural competitive metaphors (red in tooth, parasite, vulture, and lion) prevailed. Similarly, a study of Tunisian students' attitudes demonstrated how they dwelled on the economic benefits of enterprise (Harbi et al., 2009). This study did, nonetheless, socially situate the role of gender in entrepreneurial opportunity. So meaning, as well as theory, is thoroughly permeated with an economistic appreciation of entrepreneurship. Language affects what people see, how they see it, and the social categories and descriptors they use to interpret their reality (Ferraro et al., 2005). It shapes what people notice and ignore and what they believe is and is not important. In this sense, entrepreneurial reality is socially constructed (Berger & Luckmann, 1996) and language plays an important role in such constructions.

The history of entrepreneurial inquiry helps explain why this economic reification has come about. Indeed, Bjerke (2013) suggests that for 250 years, only economists were interested in entrepreneurship. Holcombe (1998) explained how the earliest of entrepreneurial scholars, Cantillon (1755), Smith (1776), Malthus (1798), and Ricardo (1821) all focused, albeit differently, on how growth occurred. For example, Stevenson and Jarillo (1990) attribute early interest in entrepreneurship to Ricardo's focus upon the economic role of the entrepreneur, rather than the individual who performs such a role. Redlich (1949) argued that following Say's (1767–1832) definition, entrepreneurship began to be considered as an economic phenomenon. It seems then that early functionalist thinking about entrepreneurship was economistically informed and shaped and that this view has become entrenched. For example, McMullen and Shepherd (2006) argue that a recurring theme in the literature is the health of the economy and how the economic system functions. But Holcombe (1998) argues economists are more ready to attack problems that fit into a general equilibrium model of the economy rather than those that are more difficult to parameterize. Certainly, Grant and Perren (2002) demonstrate the dominance of the functionalist paradigm that pervades the leading entrepreneurship journals.

Of course, despite my critique about understanding rather than explaining, we cannot ignore the substantial contribution of this economistic thinking. As Minniti (2005) explains, the methodological subjectivism of the Austrian Economic School (Kirzner, Schumpeter, and Knight) has demonstrated the power and usefulness of concepts such as innovation and opportunities. Economic thinking is responsible for us seeing how innovation as a quintessential property of enterprise (Drucker, 1985). More recently, we see how context manifest

48 *Alistair R. Anderson*

as institutions is recognized by economists to shape forms of entrepreneurship (Harbi & Anderson, 2010). Moreover, the evolutionary economic perspective shows us how the aggregation of new business formation is akin to a great experiment, as those who get it right succeed and those who don't, fail (Anderson et al., 2012). This sort of economic perspective shows us a system and how it is coordinated to produce economic outcomes. It reflects what Wohl (1954) argues is the economist's "entrepreneurial" problematic: discovering how the diverse and separate activities of a multitude of firms can explain the development of a nation.

Problems and gaps in the economistic view

Foss et al. (2008) argue that the classic contributions to the theory of entrepreneurship economists tend to portray entrepreneurial activity as an individual endeavour, and neglect how entrepreneurial judgment and the recognition and enactment of opportunities may be derived from social processes, such as dynamic interactions. Drakopoulou Dodd and Anderson (2007) make the same point about entrepreneurship as a socialized activity. Pittaway and Rose (2006) question the individualism in entrepreneurship, whilst Jones and Conway (2000) deconstruct the myth of the entrepreneur as a heroic individual. Nijkamp (2003) noted that the idea of the individual entrepreneurial hero had permeated the literature on small and medium-sized enterprises (SMEs), but suggests that in more recent developments the social embeddedness has challenged the position of the 'entrepreneurial hero'. Importantly, Samuels (1990) reminds us that economics is a discourse in itself, one bound up with specific ideologies. Hence the idea of autonomous entrepreneurial individuals fits well with particular ideologies. But in turn this highlights the problem identified by Bruyat and Julien (2001) of an epistemological rupture between the general meaning of the words and their scientific meaning.

Economists give analytical primacy to environmental factors in a systems approach (Bouchikhi, 1993) that prioritizes outcomes rather than process. McMullen and Shepherd (2006) argue that this system level approach is concerned primarily with how the economic system functions. Lipman (2003) explains how economics attempts to explain social institutions as regularities deriving from the optimization of certain functions. However, Minniti (2005) emphasizes how economic variables have failed to fully explain entrepreneurial variations and suggests that to better understand entrepreneurial behaviour one must look at the importance of the local social environment (Jack &Anderson, 2002). Thus, actual or potential economic conditions cannot be the entire story (Welter, 2011). Anecdotally, Zahra (2007) comments that when reading entrepreneurship papers, one rarely gets a sense of the substance, magnitude, or dynamics of the research context. Furthermore, this systems approach ignores the importance of human emotions (Goss, 2005). Pain and passion, perhaps even love; joy and despondency, all play a role in entrepreneurship process and practices; but they sit uneasily as a utility function or as an economic variable.

Economistic thinking thus seems to leave out the human and contextual contingency (Sarasvathy, 2001) that enables entrepreneurship to create the future (Drakopoulou Dodd et al., 2013).

Moreover, the logic of economics is self-interest. (Sen, 1997: 317) claims: "The first principle of economics is that every agent is actuated only by self interest." But the socialized practices of entrepreneurship seem to contradict this argument (Anderson & McAuley, 1999). Moreover entrepreneurial practices, even entrepreneurs themselves, are only socially "approved" when they are deemed to be acting morally (Anderson & Smith, 2007). This notion then of the primacy of entrepreneurial self-interest appears flawed, yet has arisen within the constrained logic of economic theorizing. Alvey (2000) suggested that the economic detachment from moral concerns is a 20th century phenomenon and attributes it to the "scientification" of economics. Historically, Banks (2006) points out that in the classical political economy portrayed by Adam Smith during the Enlightenment, economic activities were seen as embedded in non-economic social relations and shaped by moral values other than instrumental rationality. In modernity notions of the economy developed as an autonomous sphere with its own internal market logic, inducing a break between economic rationality and society. Solow, the Nobel Prize winning economist (1997), claims that by 1940, economics had become a technical subject whereby efficiency was prioritized over other values. However, it is these very same values, but especially social concern, often manifest as cultural and social capital, that drive social enterprise and also help configure entrepreneurship more generally (Fuller & Tian, 2006).

Entrepreneurship and economics: the paradox

Inherent in the economistic perception of entrepreneurship is a paradox. Entrepreneurship is not part of mainstream economics. Klein (2008) notes how it is largely absent from contemporary economic theory. Ironically, although we see lots of attempts to explain entrepreneurship by economic thinking, we see little economic thinking about entrepreneurship! Classically Baumol (1968) explains, the theoretical firm is entrepreneurless – the Prince of Denmark has been expunged from the discussion of Hamlet.

He explains the entrepreneur is a shadowy entity in economic theory without clearly defined form or function. Moreover, that economic theory is unlikely to develop a formal illuminating analysis of entrepreneurship. Wennekers and Thurik (1999: 32): "The neo-classical model, with its production function, the internal logic of rational choice and perfect information, leaves no room for an active entrepreneur. As neo-classical economics became more formalized and as the mathematics of equilibrium theory became more important, references to the entrepreneur receded from the micro textbooks. The model left no room for aspects like initiative, charisma, stubbornness, and the struggle with

50 *Alistair R. Anderson*

new ideas and uncertainty. The entrepreneur disappeared from microeconomic theory (Barreto, 1989).

Recently, Bianchi and Henrekson (2005) asked if neo-classic economics remains entrepreneurless. They found that entrepreneurship remains defined narrowly and cannot capture the wide-ranging and complex functions suggested outside mainstream economics. They conclude that rather than providing an exhaustive theory, the economic contributions should be viewed as pieces of a complex puzzle. They conclude that an individual real-world entrepreneur, even if highly stylized, cannot be modeled in mainstream economics, since she eludes analytical tractability. In this sense, the neoclassical entrepreneur is (still) not entrepreneurial. It seems then that economic theory is hardly a comprehensive lens to understand entrepreneurship. It follows then that it is paradoxical that it has so profoundly shaped entrepreneurial theorizing and our methodological approaches to entrepreneurship.

Towards a more socialized conception of entrepreneurship

I want to argue that it may be better to try to understand entrepreneurship as a social phenomenon, albeit one with economic outcomes. I have tried to demonstrate that economic ways of looking at the phenomenon tell us very little about how entrepreneurship emerges. In "explaining" entrepreneurship through components and variables, economic thinking misses the importance of context and contingency in understanding the process. Economic explanations carry with them the loss of understanding of how entrepreneurship is planted strongly in life *tout court* (Steyaert & Katz, 2004) rather than simply in economic life (Hjorth et al., 2003). Indeed, entrepreneurship can be viewed as an expression of the interaction among individuals, social communities, and the whole of society (Ebner, 2005). For Zafirovski (1999) this indicates the inadequacy of a 'pure' economic theory of entrepreneurship.

We see this issue as a problem manifest in our thinking about entrepreneurship, in that current economic theorizing seems unable to cope very well with how entrepreneurship is practiced and presented. It seems the economic lens focuses too much on entrepreneurial economic outcomes and consequently neglects processes and inputs. An economist's lens is good for looking at entrepreneurial outcomes, but it provides us with poor explanations of the socialized inputs, or the precedents of entrepreneurship. In contrast, a social lens gives explanatory power to context, the nature of society, and the qualities of society that allows us to understand how these things come together, the self and the entrepreneurial context (Anderson, 2000). A social lens enables us to see both how and why people are motivated to become entrepreneurial. Rather than crudely categorizing entrepreneurship as desirable opportunity entrepreneurship, or dismissing it as necessity entrepreneurship, a social lens shows us how context shapes what is desirable and what is possible and helps to explain the contingency of entrepreneurship. Of course motivation can be economic, but for every entrepreneur I have ever spoken to, financial considerations are pretty low in the ranking of motivation. They may want to make a difference, they might want to be successful, but they don't just want to make money.

The importance of a more socialized view

Following Gartner (2001: 27), it is important in entrepreneurship to examine and articulate the "assumptions we make about this phenomenon." Lindgren and Packendorff (2009) identify this as a problem because the lack of explicit discussion on underlying basic assumptions in entrepreneurship research implies an unreflective attitude to the hidden claims and perspectives. The assumptions that were challenged earlier all related to an economistic view of the entrepreneurial world. As an economic phenomenon, the entrepreneur is undersocialized and the concept too embedded in ideological individualism. In contrast, we claim that entrepreneurship is enacted socially, using socially informed actors to engage within a milieu that can be understood socially. Furthermore, entrepreneurship processes have social outcomes that may well be just as important as the economic outcomes. Thus, we argue that the social plays a role at several different levels of entrepreneurial analysis. At the very least, enacting entrepreneurship engages in the social and produces some social outcomes.

This dominance of economistic thinking is important because scholarship tends to follow the path that is illuminated by that light (Steyaert & Katz, 2004). Aldrich and Martinez (2002) warn that paradigms (such as the economic paradigm) serve as a siren song, tempting new generations of researchers to follow, regardless of any serious methodological problems. There are isomorphic pressures and deep-seated temptations to imitate. Consequently this issue of the domination of economics in entrepreneurship is neither trivial nor arcane, but of significant importance.

Conclusion

One effect of the dominance of the reductionist economic view is in how it has percolated into and shaped broad awareness of entrepreneurship. There has been a conceptual overflow from the dominant economic paradigm, such that how we present, how we appreciate, and how we perpetuate our popular grasp of entrepreneurship has been afflicted by this economic mode of thinking. Words are how we communicate meaning, but there is an economic, individualistic bias in entrepreneurial words that masks other ways of understanding entrepreneurship.

The social as configuring entrepreneurial process is most evident in the embedded literature (Aldrich & Zimmer, 1985). Almost as a response to the undersocialized entrepreneur, this growing volume of literature shows how social values configure entrepreneurial practices. In this view entrepreneurship arises in a social context and is shaped, enabled, or constrained by the social context. Seen in this way, entrepreneurship is anchored in the social. A

52 *Alistair R. Anderson*

closely related theme is that of social capital. Social capital is seen as a social resource that usually enables enterprise (Jack et al., 2010). Social capital can be seen as a relational artefact (Anderson et al., 2007) and as inhering in social relationships. Networks are a forum for, and probably of, social capital. Importantly, the network literature demonstrates how entrepreneurship is a socialized practice.

Finally we cannot ignore the number of calls to recognize the concept of entrepreneurship as a social construction (Fletcher, 2006; Anderson & Starnawska, 2008). The underpinning argument is that entrepreneurship is to be understood as a universal and that different members of society, in different roles in society, understand it differently. Moreover, Aldrich and Martinez (2002: 387) are firm believers in the social in entrepreneurship, "in a fundamental sense, then, entrepreneurship involves the social construction of new social entities." So we have made some progress in that the economic discourse and paradigm are not hegemonic, but nonetheless remain pervasive.

In reviewing the explanatory power of the economic the paper has tried to show the importance of the social in understanding entrepreneurship and for explaining enterprising practices. Entrepreneurship is too deeply enmeshed with society to allow us to stand sufficiently outside to view it only as economic. Entrepreneurship is much too profoundly engaged in society to allow us to neglect the social. A pure economic view simplifies, but yet insulates our theorizing from the complex and dynamic meshing of the entrepreneur in the society in which she operates and within which enterprise is drawn and formed. The laudable outcomes of entrepreneurship are undoubtedly amenable to economic forms of measurement, but the processes that create these outcomes are profoundly social. Too often our views, our understanding, and our appreciation of the nature of entrepreneurship are prejudiced towards a narrow economic approbation. A social ontology of entrepreneurship is required.

References

Aldrich, H. and Zimmer, C. (1985). Entrepreneurship through social networks. In D. Sexton & R. Smilor (eds.), *The Art and Science of Entrepreneurship* (pp. 3–24). New York: Ballinger.

Aldrich, H. E. & Martinez, M. (2002). Entrepreneurship as social construction: A multi-level evolutionary approach. In Z. J. Acs and D. Audretsch (eds.), *Handbook of Entrepreneurship Research*. Norwell, MA: Kluwer.

Alvey, J. E. (2000). An introduction to economics as a moral science. *International Journal of Social Economics*, 27(12): 1231–1252.

Anderson, A. R. & Smith, R., (2007). The moral space in entrepreneurship: An exploration of ethical imperatives and the moral legitimacy of being enterprising. *Entrepreneurship and Regional Development*, 19(6): 479–497.

Anderson, A. R. & McAuley, A. (1999). Marketing landscapes: The social context. *Qualitative Market Research: An International Journal*, 2(3): 176–188.

Anderson, A. R., Dodd, S. D., & Jack, S. L. (2010). Network practices and entrepreneurial growth. *Scandinavian Journal of Management*, 26(2): 121–133.

Anderson, A. R., Dodd, S. D., & Jack, S. L. (2012). Entrepreneurship as connecting: Some implications for theorising and practice. *Management Decision*, 50(5): 958–971.

Anderson, A. R. (2000). The protean entrepreneur: The entrepreneurial process as fitting self and circumstance. *Journal of Enterprising Culture*, 8: 201–234.

Anderson, A. R. (2015). Conceptualising entrepreneurship as economic "explanation" and the consequent loss of "understanding". *International Journal of Business and Globalisation*, 14(2): 145–157.

Anderson, A. R., Drakopoulou Dodd, S., & Jack, S. L. (2009). Aggressors; winners; victims and outsiders: European schools' social construction of the entrepreneur. *International Small Business Journal*, 27(1): 126–136.

Anderson, A. R., Park, J., & Jack, S. (2007). Entrepreneurial social capital: Conceptualising social capital in new high-tech firms. *International Small Business Journal*, 25(3): 243–67.

Anderson, A. R. & Starnawska, M. (2008). Research practices in entrepreneurship; problems of definition, description and meaning. *International Journal of Entrepreneurship and Innovation*, 9(4): 221–230.

Anderson, A. R. & Warren, L. (2011). The entrepreneur as hero and jester: Enacting the entrepreneurial discourse. *International Small Business Journal*, 29(6): 589–609.

Anderson, A. R. & Ullah, F. (2014). The condition of smallness: How what it means to be small deters firms from getting bigger. *Management Decision*, 52(2): 326–349.

Austin, J. L. (1962). *How to Do Things with Words*. Wm. James lectures. Clarendon: Oxford.

Banks, M. (2006). Moral economy and cultural work. *Sociology*, 40(3): 455–472.

Barreto, H. (1989). *The Entrepreneur in Micro-Economic Theory: Disappearance and Explanation*. New York: Routledge.

Baumol, W. J. (1968). Entrepreneurship in economic theory. *American Economic Review*, 58(2): 64–71.

Berger, P. L. & Luckmann, T. (1996). *The Social Construction of Reality: A Treatise in the Sociology of Knowledge*. Harmondsworth: Penguin Books.

Bjerke, B. (2013). *About Entrepreneurship*. Cheltenham: Edward Elgar Publishing.

Bianchi, M. & Henrekson, M. (2005). Is neoclassical economics still entrepreneurless? *Kyklos*, 58(3): 353–377.

Bruyat, C. & Julien, P. A. (2001). Defining the field of research in entrepreneurship. *Journal of Business Venturing*, 16(2): 165–180.

Bygrave, W. D. & Hofer, C. W. (1991). Theorizing about entrepreneurship. *Entrepreneurship Theory and Practice*, 16(2): 13–22.

Bouchikhi, H. (1993). A constructivist framework for understanding entrepreneurship performance. *Organization Studies*, 14(4): 549–570.

Chell, E. (2000). Towards researching the 'opportunistic entrepreneur': A review and some theoretical developments. *European Journal of Work and Organisational Psychology*, 9: 63–80.

Clark, G. L. & Dear, M. (1984). *State Apparatus: Structures and Language of Legitimacy*. New York: Allen and Unwin.

Dean, T. J. & McMullen, J. S. (2007). Toward a theory of sustainable entrepreneurship: Reducing environmental degradation through entrepreneurial action. *Journal of Business Venturing*, 22(1): 50–76.

Diochon, M. & Anderson, A. R. (2009). Social enterprise and effectiveness: A process typology. *Social Enterprise Journal*, 5(1): 7–29.

Diochon, M. & Anderson, A. R. (2011). Ambivalence and ambiguity in social enterprise: narratives about values in reconciling purpose and practices. *International Entrepreneurship and Management Journal*, 7(1): 93–109.

54 *Alistair R. Anderson*

Downing, S. (2005). The social construction of entrepreneurship: Narrative and dramatic processes in the coproduction of organizations and identities. *Entrepreneurship Theory and Practice,* 29(2): 185–204.

Drakopoulou Dodd, S. & Anderson A. R. (2007). Mumpsimus and the mything of the individualistic entrepreneur. *International Small Business Journal,* 25(4): 341–360.

Drakopoulou Dodd, S., Anderson, A., & Jack, S. (2013). Being in time and the family owned firm. *Scandinavian Journal of Management,* 29(1): 35–47.

Drakopoulou Dodd, S. D., Jack, S. & Anderson, A. R. (2013a). From admiration to abhorrence: the contentious appeal of entrepreneurship across Europe. *Entrepreneurship and Regional Development,* 25(1–2): 69–89.

Drucker, P. F. (1985). The discipline of innovation. *Harvard Business Review,* 63(3): 67.

Ebner, A. (2005). Entrepreneurship and economic development: From classical political economy to economic sociology. *Journal of Economic Studies,* 32(3): 256–274.

Ferraro, F., Pfeffer, J., & Sutton, R. I. (2005). Economics language and assumptions: How theories can become self-fulfilling. *Academy of Management Review,* 30(1): 8–24.

Fletcher, D. E. (2006). Entrepreneurial processes and the social construction of opportunity. *Entrepreneurship and Regional Development,* 18(5): 421–440.

Foss, N. J., Klein, P. G., Kor, Y. Y., & Mahoney, J. T. (2008). Entrepreneurship, subjectivism, and the resource-based view: Toward a new synthesis. *Strategic Entrepreneurship Journal,* 2(1): 73–94.

Fuller, T. & Tian, Y. (2006). Social and symbolic capital and responsible entrepreneurship: An empirical investigation of SME narratives. *Journal of Business Ethics,* 67(3): 287–304.

Gartner,W. B. (2001). Is there an elephant in entrepreneurship? Blind assumptions in theory development. *Entrepreneurship Theory and Practice,* 25(4): 27.

Goss, D. (2005). Entrepreneurship and 'the social': Towards a deference-emotion theory. *Human Relations,* 58(5): 617–636.

Granovetter, M. (1992). Economic institutions as social constructions: A framework for analysis. *Acta Sociologica,* 35(1): 3–11.

Grant, P. & Perren, L. (2002). Small business and entrepreneurial research: Meta-theories, paradigms and prejudices. *International Small Business Journal,* 20(2): 185–211.

Harbi, S., Amamou, M., & Anderson, A. R. (2009). Establishing high-tech industry: The Tunisian ICT experience. *Technovation,* 29(6/7): 465–481.

Harbi, S. & Anderson, A. R. (2010). Institutions and the shaping of different forms of entrepreneurship. *Journal of Socio-Economics,* 39(3): 436–444.

Hébert, R. F. & Link, A. N. (1989). In search of the meaning of entrepreneurship. *Small Business Economics,* 1(1): 39–49.

Hirshleifer, J. (1985). The expanding domain of economics. *American Economic Review,* 85: 53–68.

Hjorth, D. (2004). Creating space for play/invention – concepts of space and organizational entrepreneurship. *Entrepreneurship and Regional Development,* 16(5): 413–432.

Hjorth, D., Johannisson, B., & Steyaert, C. (2003). Entrepreneurship as discourse and life style. In B. Czarniawska & G. Sevon (eds.), *Northern Lights* (pp. 91–110). Malmö: Liber.

Holcombe, R. G. (1998). Entrepreneurship and economic growth. *Quarterly Journal of Austrian Economics,* 1(2): 45–62.

Ireland, R. D., Reutzel, C. R., & Webb, J. W. (2005). From the editors: Entrepreneurship research in AMJ: What has been published, and what might the future hold? *Academy of Management Journal,* 48: 556–564.

Johansson, D. (2004). Economics without entrepreneurship or institutions: A vocabulary analysis of graduate textbooks. *Economic Journal Watch*, 1(3): 515–538.

Jack, S. L. & Anderson, A. R. (2002). The effects of embeddedness on the entrepreneurial process. *Journal of Business Venturing*, 17(5): 467–487.

Jack, S., Anderson, & A. R. Drakopoulou-Dodd, S. (2008). Time and contingency in the development of entrepreneurial networks. *Entrepreneurship and Regional Development*, 20(2): 125–159.

Jack, S. L., Moult, S., Anderson, A. R., & Drakopoulou Dodd, S. (2010). An entrepreneurial network evolving: Patterns of change. *International Small Business Journal*, 28(4): 315–337.

Johannisson, B. (1990). Community entrepreneurship – cases and conceptualization. *Entrepreneurship & Regional Development*, 2(1): 71–88.

Jones, O. & Conway, S. (2000). *The Social Embeddedness of Entrepreneurs: A Re-Reading of 'Against the Odds.'* RP 0023, Birmingham: Aston Business School Research Institute.

Karp, T. (2006). The inner entrepreneur: A constructivist view of entrepreneurial reality construction. *Journal of Change Management*, 6(3): 291–304.

Klein, P. G. (2008). Opportunity discovery, entrepreneurial action, and economic organization. *Strategic Entrepreneurship Journal*, 2(3): 175–190.

Korsgaard, S. & Anderson, A. R. (2011). Enacting entrepreneurship as social value creation. *International Small Business Journal*, 29(2): 135–151.

Keynes, J. M. (1936). *The General Theory of Employment, Interest and Money*. London: Macmillan Press.

Lindgren, M. & Packendorff, J. (2009). Social constructionism and entrepreneurship: Basic assumptions and consequences for theory and research. *International Journal of Entrepreneurial Behaviour & Research*, 15(1): 25–47.

Lipman, B. L. (2003). Language and economics. In Marcelo Basili, Nicola Dimitri, & Itzchak Gilboa (eds.), *Cognitive Processes and Rationality in Economics*. London: Routledge.

McDonald, S., Ching Gan, B., Fraser, S., Oke, A., & Anderson, A. R. (2015). Towards a multiple perspective view of entrepreneurship. *International Journal of Entrepreneurship Behaviour and Research*, 21(3): 291–315.

McMullen, J. S. & Shepherd, D. A. (2006). Entrepreneurial action and the role of uncertainty in the theory of the entrepreneur. *Academy of Management Review*, 31(1): 132–152.

Malthus, T. R. (1798). *An Essay on the Principle of Population*. Printed for J. Johnson, in St. Paul's Church-Yard, London.

Minniti, M. (2005). Entrepreneurship and network externalities. *Journal of Economic Behavior & Organization*, 57(1): 1–27.

Minniti, M. & Lévesque, M. (2008). Recent developments in the economics of entrepreneurship. *Journal of Business Venturing*, 23(6): 603–612.

Mises, L. v. [1949] 1966. *Human Action: A Treatise on Economics*. Chicago: Henry Regnery.

Nijkamp, P. (2003). Entrepreneurship in a modern network economy. *Regional Studies*, 37(4): 395–405.

Pittaway, L. & Rose, M. (2006). Learning and relationships in small firms: Introduction to the special issue. *International Small Business Journal*, 24(3): 227–231.

Redlich, F., (1949). The origin of the concepts of "entrepreneur" and "creative entrepreneur". *Explorations in Entrepreneurial History*, 1(2): 1–7.

Ricardo, D. (1821). *On the Principles of Political Economy and Taxation*. J.M. Dent, London.

Samuels, W. J. (ed.) (1990). *Economics as Discourse: An Analysis of the Language of Economists*. Boston: Kluwer Academic.

Sarasvathy, S. D. (2010). Entrepreneurship as economics with imagination. *The Ruffin Series of the Society for Business Ethics*, 3: 95–112.

Sarasvathy, S. D. (2001). Causation and effectuation: Toward a theoretical shift from economic inevitability to entrepreneurial contingency. *Academy of Management Review*, 26(2): 243–264.

Sen, A. (1997). Economics, business principles and moral sentiments. *Business Ethics Quarterly*, 7(3): 5–15.

Solow, R. M. (1997). How did economics get that way and what way did it get? *Daedalus*, 126(1): 39–58.

Smith, A. (1776). *An Inquiry into the Nature and Causes of the Wealth of Nations*. London: George Routledge and Sons.

Stanworth, M.J.K. & Curran, J. (1976). Growth and the small firm – an alternative view. *Journal of Management Studies*, 13(2): 95–110.

Stevenson, H. H. & Jarillo, J. C. (1990). A paradigm of entrepreneurship: Entrepreneurial management. *Strategic Management Journal*, 11(5): 17–27.

Steyaert, C. & Katz, J. (2004). Reclaiming the space of entrepreneurship in society: Geographical, discursive and social dimensions. *Entrepreneurship & Regional Development*, 16(3): 179–196.

Steyaert, C. & Hjorth, D. (eds.) (2007). Introduction: What is social in social entrepreneurship? In *Entrepreneurship as Social Change: A Third New Movements In Entrepreneurship Book* (pp. 1–18). Cheltenham: Edward Elgar Publishing.

Street, C. T. & Cameron, A. F. (2007). External relationships and the small business: A review of small business alliance and network research. *Journal of Small Business Management*, 45(2): 239–266.

Van Praag, C. M., & Versloot, P. H. (2007). What is the value of entrepreneurship? A review of recent research. *Small Business Economics*, 29(4): 351–382.

Welter, F. (2011). Contextualizing entrepreneurship – conceptual challenges and ways forward. *Entrepreneurship Theory and Practice*, 35(1): 165–184.

Wennekers, S. & Thurik, R. (1999). Linking entrepreneurship and economic growth. *Small Business Economics*, 13(1): 27–56.

Wohl, R. R. (1954). The significance of business history. *Business History Review*, 28(2): 128–140.

Zafirovski, M. (1999). Probing into the social layers of entrepreneurship: Outlines of the sociology of enterprise. *Entrepreneurship & Regional Development*, 11(4): 351–371.

Zahra, S. A. (2007). Contextualizing theory building in entrepreneurship research. *Journal of Business Venturing*, 22(3): 443–452.

Zontanos, G., & Anderson, A. R. (2004). Relationships, marketing and small business: An exploration of links in theory and practice. *Qualitative Market Research: An International Journal*, 7(3): 228–236.

5 Social entrepreneurship
To defend society from itself

Karin Berglund and Annika Skoglund

> In the name of empowering both the individual and the community, parties of both right and left advocate the removal of aspects of welfare and security from State control and supply.
>
> (Barry et al., 1996a: 1)

Introduction

In this chapter the reader will encounter three forms of entrepreneurship that have been implemented in Sweden. The first takes place through the formation of a network for ex-criminals who are to become 'Creative Honest Entrepreneurs' (CHF) supported by the NGO Criminals Return Into Society (CRIS). The second is pursued as education in entrepreneurship for the transformation of teenage girls into 'Stoned Unquenchable Souls'. Lastly, the third form of entrepreneurship is situated in the context of immigrant women who form a Network of Entrepreneurs from Ethnic Minorities (NEEM).

These three examples share a common assumption, namely that entrepreneurship is the solution to various social problems and can serve as protection against present insecurities and uncertain futures. Within these seemingly positive and friendly initiatives, which open up for new forms of entrepreneurships, it will be illustrated that there is a battle taking place. This battle is, however, not only about removing barriers to entrepreneurship and releasing a suppressed entrepreneurial potential among these groups. Rather, we will show how these entrepreneurships relate to a shift in social security, which targets the citizen, with all his or her imperfections and deviating behaviour, assumed to be a threat to society itself. The goal of this battle against the human is to make everyone believe that they have the abilities required to transform themselves into some type of entrepreneur.

This chapter aims to explore how forms of entrepreneurships are disseminated and how entrepreneurship is refined and unfolds on new terrains, often with quite intricate targets. To be more specific, our aim is to unravel and scrutinize the potential effects of entrepreneurships, and in particular social entrepreneurship. This requires an analysis that recognizes the shift from direct state interventions to a neoliberal ideal of indirect governing via 'the social entrepreneur', who seeks to reinvest in social security in the form of social entrepreneurship. Through conceptualizing 'entrepreneurial security', we are better able to distinguish and highlight the effects of this shift and its transformation of individuals into social entrepreneurs. Additionally, the introduction of 'entrepreneurial security' makes it possible to theorize and perform research into entrepreneurship – social or other – with the help of new perspectives.

The transformation from entrepreneurship to more social entrepreneurships should, however, not be considered mainly as a debate among entrepreneurship scholars, looking for more precise definitions, or to develop the field. Rather, this transformation corresponds well with general social and political changes, which means that the role, sense and function of entrepreneurship must be academically reassessed. The broader aim of this chapter is to open up for a rethinking of entrepreneurship through discussing the effects of the transformation from 'conventional' entrepreneurship to entrepreneurships.

We start by illustrating the shift from entrepreneurship to entrepreneurships, whereafter we contextualize this in relation to post-Foucauldian studies of 'security'. More specifically, we turn to post-Foucauldian literature to investigate how the wishes and ambitions of the social entrepreneur are in line with overall neoliberal norms of self-management, self-reliance, and self-security. This theoretical framework facilitates our attempted meta-perspective on the effects of entrepreneurships. Subsequently, we use the Swedish cases as a vehicle for our analysis of how social entrepreneurs are situated at the crossroads of business, NGOs, and the enabling state. To end, we discuss how this contributes to knowledge about how the already developed and rich neoliberal citizen is formed to work on itself through calls for social entrepreneurship, first and foremost in efforts to reduce marginalized and dangerous elements within society, and defend society from itself.

From entrepreneurship to entrepreneurships

Today entrepreneurship is taking on new forms, as illustrated by the increasing number of prefixes, as in, for example social, green, political and sustainable entrepreneurship. CRIS, the Unquenchable Souls, and Neem are usually referred to as social entrepreneurship, entrepreneurship education, and immigrant women's entrepreneurship respectively. The policy and research community has not been slow to pick up and further the plethora of emerging entrepreneurships, framed as a promising way to break with economic and instrumental entrepreneurship discourses (e.g. Austin, Stevenson, & Wei-Skillern, 2006; Berglund, Johannisson, & Schwartz, 2012; Dacin, Dacin, & Matear, 2010; Shaker et al., 2009; Hjorth & Steyaert, 2006). Entrepreneurship is seen to be situated in the midst of – or even locked in by – the economic domain, which hampers the potential of more social entrepreneurships to emerge and solve problems, not only in the market domain, but also on social terrains (Steyaert & Katz, 2004). Entrepreneurship is today under pressure to bring about not only economic growth, but also social change.

The new types of entrepreneurships that have emerged have not only been received positively, but have also been seen as the solution to how social problems can be successfully dealt with (e.g. Mair & Martí, 2006). By conceptualizing entrepreneurship as a social phenomenon, it is also argued that it is possible to achieve a better, richer, and more complete understanding of how entrepreneurship is enacted among individuals, social communities, and society as a whole (Ebner, 2005; Steyaert & Hjorth, 2006). As Anderson (2013) states in a preliminary draft to his chapter in this book, entrepreneurship is still 'economically constructed', although the 'social turn is growing stronger, but it is not yet strong enough'. Hence, it seems as if entrepreneurship has reached a state where it must be defended, to become more ingrained in the everyday life of the social citizen. This, in turn, makes entrepreneurship a moving target, hard to grasp, seemingly impossible to pin down analytically, and with effects unknown to us.

Moreover, social entrepreneurship has been recognized as disseminating a neoliberal market rationality in order to tackle social issues (Dempsey & Sanders, 2010). Eikenberry and Kluwer (2004) argue that this resembles a typical effort to marketize society. These criticisms of social entrepreneurship have not only highlighted how the rationality and business logic proceeds (cf. Nicholls, 2010), but also how attempts are made to hide this under the label of 'the social' in a more general attempt to target the 'becoming' of the neoliberal democratic citizen.

Neoliberal transformations of entrepreneurship in relation to 'security'

Entrepreneurial security has been theorized in relation to capitalistic entrepreneurship. Easterbrook provided a definition as early as 1949: 'The first and most obvious manifestation of security I shall label 'entrepreneurial security,' this referring to the freedom of the businessman to take 'the ordinary and legitimate risks of doing business' or what the late Henry C. Simons described as 'risks of investing in the wrong places – risks of demand changes, of technical obsolescence in plant facilities, and of guessing badly only because too many others guessed the same way.' (Easterbrook, 1949: 328). However, it is unclear how 'entrepreneurial security' can be conceptualized today, as we see the proliferation of security-seeking through the caring and friendly endeavors of 'social entrepreneurship'.

This reinvestment in social security in the form of social entrepreneurship can be linked to a general shift in how contemporary neoliberal societies are sought to be governed. Neoliberalism has not only thrived on entrepreneurship as we usually discuss it – in economic terms – but has also operationalized population management through individualist and flexible approaches to shape an entrepreneurial citizen. This exemplifies the traditional liberal quest: to regularize the circulation of freedom.

The biopolitical focus on regularizing circulation and aleatory aspects of life at an aggregate level was optimized by strategies and technologies that spurred subjectification and self-regulation (Foucault, 1979/2010). As Foucault clarified in the 'Society must be defended' lectures (Foucault, 1997/2004: 246), liberal modernity targeted 'the population', and specifically biological accounts of life, in relation to security. Here, he outlines the shift in security discourse: from the sovereign power to kill and make live, to the biopolitics of make live and let die. War, previously understood as something fought at territorial borders, can in these lectures be understood as something fought through political means within and beyond borders. The population, as statistical categories that inhabit a territory, became the reference object of this liberal government where certain life and ways of living were to be fostered and produced.

Hence, from the eighteenth century, global liberal governance has been spread through a will to examine 'the detailed properties and dynamics of populations so that they can be better managed with respect to their many needs and life chances' (Dillon & Reid, 2001: 41). Population management, biopolitics, unfolds through the way in which the biological body *en masse* is explored as a productive force which can be optimized for more than economic reasons, such as the right type of reproduction and opening up for refinement of the species, whereby those elements of life that posed a threat to life were to be eliminated. Not only are biological and environmental threats to the human species targeted, but those ways of life that do not fit the vital norms that arise are to be effectively intruded upon. That is, while seeking to protect future life, '[c]ertain lives may have to be abandoned, damaged or destroyed in order to protect, save or care for life' (Anderson, 2010: 780). It thus became important to work on the optimization of one's own self-protection in order to ensure an optimization of the vitality of the population.

Biopolitics has thus been perceived as producing life with racial effects – 'biopolitics is the pursuit of war by other means' (Dillon & Reid, 2001: 42). Biopolitics grew as a positive way of supporting certain life whilst eliminating other, to handle the circulation of freedom, chance and uncertainties, and thus defend society from itself. This also implies that 'almost all of the Foucault-informed scholarship within areas of sociology, neglects [is] the role of the military dimension of society in Foucault's analysis of liberal regimes' (Reid, 2006: 21). For example, the logistics of individuals became an important preoccupation of liberal regimes in their effort to regularize circulation and aleatory aspects of life (ibid).

Furthermore, liberal security was formed through freedom as a technology of power, where the security apparatus can only operate well under the 'condition that it is given freedom, in the modern sense that [the word] acquired in the eighteenth century: no longer the exemptions and privileges attached to a person, but the possibility of movement, change of place, and processes of circulation of both people and things' (Foucault, 1977–78/2007: 48–49). Government became questionable as 'Why should one govern?' (Foucault, 1979/1997: 74f).

Facilitation of self-government is thus crucial within the liberal form of social regulation that human biopolitics supports (e.g. see Lemke, 2011: 34).

Social entrepreneurship 61

Nowadays, the question of how one shapes one's life or oneself is often linked to some expertise and a liberal governmental rationality that seeks to work through the choices of individuals and groups (Dean, 2013). Individuals are not only formed into choosing, consuming citizens, but introduced to entrepreneurial ways of life, even in the education of preschoolers (Berglund, 2012). As has been richly illustrated, former publicly organized social welfare has been exposed to the logic of private sector competition, calling for subjects to be 'free' but 'responsibilized' in a certain way (Rose, 1996).

Whilst violent exercising of sovereign power had led to resistance, the launch of a politics productive of life through 'friendly' life-supportive mechanisms also eluded potential internal resistance to sovereign power. People were targeted for inclusion in the governing procedures in seemingly non-oppressive ways, invited to become competent participants to address themselves as solutions to various problems. This was done first and foremost to foster certain capabilities, or elements, assumed to be 'within themselves', and let others die.

One widely promoted capability of individuals in liberal modernity is responsibility. Power relations changed as a result of the way in which promotion of freedom was coupled to a dissemination of responsibility where the promotion of freedom exemplifies a liberal technology of governing at a distance (Barry et al., 1996b; Rose, 1999; Miller & Rose, 2008), and various entities, such as the family, community, NGO, hospital and workplace, are formed to 'govern without governing "society"' to secure security in a variation of ways' (Lentzos & Rose, 2009: 233). Making subjects prone to secure themselves includes, the authors argue, a mobilization of subjectivities of doubt and anxiety, through which preparedness and preemption can be conjured. For example, resilience is pointed out as being a logic that aims to meet disturbances wrought by complex worlds, to 'live freely and with confidence in a world of potential risk' (Lentzos & Rose, 2009: 243).

This emphasis on how to live well in insecurities resembles Reid's (2012) derivation of how security issues have been remoulded with ecological reason to form a resilient subject (also see Evans & Reid, 2013). It is a subject that must bear disaster on its own shoulders as a requirement for reaching future prosperity. 'The human here is conceived as resilient in so far as it adapts to rather than resists the conditions of its suffering in the world. To be resilient is to forego the very power of resistance' (Reid, 2012:76). Consequently, the resilient subject is attuned to support the rule to which it is subjected.

The shift from security to resilience has been genealogically elaborated on in the case of liberal 19th-century development doctrine and the recent shift into sustainable development (Duffield, 2007). Duffield explains how sustainable development promotes people, and not the state, to support life. Consequently, sustainable development exemplifies a neoliberal political agenda that reconfigures the population 'in risk management terms as social entrepreneurs or active citizens' (Duffield, 2007: 69). In the case of development interventions in countries termed underdeveloped, he shows how enabling choices and opportunities are created for such entrepreneurial selves, so that they may improve their individual and collective self-reliance. Duffield derives that sustainable development requires that 'people abandon the idea of state-led modernization strategies and practice' (Reid, 2013: 357). Self-reliant communities are formed, wherein the poor are expected to change behaviours and attitudes to continue life 'within their own powers of self-reliance' (Duffield, 2007: 68). The colonial debt is here formulated in terms of a shift from ruling to helping, advising, and empowering, effectively operationalized through the NGO sector (cf. Karim, 2008). The NGO movement has also expanded, and with it the biopolitics that it exercises (Duffield, 2007: 56).

In comparison, the already 'developed' subject in advanced liberal democracies may be offered alternative ways to bear insecurities and become self-reliant. In such a context, social entrepreneurship can potentially function as a security technology that addresses the relationship between the active citizen and the outspoken criticism of the prevailing neoliberal economic crisis. That is to say, the active self-regulating citizen, already shaped and empowered in social liberal democracies, may be expanded and reinvested in through the deployment of social entrepreneurship policies, education, and ventures. Through these, we may be offered alternatives to capitalist entrepreneurship that also respond to the withdrawal of state security. It is a response to crisis that offers citizens the opportunity to adjust their expectations by embracing social entrepreneurship as a way to constantly work on their own capability to self-secure, collectively or individually.

Social entrepreneurship is thus a new way for neoliberal regimes to problematize the balance between freedom and security, at the same time as it fulfils the ambitions of neoliberal states to face insecurities indirectly and flexibly. Hence, social entrepreneurship can be analysed in relation to how it functions as a security technology which mainly targets marginalized and/or potentially 'dangerous' populations, or those elements identified 'within individuals' as threatening. This politics of social entrepreneurship will be further explored with help of the three cases.

Cases of social entrepreneurship

This section presents an analysis of the three examples of social entrepreneurship – CRIS, the Unquenchable Souls, and Neem – with the focus on how social entrepreneurship functions as a 'security technology'. All three examples build on previous ethnographic studies. Two of the examples, the Unquenchable Souls and Neem, have been studied by one of the authors. The Unquenchable Souls were primarily followed in 2009, when observations, interviews, and focus group interviews took place. Neem has been followed over a longer period, from its emergence in 2002 through to 2008 (Berglund, 2007/2012, 2008). The CHF example was conducted by Malin Gawell (2012) during the period 2009–2011. In addition to Gawell's work on CHF and CRIS, we have adopted an ethnographic approach through which we were able to make use of stories, movies, and discussions of and by participants in CHF, on different websites in general and on YouTube in particular (cf. Murthy, 2008).

Stoned Unquenchable Souls

A forerunner to the growing institutional support to teachers and students in forming their entrepreneurial selves through education programmes is 'Health and Leadership' in Sunne, Sweden. In this programme, the teachers had the opportunity to freely frame an entrepreneurial approach, with regard to both content and overall structure. This resulted in widespread recognition and they were invited by the Swedish Agency for Economic and Regional Growth to write a book about their educational approach. According to a government official, this book, *Så tänds eldsjälar* [So Are Enthusiastic Souls Lit], written by two of the teachers, Westlund & Westlund (2007), became a bestseller and was referred to as an example of best practice in entrepreneurship education.

In the book, Westlund & Westlund explain how they became motivated to engage in entrepreneurship education, to counter the problem they call 'learned helplessness'. They define this as a state in which young people become imprisoned in the educational system, making it difficult for them to see how their actions have consequences not only for their own lives, but also for society at large. Westlund & Westlund view entrepreneurship education as an 'excellent pedagogical form' (ibid: 18) to combat learned helplessness and to reinvent the connection between the individual and society. This learned helplessness, furthermore, arises when the students meet reality, which they argue in another book is much more complex:

> 'The present and the future are so much more complex and unpredictable than a few decades ago. A lot of people rely on the old principles of security, but these do not work for the generations that are growing up today. Governance, control and classic authoritarian methods only provide educators and students with a false sense of security to lean on for a limited time. Now we need a different starting point, where students are taught to meet new situations and constant change, to find security therein. In this context, the concept of competence is central; to be able to make their knowledge applicable, valuable and useful for the self and others'.
>
> (POS, 2007: 10)

This quote is part of a foreword to a book, written by their very first class of students, called Stoned Unquenchable Souls, published at approximately the same time as *Så tänds eldsjälar*. In this quote, the teachers turn away from classic authoritarian educative methods, since these are assumed to provide a false sense of security in a reality where 'the present and the future are so much more complex and unpredictable'. Hence, they provide their students with a reality full of insecurities, and, consequently, the students need to become adaptable to constant change. From the point of view of the teachers, it is not complexity that brings insecurity, but an inability to handle complexity individually. Sovereign forms of power are thus to be unequivocally abandoned, since that traditional provision of security is the very reason for a self being deprived of any possibility to secure itself. Hence, the teachers pose a very common form of neoliberal criticism of the state and seek a self-reliant individual able to navigate well in the complex waters one takes for granted as determining the world (Evans & Reid, 2013). So what passes unnoticed by the teachers is how they place the teenage girls in a reality where they will perceive themselves as vulnerable, since their misfit qualities do not prepare them to meet an unknown complex future. First they must grasp this vulnerability, given to them by portraying the impossibility of actually being provided with any form of security in today's society, except for the security of self-reliance that entrepreneurship education promises.

The book Stoned Unquenchable Souls aims to tell the students' own stories of how they developed as individuals, and to inspire others to take part in an entrepreneurial education. 'We often felt like curling stones,' they say and describe themselves as 'school-damaged' prior to their experience of participating in this particular entrepreneurship education.

> 'We have been given an experience of what school and learning can be like, that is why we want to give you the same opportunities to get an insight into how we work. Our vision is to contribute to school managers, principals, teachers and decision makers introducing entrepreneurship education early in school'.
>
> (POS, 2007:15)

From an analytical point of view, the vulnerability is here turned into some invincible capacities to spread a specific way of thinking to others. They are thus convinced that the traditional school system had destroyed their abilities to become secure. Willingly, they now position themselves in a more correct description of reality, the one that is continuously insecure, to spread the solution to this state of the world: entrepreneurship. Hence, entrepreneurship education is discussed frankly by the teachers and students in chorus as a way to provide society with a real sense of security. However, this belief in contemporary insecurities and the provision of invincible capacities to meet it has been obtained through certain practices, as is vividly illustrated by the students.

The first few weeks of the programme, they explain, were arranged in a way designed to create a definitive break from the traditional school. The students were given their own classroom as a 'home base'. 'Like in first grade,' they comment. This classroom was not to be furnished like traditional classrooms. Instead, the students were told to reorganize the furniture. 'This was not only the first reorganization of the classroom, it was also the beginning of a big reorganization of our lives' (POS, 2007: 14). After the reorganization, they gathered in a circular seating arrangement several times a day to discuss what they were doing, encouraged to share their thoughts and inner experiences.

They had no ordinary schedule to rely on. Basically, everything was turned upside down compared with ordinary school. This, they explain, took them by surprise. They all expected a 'normal' upper-secondary school programme, and none of them had any prior knowledge about health, leadership – or entrepreneurship. The students describe how they found the circle sessions really uncomfortable as they were used to hiding behind an ordinary school desk. The circle soon became a natural part of their daily routine and they used it to get started and to close the day, but also to make presentations, get help with difficulties, and resolve conflicts.

Another challenge was the lack of a schedule. They had to make up their own. They were given the task of planning part of their courses in their first year, and as their education progressed they assumed more and more responsibility and ended up planning the last semester and the exam project entirely on their own. This included contacting organizations to interview, visit, or co-operate with. This is described as a huge step for some students, but as they overcame their fear, so they grew in confidence and began to take charge, the story continues. The students also state that they no longer expect other people – teachers or parents – to make decisions for them. Instead, they have learned to take responsibility for creating their own futures. Moreover, with the help of the education programme and its specific practices follow opportunities for self-narratives that address the transformed and new version of the collective self:

> 'Today, we have an enlarged responsibility field and it has become a natural part of our everyday lives. Now, we are not only responsible for bringing the right clothes for sports lessons, but for everything we do. Because we have our own business, this means that we must take a lot of responsibility for economic aspects, keeping deadlines, and for taking important decisions. We do not want things served up any longer, but like to help ourselves and take responsibility for our own jobs and ourselves. This also means that we have matured tremendously during the time of this programme, which is positive. For us, taking responsibility means that we can take the initiative and decisions, in particular concerning ourselves. Responsibility also means that we can use the time more effectively, which we have become much better at'.
>
> (POS, 2007: 28)

The self-narrative exemplifies the constitution of a subject responsible for its own future, in relation to both economic prosperity and logistical efficiency for overall productivity. It resembles other entrepreneurship programmes in the way in which young people are encouraged to be creative, take their own initiatives, look for opportunities, and have a positive outlook on life (e.g. Berglund & Holmgren, 2007). To accomplish this, entrepreneurial educational tools are often offered to entice young people to take part in enterprising activities in a playful way. This is in line with research where the playing human – *homo ludens* – has been proposed as an archetype of the entrepreneur (e.g. Hjorth, 2004; Johannisson, 2010). It also aligns very well with contemporary pedagogical expertise on 'the competent child'. This child is given the opportunity, sometimes even obliged, to become an active participant and raise its voice to engage in various political issues (Skoglund & Börjesson, 2014).

CRIS – transform and have your revenge

'Criminals Return Into Society' (CRIS) is an association started by criminals and/or drug addicts for criminals and/or drug addicts. The main target group is people recently released from prison, who are provided with a network that can help them to start a new life. In the direct translation from Swedish, the name CRIS in fact stands for 'criminals' revenge on society'.

Between 2009 and 2011, Gawell studied CRIS and its initiative Creative Honest Entrepreneurs (CHE) – an entrepreneurship training programme carried out by and for former criminals and/or drug abusers (www.kris.a.se). The training programme was launched as a solution to the difficulties former criminals met when trying to find an honest way to make a living, and aims primarily to deliver tangible benefits for society through providing skills development, along with social enterprise and entrepreneurship education, to participants who have a hard time in the labor market. It is claimed that CHE gave ex-criminals the space to develop skills so they could function as motivators and enthusiasts, and disseminate their knowledge regarding entrepreneurship to social groups in need of empowerment (Gawell, 2011).

With funding from the European Social Fund, CHE was set up to offer CRIS members 'personal development training' linked to entrepreneurship training. The CHE programme was quite extensive and gathered people from local branches for one week per month for a whole year. Gawell explains (2011, 2012a) that in order to transform oneself and become an ex-criminal, innovation had to occur on a personal level. In a YouTube clip, three of the leaders involved in CHE reflect on the programme and what it has meant for them and for the participants after a year of activities. They discuss the fact that CHE is about more than accounting and must be put in a broader societal perspective where ex-criminals have been engaged in giving a deeper meaning to the notions of trust, honesty, and entrepreneurship. They also agree that CHE is mainly about personal development:

> 'Today, I see Creative Honest Entrepreneurs more like a human development project that is about creating energetic people through entrepreneurship – or to empower these people to become entrepreneurs to take command of their lives. Entrepreneurship does not necessarily only mean starting new businesses, it also means taking responsibility for the situation you are in. For how to live'.
>
> (KRIS at Youtube, 2011a)

The organization thus profiled decisiveness as a quality you had to acquire, since a long journey with yourself was to be expected. Several YouTube movie clips also describe how they engaged in dramas and scenarios where the ex-criminals could express their feelings and get to know themselves in new ways. Humor and laughter is often mixed with serious matters such as trust and honesty. One example is a sequence where a lecture on accounting is interrupted by a false robbery. The participants express this mix of feelings as a means to

Social entrepreneurship 67

open up for talking about their former experiences and move forward. The following quote is from a YouTube movie clip by one of the participants who talks about her experiences with CHE. The movie opens with her saying, 'I can see how much I'm worth, I couldn't do that before.' She then continues:

> 'Here at CHF we learn to communicate. We learn a lot about our emotions and reactions and how that affects some of our behavior. For my part this . . . education here is really nice because I [laughs] feel stronger as a person. I can look at my work now and see that it is worth something . . .'

(KRIS at Youtube, 2011a)

In another film clip, two men talk about the process simulation exercise of starting up a new rehabilitation home. One of them describes how he was obsessed by thoughts of escaping during the first week. His only thought was how to get out. 'But,' he continues, 'I decided to stay and now I can see that I developed enormously. I was terrified to start with, but when I was in the middle of it, I enjoyed it to the full. My first thought was that I would never manage this, but with hindsight, we solved it really well. And I have found peace with myself' (KRIS at Youtube, 2011a).

This decisive relationship with yourself was also to be extended to other groups in society, as well as the family, Gawell (2011: 28–29) explains that the aim of the project is to manage to reach a durable position where it is not only possible to help oneself but also to help others. Helping oneself through helping others can indeed be achieved through practicing entrepreneurship, Peter Söderlund, an ex-criminal, maintains in an interview in the Swedish magazine *Manager*. The article tells the story of Peter, his 'colorful past', and his 'entrepreneurial journey through life'. It describes how he started drinking alcohol when he was 10 years old, how at 13 he took hashish, and how at the age of 18 he started his own business. After that he went down a criminal path, lined with robberies and thefts. At 47 he is no longer a criminal, but an ex-criminal working as a national coordinator of CRIS and also as project leader at a furniture company that employs ex-criminals. He explains how important, yet difficult, it can be for people who have lived with crime and drugs for a long time to break with the norm of being 'a criminal'—but also how, if offered a chance to develop, they can move on, either through self-employment or through employment. 'I wish that more companies supported the voluntary sector much more,' he says and continues:

> 'As long as you are a criminal the government invests a lot of money, for example in prison and rehabilitation. But when criminals quit, the state does not support that process. We figured that we must build our own system. We wanted to create a product that can provide employment for ex-criminals. Once they have found work they can then reintegrate into society. We found a gap in the outdoor furniture market. There was no strong brand, so we decided to go for it. . . . Behind the companies there

68   *Karin Berglund and Annika Skoglund*

are people. Behind humans there are problems. Through helping others you get more insight into the problem. Besides, the state cannot prevent addiction and crime. We can see that clearly. This means that companies need to help out. If companies employ ex-criminals, they also help to reduce crime in their own neighborhood'.

(Chef, 2008)

Crime prevention has been widely studied as an example of neoliberal government in 'risk society' (e.g. see O'Malley & Hutchinson, 2007). Here, civil society became increasingly important for crime control through mundane ways of making people conform to orderly behaviour, i.e. not disciplining, but 'regulating mass distributions and flows', similar to designs of urban security (O'Malley & Hutchinson, 2007: 373). However, CRIS targets the newly released criminals 'at risk' directly, to work on their future free circulation among more 'normal' social elements. A presumed relapse into crime and drug abuse will not only be overcome by reaching for the creativity and the taken-for-granted 'entrepreneurial spirit' within the criminal; it will also be achieved through the creation of personal networks and new moral attachments. The desired transformation of the criminal 'at risk' is linked to an obligation to work hard on, and reform, relationships with others, specifically relatives and the family. CRIS emphasizes that a readjustment needs decisive work with oneself in relation to those social elements that can provide stability. Even if drug abuse is strictly forbidden in disciplining terminologies, general aberration is to be erased by reaching out for more secure behaviours found in non-criminogenic sites. We can see this positive embracement of the self-securing individual in another section found on their website:

'CRIS mainly looks upon a human being positively. All humans have an inner force and an ability to change their life for the better. It is important to point out that you and nobody but you is responsible for your own life, but that we also have a responsibility towards one another. We are not interested in what people have done in their past but what they can do with their future!'

(KRIS, 2013)

The talk about responsibility is, of course, very familiar in the neoliberal era. The price of freedom to circulate is, as a matter of speaking, responsibility. The positive approach to an essentialist definition of an 'inner force' also tells us that the reference object of security is the individual in the network. 'Nobody but you' is responsible 'for your own life' reduces the question of security to a question of fostering self-reliance. Furthermore, being diligent regarding self-security and volunteer subjectification to self-reliance may lead to class transition, as CRIS continues:

'We won't settle for the fact that drug addicts are viewed as second-class citizens. Our goal is to make everyone free, independent, and full good members of society. We claim that this is possible to achieve and this is something we wish should happen to all drug addicts!'

(KRIS, 2013)

CRIS exemplifies well what Gawell (2012a: 1) proposes, namely that social enterprises use 'different methods of empowerment [. . .] to strengthen individuals that many times are both unemployed and troubled by some kind of mental and/or social impairment, former drug abuse and/or criminals.' However, she does not explore the transformation of the criminals in relation to security; how a transformation of the unfavorable into the more favorable is accomplished by membership of CRIS and an extended network, where those classified as risky individuals are taught to apply themselves as a solution to the problem of criminality. CRIS seeks to shape the risky individuals into more non-threatening elements, to erase the phenomenon of criminality by erasing the criminal subject. Those who deviate from normality are thus normalized through the application of 'social' entrepreneurship as a way to regularize the free circulation of ex-criminals.

Microcredit – a way to integration

The NGO Network of Entrepreneurs from Ethnic Minorities (Neem) was established in 2002, as a result of the European Union project Diversity in Entrepreneurship (DiE). DiE was a project within the Equal programme and aimed at changing discrimination and exclusion in relation to the labor market. DiE described itself as wanting to change the old business support system to create recognition for specific target groups, namely immigrant women, disabled people, young people, and cultural workers. 'The experts', as the team leaders in DiE often point out, were 'not the advisers in the system, but the participants themselves' (field notes, 30 September 2002). Furthermore, the target groups were called 'mobilizing groups', and the aim was to make them mobilize their entrepreneurial capabilities. Mobilization was described as a process that preceded entrepreneurial activity, such as starting a business, and aimed at discussing, highlighting, and evaluating the participants' experiences and knowledge (Berglund, 2007/2012: 249). By constructing this as an unfolding process, and situating the participants within it, it was assumed that business and entrepreneurship would automatically follow as the next step. Entrepreneurship and its correlating entrepreneurs were thus to be processed.

Women from ethnic minorities were one of four groups recognized as invisible entrepreneurs; in other words, they had been largely neglected by the business promotion structure but could be enlightened about their hidden entrepreneurial capacities. At the start of the project, however, the women did not see themselves as being in need of any help to accomplish entrepreneurship. They responded to the programme with surprise and resistance and were unable to understand why they should be involved in an entrepreneurship project: 'I don't understand why I should be part of this – an entrepreneurship project? What I need is a job!' (field notes, 28 November 2002). At this point they expressed faith in 'the welfare system' and how they expected to be treated as equals by the Swedish labor market. Many testified to how they had both education and experience but had been directed to different labor market measures that seldom resulted in employment, but rather in a step back to square one as unemployed and reliant on benefits. The coordinator, who had been working with several immigrant projects, was struck by how immigrant women in particular were subjected to specific measures and occupations, such as sewing projects or working in health care or with child care. 'It's high time that we begin to ask what the women want instead of telling them what to do' (field notes, 17 January 2003).

The dissatisfaction with a malfunctioning social welfare system also spurred the women's interest in entrepreneurship since it was portrayed as the means to pave the way for changing their situation. A passionate team leader, herself an immigrant woman with a background in entrepreneurship from Tanzania, took time to listen to the women's frustration at a dysfunctional system and succeeded to slowly turn around their resistance. She appealed to the solidarity of being an immigrant woman and reminded the participants about what could be achieved if they acted together. Her main arguments were centred around resistance towards the male hegemonic entrepreneurial norms, effectiveness of microcredits, and the inner power to be released within women. The patriarchal, male-dominated, and discriminating business support system was also criticized in the DiE project.

A growing number of women also became interested and started to attend the meetings, where they were taught more about entrepreneurship, including that it did not require any extraordinary strength, but that it was mainly about simply having an idea. 'I did not know that entrepreneurship could be something so simple! I realized that everyone has an idea that can be realized' (field notes, 5 September 2003). As entrepreneurship was opened up and not just portrayed as a heroic exercise, it could also be communicated to the immigrant women in a less rigid form; as doing something with one's life, or the commercialization of a simple idea. This, it was believed, would have a more direct appeal to the women. In line with this, the women also started to formulate business ideas and took a more positive stance towards entrepreneurship. However, several practices had to be launched to facilitate the process. Specifically, they were helped to realize their ideas through the launch of events such as bazaars and market places. These staged particular themes – often to promote handicraft products and the offering of food from the countries where the women originated. Moreover, creative workshops were organized where the women were trained to support each other, conferences were staged for them to visualize and sell their ideas, and cooperation took place with an international women's network to spread, support, and share their entrepreneurial spirit.

The initial resistance was now overcome and the women took it into their own hands to set up a new support system by establishing Neem, an NGO that persisted in working with finding innovative solutions for integration and social change, focusing in particular on women with an international background

Social entrepreneurship 71

who were categorized as inactive. 'We want to highlight these women's skills and entrepreneurial drive,' it states on their website (www.neem.se). A part of supporting this group's entrepreneurship was that they recognized that their members did not have a financial buffer, but often had an income that for the most part consisted of public allowances. For this reason, problems arose when they went to present their business ideas to the bank, as they were not seen as creditworthy. They were even termed non-bankable subjects (Berglund & Johansson, 2007). As early as in the initial discussion in DiE in 2002, micro-credit was formulated as a promising solution. Six years later, in 2008, Neem took a lead in launching the first Micro Finance Institute (MFI) in Sweden to support their members, aiming to extend financial services for start-ups or developing companies for those groups, particularly immigrant women, who had no access to finances in the process: from idea to business.

The women in Neem soon got to know each other well and supported, indeed mobilized, each other in their entrepreneurial processes, in meetings with suppliers, customers, and other stakeholders and in everyday life, with all that it entailed. Friendly support was given when it was needed and views were shared on how to mobilize oneself in more efficient ways. These discussions could also revolve around how the women related to their entrepreneurial project and in balance with domestic tasks and family obligations. Usually the women corrected each other if the responsibilities for the household intruded too much on the entrepreneurial process. When someone did not show up to a meeting, or if someone had a problem with household chores or a controlling husband, some women got together to visit the woman 'in need'. The women began to discuss how they could mobilize their husbands to believe more in themselves – and in their wives. Hence, instead of having the entrepreneurial process disrupted by disinterested husbands, they were to be processed in tandem. As is testified during a meeting when a woman shares how she has mobilized her husband: 'Everything does not have to be safe! In the past, he wanted to have the family budget secured a year ahead. He does not dare to take risks, or take a chance . . . but now he does!' Another woman then replied: 'My husband was the same,' and the third one reflected how 'the men should loosen up a little more, go their own way and just try it out!' (focus group interview, September 2007). Tellingly, the patriarchal sovereign form of security is here downgraded in favor of risk taking as part of how entrepreneurship should be processed into being.

By establishing new close friends and less resistant men, the women were to make something out of their own lives through corrections, complaints, suggestions, and hands-on help. These exercises of governing – one's self and others in conjunction – were increasingly apparent as the process progressed. This transformation of the 'social' well resembles the Bangladeshi context, the origin of microcredits (Karim, 2008), where women lenders who failed to make repayments to their group received questions such as: Why did you eat chicken yesterday? Why did you send your son to see a movie? Why did you buy new clothes? Why are you arranging the wedding for your daughter? (Fernando, 1997: 171). These kinds of questions use shaming as an instrument of social

72 *Karin Berglund and Annika Skoglund*

control among the poor, and in particular among poor women (Karim, 2008). Local norms of cohesion and community are violated in the furtherance of the capitalist goals of microcredits (ibid., p. 6). In comparison with Bangladesh, the ability to create equal relationships and improve oneself and others as entrepreneurs was governed in the Swedish context, whilst the economically responsible housewife was governed in the Bangladeshi context. Hence, entrepreneurship processes introduce governing of the self and others, albeit in different ways. Moreover, empowerment processes increased the exertion of control by husbands or men close to the women in both contexts. Violence in the household also appears to be an unexpected, and often unspoken, effect of women's empowerment (cf. Fernando, 1997: 163).

By taking the offer to exclude themselves from the social welfare system seriously, the immigrant women now seem to have fulfilled a general aim found within Western development policy that targets non-Western subjects: to form self-reliant communities (Duffield, 2007: 18). However, since Neem seems to deploy a development strategy and situate it in a Swedish context, instead of bringing it into the developing world, the differences with other microcredit initiatives also surface. The social intervention, i.e. the social goals to be met by the formation of this specific community, has in our case come much further in a 'Westernization' of the family relations. The aim to bring basic needs, such as sewing and cooking, into an entrepreneurial process, so as to make the immigrant women into economic subjects, continues with work on the husband and his inability to acknowledge the new neoliberal life of his woman, who now belongs to 'social' entrepreneurship.

As many of the success stories in relation to Neem and the new microcredit systems in Sweden show, Neem succeeds in transferring the immigrant woman from the place of discrimination in a malfunctioning welfare system to a place which provides 'happiness' through microcredit funding and running your own company. Again, it is assumed to be impossible to provide security through some sort of sovereign provision of help. Instead, Neem is expanding and now, after ten years of operations, it continues to work with mobilization, coaching, and follow-up of the entrepreneurs' businesses as well as provisions of social performance management.

Conclusions

In this chapter, we have shown how social entrepreneurship unfolds as a security technology, launched to target both the individual citizen and communities in relation to prevailing insecurities. Looking at social entrepreneurship as a 'security technology' calls for a new understanding of entrepreneurial security that Easterbrook, in 1949, saw as the freedom of the businessman to take risks (Easterbrook, 1949). In contrast, the social entrepreneur is to practice her or his freedom by embracing insecurities and engaging in traditional governmental problems. Entrepreneurial security is thus offered to us as the natural way to form self-confidence through a continuous exploration of new ways to self-secure. The exposure to neoliberal economic crisis and the lack of

Social entrepreneurship   73

state security are regarded by social entrepreneurship (proponents) as positive for the constitution of new 'social' opportunities. The three examples in this chapter demonstrate clearly the flexibility with which social entrepreneurship initiatives respond to crisis and unwanted elements, whether within the targeted individuals or in their communities. Through their engagement with entrepreneurial opportunities, the social is continuously secured in various innovative ways.

At the same time as the social entrepreneur is called on to solve previous governmental problems, she or he responds to the criticism of capitalistic entrepreneurship. To be prosperous as a social entrepreneur is to succeed in taking upon oneself the responsibility to establish security for others. 'Entrepreneurial security' is to be executed through friendly and caring forms of endeavors that link the private and the social, through these new 'welfare' providers. Security, in this sense, is not to be provided by the state, but by how the students, ex-criminals, and ethnic minorities ensure that others are encouraged to accept insecurities, take action, and change their behaviour.

The target groups that the social entrepreneur addresses are governed at the same time as the social entrepreneur governs him/herself through a conviction that an entrepreneur should possess different qualities in comparison to a capitalist. The social entrepreneur is, for example, construed as more vigilant in adapting to disturbances and as better able at prospering in the taken-for-granted, complex world we now live in. The subject who is shaped through social entrepreneurship thus has some resemblance to the resilient subject illustrated by Reid (2012), as it is taught to accept insecurities instead of resisting this condition. Hence, social entrepreneurship alters the apparatus of security by how it wages a war on those forms of subjectivity that turn to the state and ask for security.

As exemplified, various practices were provided to stimulate individuals to turn to themselves for help. They were, in all cases, activated to help each other to become more socially enterprising. With the aid of specific techniques and ideas on how to live well, the targeted subjects were to be transferred from one place to another. First, we had the unwanted place of criminality; second, the ridiculed place of those damaged by school; and third, the abandoned place for ethnic discrimination.

The transfer to a new place, not determined by crime, was never really completed in the case of CRIS. The ex-criminals were presumed to be vulnerable to a relapse into crime and had to carry around a virtual imprisonment, pretending that the fence and restrictions were somehow still attendant. This included the categorization of them as ex-criminals, keeping in mind that the 'ex' before 'criminal' is an utterly precarious condition. The new place is, it could be said, only accessible in the form of a negative connotation of ex-criminality. Social entrepreneurship, therefore, could only partly provide a solution to the security problem that arose as newly released criminals were to be treated as freely circulating social entities.

Turning to the teenage girls, their collective self-narrative illustrated how they leave the place of traditional education and reach a place inside themselves, the stoned unquenchable soul. This place, it was assumed, would bring

74 *Karin Berglund and Annika Skoglund*

real security. However, it was a form of security that needed constant adjustments to fit a changing world. To live processually and follow the complexities of the world thus demands a subject attuned to resilience.

In the case of the women from ethnic minorities, these were to be transferred from discrimination to a place of non-discrimination. Social entrepreneurship did, here, unfold as a new community consisting of tight friendships. This new place, however, only transferred the women away from a faith in Swedish social security to a place filled with neoliberal development doctrine. The idea of microcredits was implemented to create community-based self-reliance, to refine entrepreneurship arising from basic needs to remould these women into economic and responsible subjects. In extension, this made their domestic situation increasingly insecure, since they had to fight patriarchal security wishes as they became obliged to include a transfer of their husbands into a more modern place.

Consequently, the place of the honest and drug-free, the unquenchable, and the non-discriminated female immigrant entrepreneur are places where you constantly need to work on yourself so as not to fall back on a more sovereign form of security. These examples of social entrepreneurship wage a war both on the self and on others, to eliminate those elements of life that are not apt to freely circulate as active participants in social entrepreneurship.

To summarize, in this chapter we have linked the spread of new forms of entrepreneurships – in particular social entrepreneurships – to neoliberal ways of life. We thus view social entrepreneurship as a security technology through which the neoliberal citizen is to embrace insecurities and engage in traditional governmental problems. This reproduces the neoliberal order and its correlating citizen, an ideal of citizenship that today not only endures in complexity but is taught to enjoy the struggles it must experience in complexity. Social entrepreneurship facilitates this contemporary form of power over life and has now altered security by implementation of 'social entrepreneurship' as a way to reach ex-criminals as material for empowerment, construe self-reliant communities to contain ethnic minorities within Western civilization, and produce invincible capacities among teenagers, all of which are devoted to spreading the entrepreneurial way of life further.

From our discussions in this chapter, we hope that social entrepreneurship can be critically assessed regarding its diverse effects. Instead of taking social entrepreneurship for granted, this chapter opens up for new avenues of research that may delve further into issues of how a dissemination of entrepreneurships may reinstall the inequality, injustice, and social exclusion which it attempts to remedy. Research on social entrepreneurship usually points to its benefits, rather than to what its assumed benefits may mean politically. Paying attention not only to the emphasis on the economic in neoliberal societies, but also to how entrepreneurial security arises as a way to govern us paves the way for a more critically informed research. Thereby, we, as entrepreneurship researchers, may lead the way towards less introspective tendencies and provide theoretical contributions that are of interest for a broader audience within the social and political sciences.

References

Anderson, A. (2013). *The Economic Reification of Entrepreneurship: Reviving the Social*. Paper presented at Babson Pre-Conference Event "Enacting Entrepreneurship out of the Box," 4 June 2013.

Anderson, B. (2010). Preemption, precaution, preparedness: Anticipatory action and future geographies. *Progress in Human Geography*, 34(6): 777–798.

Austin, J., Stevenson, H., & Wei-Skillern, J. (2006). Social and commercial entrepreneurship: Same, different, or both? *Entrepreneurship Theory and Practice*, 30(1): 1–22.

Barry, A., Osborne, T., & Rose, N. (1996a). Introduction. In A. Barry, T. Osborne, & N. Rose (eds.), *Foucault and Political Reason*. London: UCL Press Ltd.

Barry, A., Osborne, T., & Rose, N. (eds.) (1996b). *Foucault and Political Reason*. London: UCL Press Ltd.

Berglund, K. (2007/2012). *Jakten på Entreprenörer – om öppningar och låsningar i Entreprenörskapsdiskursen* [The hunt for Entrepreneurs – on openings and closures in the entrepreneurship discourse]. Stockholm: Santérus Academic Press.

Berglund K. (2008). Mikrokrediter! – Ett sätt att mobilisera kvinnors entreprenörskap? In K. Berglund & A. W. Johansson (eds.), *Arenor för Entreprenörskap*. Örebro: FSF Förlag.

Berglund, K. (2012). Friends, feelings, and fantasy: The entrepreneurial approach as conceptualized by preschool teachers, In K. Berglund, B. Johannisson, & B. Schwartz, (eds.), *Societal entrepreneurship: Positioning, Penetrating, Promoting* (pp. 191–213). Cheltenham: Edward Elgar.

Berglund, K. & Holmgren, C. (2007). *Entreprenörskap and Skolan – Vad berättar lärare att de gör lärare när de gör entreprenörskap i skolan?* [Entrepreneurship and School – What do teacher say they do when they do entrepreneurship in school?]. Örebro: FSF Förlag.

Berglund, K. & Holmgren, C. (2013). Entrepreneurship education in policy and practice – On tensions and conflicts in processes of implementing entrepreneurship education. *International Journal of Entrepreneurial Venturing*, 5(1), 9–27.

Berglund, K. & Johansson, A. W. (2007). Entrepreneurship, discourses and conscientization in processes of regional development. *Entrepreneurship and Regional Development*, 19(6): 499–525.

Berglund, K., Johannisson, B., & Schwartz, B. (eds.) (2012). *Societal Entrepreneurship: Positioning, Penetrating, Promoting*. Cheltenham, UK: Edward Elgar.

Chef (2008) Man måste öppna armarna [You need to open your arms]. http://chef.se/kicken-aer-att-se-maenniskor-resa-sig [accessed 4-20-2014].

Dacin, P. A., Dacin, M. T., & Matear, M. (2010). Social Entrepreneurship: Why we don't need a new theory and how we move forward from here. *Academy of Management Perspectives*, 24(3): 37–57.

Dean, M. (2013). *The Signature of Power: Sovereignty, Governmentality and Biopolitics*. London: Sage.

Dempsey, S. E. & Sanders, M. L. (2010), Meaningful work? Nonprofit marketization and work/life imbalance in popular autobiographies of social entrepreneurship. *Organization*, 17: 437.

Dillon, M. & Reid, J. (2001). Global liberal governance: Biopolitics, security and war. *Millennium – Journal of International Studies*, 30(1): 41–66.

Duffield, M. (2007). *Development, Security and Unending War, Governing the World of Peoples*. Cambridge: Polity Press.

Easterbrook, W. T. (1949). Possibilities for a realistic theory of entrepreneurship – the climate of enterprise. *American Economic Review*, 39(3): 322–335.

76   Karin Berglund and Annika Skoglund

Ebner, A. (2005). Entrepreneurship and economic development: From classical political economy to economic sociology. *Journal of Economic Studies*, 32(3): 256–274.

Eikenberry, A. M. & Kluver, J. D. (2004). The marketization of the nonprofit sector: Civil society at risk? *Public Administration Review*, 64(2): 132–140.

Evans, B. & Reid, J. (2013). Dangerously exposed: The life and death of the resilient subject. *Resilience: International Policies, Practices and Discourses*, 1(2): 83–98.

Fernando, J. L. (1997). Nongovernmental organizations, micro-credit, and empowerment of women. *Annals of the American Academy of Political and Social Science*, 554: 150–177.

Foucault, M. (1979/1997). The birth of biopolitics. In P. Rabinow (ed.), *Michel Foucault, Ethics Subjectivity and Truth, Essential Works of Michel Foucault 1954–1984* (pp. 73–79). New York: The New Press.

Foucault, M. (1997/2004). *Society Must Be Defended*. London: Penguin.

Foucault, M. (1977–78/2007). *Security, Territory, Population*. New York: Palgrave Macmillan.

Foucault, M. (1979/2010). *The Birth of Biopolitics* (G. Burchell, Trans.) Hampshire: Palgrave Macmillan.

Gawell, M. (2011). Inte vilket entreprenörskap och företagande som helst: en fältstudie av 7 projekt med finansiering från Europeiska socialfonden[Not any entrepreneurship or business: a field study of seven projects funded by the European Social Fund Stockholm: Swedish Agency for Economic and Regional Growth.]

Gawell, M. (2012a). *Emerging Markets and Policies for Social Entrepreneurship*. http://sernoc. ruc.dk/wp-content/uploads/2011/11/Gawell_M_2-EmergingSE-market-and-pol.pdf

Gawell, M. (2012b). *Social Entrepreneurship – Action Grounded in Needs, Opportunities and/or Perceived Necessities? VOLUNTAS: International Journal of Voluntary and Nonprofit Organizations*. doi: 10.1007/s11266-012-9301-1.

Hjorth, D. (2004). Creating space for play/invention – concepts of space and organizational entrepreneurship. *Entrepreneurship & Regional Development*, 16(5): 413–432.

Johannisson, B. (2010). In the beginning was entrepreneuring. In F. Bill, B. Bjerke, & A. W. Johansson (eds.), *(De)mobilizing Entrepreneurship: Exploring Entrepreneurial Thinking and Action*. Cheltenham, UK and Northampton, MA: Edward Elgar.

Karim, L. (2008). Demystifying micro-credit: The Grameen bank, NGOs, and neoliberalism in Bangladesh. *Cultural Dynamics*, 20(1): 5–29.

KRIS at Youtube. (2010). Malin about the KHF project, www.youtube.com/watch?v= PTGuVbI-B7U [Accessed 2010-05-02].

KRIS at Youtube. (2011a). Kreativa Hederliga Företagare: Göran Urban och Bengt delar sina intryck och tankar om KHF (1/3) www.youtube.com/watch?v=lmwDemRrfbc [Accessed 2011-08-10].

Kris at Youtube. (2011b). KHF Kreativa Hederliga Företagare: Processimulering Reflektioner 1, www.youtube.com/watch?v=w81R9L8KoU8, [2011-08-18].

KRIS, 2013 KRIS. (2013). Kris [Criminals revenge in society]. http://kris.a.se/in-english/ [Accessed 2013-10-11].

Lemke, T. (2011). *Bio-politics – An Advanced Introduction*. New York and London: New York University Press.

Lentzos, F. & Rose, N. (2009). Governing insecurity: Contingency planning, protection, resilience. *Economy and Society*, 38(2): 230–254.

Mair, J. & Martí, I. (2006). Social entrepreneurship research: A source of explanation, prediction, and delight. *Journal of World Business*, 41: 36–44.

Miller, P. & Rose, N. (2008). *Governing the Present*. Cambridge: Polity Press.

Murthy, D. (2008) Digital ethnography: An examination of the use of new technologies for social research. *Sociology*, 42: 837–855.

Nicholls, A. (2010). The legitimacy of social entrepreneurship: Reflexive isomorphism in a pre-paradigmatic field. *Entrepreneurship theory and practice*, 34(4): 611–633.

O'Malley, P. & Hutchinson, S. (2007). Reinventing prevention – why did 'crime prevention' develop so late? *British Journal of Criminology*, 47(3): 373–389.

POS (2007). *Påtända osläckbara själar* [Stoned Unquenchable Souls] Idéskaparna: Falun Scandbook.

Reid, J. (2006). *The Biopolitics of the War on Terror, Life Struggles, Liberal Modernity, and the Defence of Logistical Societies*. Manchester: Manchester University Press.

Reid, J. (2012). The disastrous and politically debased subject of resilience. *Development Dialogue – The End of the Security-Development Nexus? The Rise of Global Disaster Management*, 58: 67–80 [accessed 2/17/2011].

Reid, J. (2013). Interrogating the neoliberal biopolitics of the sustainable development-resilience nexus. *International Political Sociology*, 7(4): 353–367.

Rose, N.S. (1996). *Inventing Our Selves: Psychology, Power, and Personhood*. New York: Cambridge University Press.

Rose, N. (1999). *Powers of Freedom – Reframing Political Thought*. Cambridge: Cambridge University Press.

Westlund, Marielle & Westlund, Christer (2007). Så tänds eldsjälar: en introduktion till entreprenöriellt lärande. 1. uppl. Stockholm: Verket för näringslivsutveckling (NUTEK).

Påtända Osläckbara Eldsjälar (POS) (2007). [Stoned Unquenchable Souls'].

Shaker A., Zahra, S. A., Gedajlovic, E., Neubaum, D.O., & Shulman, J. M. (2009). A typology of social entrepreneurs: Motives, search processes and ethical challenges. *Journal of Business Venturing*, 24: 519–532.

Skoglund, A. & Börjesson, M. (2014). Mobilizing 'juvenocratic spaces' by the biopoliticization of children through sustainability. *Children's Geographies*, 12(4): 429–446.

Steyaert, C. & Hjorth, D. (eds.) (2006). *Entrepreneurship as Social Change: A Third Movements in Entrepreneurship Book*. Cheltenham: Edward Elgar.

Steyaert, C. & Katz, J. (2004). Reclaiming the space of entrepreneurship in society: Geographical, discursive and social dimensions. *Entrepreneurship & Regional Development*, 16: 179–196.

6 Is international entrepreneurship research a viable spin-off from its parent disciplines?

Nicole E. Coviello, Marian V. Jones, and Patricia P. McDougall-Covin

Introduction

Hambrick and Chen (2008) argue that new academic fields are advanced through the process of differentiation, mobilization, and legitimacy building. They suggest that some of the signals used to establish a field will include the adoption of a 'name' for the field, members refer to it as such, and efforts are made to develop community structures. As observed by Coviello, McDougall, and Oviatt (2011), research in International Entrepreneurship (IE) seems to have followed such a pattern, beginning with early efforts to position itself at the interface of entrepreneurship and international business (IB). Our objectives with this chapter are to: 1) extend aspects of Coviello et al. (2011) and the ontological review of IE by Jones, Coviello, and Tang (2011), and then 2) use this information to assess if IE research is a viable spin-off of its parent disciplines. That is: is it a field? To facilitate this, we assess IE relative to the criteria proposed by Hambrick and Chen (2008: 32) in the model they develop to explain the rise of new academic fields as part of an "admittance-seeking social movement." We begin by discussing the origins and evolution of IE.

The origins of IE research

In the late 1980s, the global economy was experiencing "momentous" change in world political and economic systems, rapid technological development, and "dramatic" advances in IT and organizational methods (Dunning & Lundan, 2008: 739). During that period, researchers around the world began to take notice of small and young firms that were successfully competing globally; competing in ways that were previously unaddressed or inadequately explained by theory in either international business or entrepreneurship.

To the best of our knowledge, the first mention of the phrase 'International Entrepreneurship' is found in a Harvard Business School dissertation by Kohn (1988): *International Entrepreneurship – Foreign Direct Investment by Small US Based Manufacturing Firms*. Also in 1988, Morrow referred to 'the age of the entrepreneur' in discussing the role of technology in dismantling international barriers. The genesis of IE as a potential field, however, was marked with

McDougall's (1989: 387) empirical comparison of domestic and international new ventures (INVs). She defined these as ". . . new ventures or start-ups that, from inception, engage in international business, thus viewing their operating domain as international from the initial stages of the firm's operation." This early work was closely followed by scholars writing about new timing and patterns of international expansion seen in young firms (e.g. Jolly, Alahunta, & Jeannet, 1992; Litvak, 1990; Rennie, 1993). Also appearing in the early 1990s were studies stimulated in part by a growing awareness of the diversity in entrepreneurial activity across countries. For example, Choy (1990) discussed different entrepreneurial financing practices at a nation level. Others focused on differences relating to culture such as studies of the cultural influences on the entrepreneur's perceptions and values (e.g. McGrath, MacMillan, & Scheinberg, 1992; McGrath et al., 1992).

By the early 1990s, research had emerged on two topics of interest that would later form clear streams of IE research. As later identified by Jones et al. (2011), these were Type A: Entrepreneurial Internationalization, and Type B: International Comparisons of Entrepreneurship. By 2001, the emergence of studies was seen comparing entrepreneurial internationalization across countries or cultures. These combined the perspectives of the first two streams and are labeled Type C (Jones et al., 2011).

The evolution of IE research

After McDougall's (1989) study, she, together with Ben Oviatt, sought out other scholars studying INVs, and found evidence from around the world of this new phenomenon. In 1994, they published two catalytic articles that provoked examination of, and challenges to, extant theory. One article (McDougall, Shane, & Oviatt, 1994) was published in entrepreneurship's premiere journal: *Journal of Business Venturing*. It used theoretical sampling to assess 24 INV case studies – 12 cases compiled by the authors and 12 cases that they had identified from academic journals and meetings – relative to various aspects of IB theory. In parallel, Oviatt and McDougall (1994) appeared in the pinnacle journal of the other parent discipline of IE: *Journal of International Business Studies*. That paper developed a four-part typology of INVs, an organizational form generally defined as "a business organization that, from inception, seeks to derive significant competitive advantage from the use of resources and sale of outputs in multiple countries" (Oviatt & McDougall, 1994: 49). As defined by them, these included global start-ups, geographically focused start-ups, export/import start-ups, and multinational traders.

Also in this time frame, Zahra (1993) offered a definition of IE that extended beyond the study of INVs (as per McDougall, 1989) to include corporate entrepreneurship. He also conceptualized a process of IE. In addition, Giamartino, McDougall, and Bird (1993) provided the first assessment of IE, from the perspective of academic researchers, while Wright and Ricks' (1994) Delphi study for the *Journal of International Business Studies* led them to argue that IE should

80　*Nicole E. Coviello et al.*

be an important area for research in international business. Also, Knight and Cavusgil (1996) published their arguments about the 'born global.'[1]

As explained by Kuhn (1996), such scholarly discourse signals a new line of inquiry, and these developments helped research in IE quickly gain momentum. The 1993 Babson Frontiers of Entrepreneurship Research Conference offered a track devoted to 'Global Entrepreneurs and International Entrepreneurship', one that was differentiated from the cross-cultural entrepreneurship stream that began in 1989.[2] In 1996, *Entrepreneurship Theory and Practice* published a special issue on IE and the McGill International Entrepreneurship Conference Series was launched by Richard Wright, Hamid Etemad, and Peter Johnson in 1998. The first of these conferences led to two special issues in the *Journal of International Marketing* (1999).

In 2000, the *Academy of Management Journal* published a special IE Research Forum. As an indication of the interest in IE, the AMJ special issue generated 34 submissions from 81 authors in 21 different countries. It also provided three specific catalysts important to researchers in IE. First, because AMJ is the premiere empirical journal in management research, its recognition of IE signaled legitimacy to other areas. Second, Zahra, Ireland, and Hitt's (2000) paper on new venture internationalization, learning, and performance received the AMJ Annual Best Paper Award. Third, McDougall and Oviatt's (2000) introduction to the special issue formally positioned IE at the intersection of research in international business and entrepreneurship. IE was defined as "a combination of innovative, proactive and risk-seeking behaviour that crosses national borders and is intended to create value in organizations" and it included "research on such behaviour and research comparing domestic entrepreneurial behaviour in many countries" (McDougall & Oviatt, 2000: 903). This definition is generally considered to be the formal 'naming' of the emerging field. Also relevant is that it established parameters for research in IE.

As understanding of IE continued to surface, Zahra and George (2002: 262) offered another definition of IE, considering it to be "the process of creatively discovering and exploiting opportunities that lie outside a firm's domestic markets in the pursuit of competitive advantage." Notable with this definition is that it exclude the international comparisons of entrepreneurial behaviour included by McDougall and Oviatt (2000).

In 2003, the *Journal of International Entrepreneurship* was launched to provide a forum for research specific to IE (rather than being an 'international journal' of entrepreneurship). In addition, special issues on IE continued to appear. Examples include: *Journal of International Management* (2001), *Entrepreneurship Theory and Practice* (2002), *Small Business Economics* (2003, 2005, 2008), *Journal of International Business Studies* (2005), *Management International Review* (2005), and *International Business Review* (2005). During this period, the Academy of International Business Annual Meetings held tracks for IE research, including a special panel session at the 2005 meeting in Quebec City.

In 2005, the *Journal of International Business Studies* awarded Oviatt and McDougall the JIBS Decade Award for their 1994 contribution, simultaneously publishing commentaries on IE by Autio (2005) and Zahra (2005). This signaled further recognition for IE among IB scholars. Similar acknowledgement came from other fields in that the *Journal of International Marketing*'s Hans B. Thorelli Award (for the most significant and long-term contribution to international marketing theory or practice) was awarded three times to IE studies: Jones (1999), Knight (2000), and Burgel and Murray (2000). Since then, the terms of the prize have changed and two more IE studies have recently received the Thorelli Award: Moen and Servais (2002), and Chetty and Campbell Hunt (2004).

Also in 2005, Oviatt and McDougall (2005: 540) offered a refined definition of IE in *Entrepreneurship Theory and Practice*. Like Zahra and George (2002), they incorporated the concept of opportunity: "International entrepreneurship is the discovery, enactment, evaluation, and exploitation of opportunities – across national borders – to create future goods and services." Notably, this definition permits – but does not require – the formation of new organizations, and allows for corporate entrepreneurship. By removing reference to the original three components of an entrepreneurial orientation (from Covin & Slevin, 1990), it opens debate on how many, or which, dimensions of entrepreneurial orientation to include. It also allows for multiple levels of research, potentially incorporating the individual entrepreneur, team, firm, and/or external actors and influences. Also important is that again, Oviatt and McDougall (2005) explain how IE research includes studies of: 1) entrepreneurship *crossing* borders, i.e. entrepreneurial internationalization, and 2) comparative studies of entrepreneurial behaviour *across* borders (i.e. in different countries and/or cultures).

From 2006 to 2009, yet more special issues on IE appeared: *International Marketing Review* (2006), *Journal of World Business* (2007), and *Strategic Entrepreneurship Journal* (2009). Notable across these and the earlier special issues is that the list includes the leading journals in Management, Entrepreneurship, International Business, International Marketing, and Small Business. IE research has also been published in numerous books.

Also in 2009 was the launch of *ie-scholars.net*, a virtual community built to support IE research globally.[3] This initiative was supported by a grant from Canada's Social Sciences and Humanities Research Council. *Ie-scholars.net* has nearly 300 research members and partner institutions in seven countries (at time of writing in early 2014). It provides support for the annual McGill International Entrepreneurship Conference and Doctoral Colloquium (rotating through Canada and other countries) and the *Journal of International Entrepreneurship*. More tangible outcomes include the five-volume SAGE book series of IE research edited by McNaughton and Bell (2009) and a six-book series edited by Etemad (published by Elgar).

Challenges to IE

By 2009, IE appeared to hold an identifiable position at the interface of international business and entrepreneurship research. A number of reviews of IE had also been published (see Coviello et al., 2011 for a summary), reviews

82 *Nicole E. Coviello et al.*

that helped signal the potential of research in the area. Some reviews assessed specific areas of interest, while others considered IE from a particular disciplinary perspective or theoretical lens. However, Zahra, Korri, and Yu (2005) suggested that IE research was mechanical, with some of it atheoretical. Then, two reviews outlined grave concerns for IE research. Keupp and Gassman (2009) conducted a review to identify the gaps, deficiencies, and inadequacies of IE. They criticized its phenomenological basis, imbalance in the theoretical integration of international business and entrepreneurship, and lack of coherence. Similar concerns were expressed by Coombs, Sadrieh, and Annavarjula (2009: 31) and they concluded that "a theoretical paucity summarizes the present state of research [in IE]."

We consider the above reviews as healthy for debate, and note they highlight certain important points (e.g. the need for multi-level research). However, although we believe that theoretical convergence is an important process in the development of a field, we follow Johnson and Duberly (2000) in arguing that a fixation on the development of theoretical models and unity in methodological approaches, constructs, and measures may result in a set of relatively inflexible 'game rules' being applied to IE (Jones et al., 2011). That is, although such milestones are important, focusing solely on them might blind researchers to a richer understanding of IE phenomena. Applying Kuhn (1996), it could also lead to IE scholars taking the phenomena and paradigmatic views that launched research in the area for granted. In addition – as noted by Jones et al. (2011) – there were a number of limitations in the parameters and search procedures of the reviews. For example, Keupp and Gassmann (2009) restricted their review to a predetermined set of 16 journals, and included teaching cases and traditional small and medium-sized enterprise (SME) export studies. In addition, it is not clear whether Keupp and Gassmann's (2009) search extended to and included cross-country and cross-cultural studies.

This led Jones et al. (2011) to conduct an extensive review of the literature, focusing on the phenomena and related issues that had been studied in IE over its full history. They reviewed the domain in a manner consistent with its defined parameters, arguing that in IE, this must include research explicitly positioned at the interface of international business and entrepreneurship. That is, integrating theory and arguments from both fields. Rather than applying a particular theoretical lens to analyze aspects of IE or using predetermined attributes to define their analysis, they used inductive thematic analysis and interpretation to identify patterns of inquiry from 1989 to 2009. This drew on procedures from the medical sciences and evidence-based management research, and facilitated a process of systematic review that was as comprehensive and inclusive as possible. The outcome was a review that, to the extent possible, covered all available IE articles published in English language journals, with selection guided by a detailed protocol for article inclusion/exclusion and assessment (see Appendices A and B in Jones et al., 2011). The result was an ontological map of IE research for the period 1989–2009. This was published in a special forum dedicated to reviews of IE in the *Journal of Business Venturing.*

IE research: 2010–2012

To this point, we have summarized the evolution of IE research from 1989 to 2009. Now, in 2013, we ask: has IE in fact, emerged as a field? To help answer this question, we take three steps. First, we apply the Jones et al. (2011) protocol to extend the literature review and identify IE research published in 2010–2012, including the parameters they used to identify what is and is not IE research (see Table 6.1). This process identified 213 empirical papers, 17 conceptual papers, 11 reviews, 5 papers focused on methodological, education, or theory-building issues, and 4 editorials with detailed commentaries. Thus, a total of 250 IE papers were published between 2010 and 2012. Second, we analyze the full set of articles (1989–2012) for evolutionary patterns. Third, we combine this information with that from earlier sections in this chapter to help assess IE relative to Hambrick and Chen (2008). Of note, Galkina (2012) also discusses IE using the Hambrick and Chen (2008) framework. Our analytic approach differs, however, in that our foundation rests on the systematic review and analysis noted above, while she offers a critical review to address whether or not IE should broaden (i.e. delimit) its domain in order to be recognized as a discrete research area.

Patterns relating to primary themes

We report the results of our preliminary analysis, focusing on how primary themes have emerged, the nature of empirical studies, and the relative influence of the parent disciplines on IE over time. To begin, we provide an overview of how IE research has developed. Figure 6.1 presents the primary IE

Table 6.1 The parameters of international entrepreneurship research

A. *Inclusion Criteria*

   1. Research that directly and explicitly integrates theory and concepts from both IB and E in one of three categories (based on the definition of IE from McDougall and Oviatt [2000] and the ontological review of Jones, Coviello, and Tang [2011]):

      a. Entrepreneurial behaviour across borders (entrepreneurial internationalization);
      b. International comparisons of entrepreneurial behaviour;
      c. Comparative studies of entrepreneurial internationalization.

B. *Exclusion Criteria by Theoretical Relevance*

   1. Studies focused on SMEs rather than IE per se, i.e. where entrepreneurship issues and theories are not integrated or addressed in the study;
   2. Studies in which the primary focus is not international entrepreneurship. E.g. studies of biotech firms in global industries or in which the focus is on technological innovation rather than business or entrepreneurial processes;
   3. Studies focused on domestic entrepreneurship in one country;
   4. Cross-cultural assessments of (e.g.) entrepreneurial orientation (EO) measures that focus on scale and measure development or validation;
   5. Studies on transnational and/or immigrant entrepreneurship.

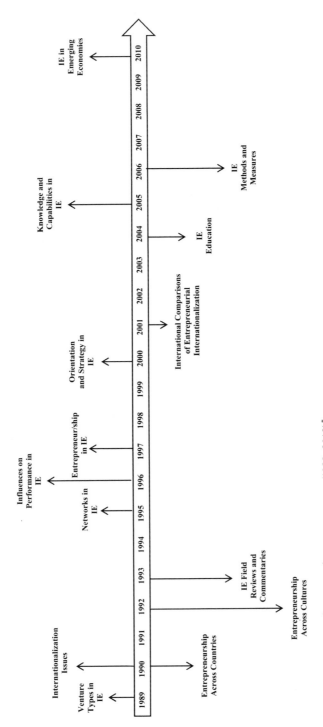

Figure 6.1 Patterns of primary theme emergence (1989–2012)*

*Themes are not mutually exclusive and reflect only what was interpreted to be the primary theme/focus for a paper. Each paper has themes at secondary and tertiary levels.

research themes in order of their emergence into the literature. The pattern begins with McDougall's (1989) study that differentiated the international and domestic new venture.

Between 1989 and 1993, the earliest themes were concerned with: 1) the type of venture and 2) internationalization. Other themes to emerge in the first five-year period are comparative studies of entrepreneurship focusing on: 3) cross-national and 4) cross-cultural differences. By 1993, it appeared that IE had promise as a field of study and the first evaluation of it was published. The period 1994–99 saw the introduction of three new themes: 1) networks, 2) influences on performance, and 3) the entrepreneur/ship focus in IE. The following five years (2000–2004) saw acceleration in published output and a further three themes: 1) orientation and strategy, 2) international comparisons of entrepreneurial internationalization, and 3) a small category we refer to as 'other' but note as dominated by educational issues for IE. Two more themes emerged in 2005–2006: 1) resources and capabilities and 2) research methods in IE.[4] In 2010, the most recent theme appeared, focused on IE research in emerging and transitional economies. In addition, there is a marked increase in Type C studies (international comparisons of entrepreneurial internationalization) in the most recent time period (2010–2012), and the Resources and Capabilities theme was dominated by research on learning and knowledge. We also note what appear to be emerging themes related to: 1) the role of the internet in IE and 2) studies of IE embedded in the context of venture capital firms and family businesses. Finally, we note with interest three papers that depart from the traditional focus on the firm or entrepreneur as unit of analysis for IE. Chandra and Coviello (2010) develop arguments regarding the 'consumer-as-international-entrepreneur', while Nasra and Dacin (2010) explore the nation-state as an international entrepreneur. In addition, Chelekis and Mudambi (2010) study how multinational corporations (MNCs) internationalizing into emerging (and rural) economies support micro-entrepreneurship

As of the end of 2012, we identify 551 IE articles for analysis. As per Jones et al. (2011), this excludes editorials. Of the 551 we analyze, 459 are empirical and 57 are conceptual. Those remaining include reviews of IE, or papers focused on issues pertaining to methodology, education or how to develop theory. Although the empirical research is dominated by Type A studies (entrepreneurial internationalization; n = 307 or 67%), international comparisons of entrepreneurial behaviour are clearly evident. By 2012, these Type B studies include 49 that emphasize cross-cultural analysis and a further 75 that assess entrepreneurship across countries. Type C research is much smaller (n = 28) but has begun to emerge more recently. In the same way that Type C research is now appearing and Type A research has shown increased interest in learning and knowledge as it pertains to IE, Type B research has been dominated in recent years by country comparisons that typically rely on secondary datasets. Examples include Stephan and Uhlaner (2010) and De Clercq, Meuleman, and Wright (2012).

General methodological patterns

Turning to the methodological patterns in IE, Table 6.2 summarizes the approaches used in the empirical studies we identified. Survey research dominates IE (47%), although qualitative (28%) and mixed method techniques (9%) are also evident. This prevalence of qualitative and mixed method approaches is particularly so for Type A (entrepreneurial internationalization) studies, and likely a result of arguments that a new field requires exploratory work. These methods provide depth and context to the understanding of IE phenomena. Table 6.2 also indicates that Type B studies make more use of secondary datasets, notably Global Entrepreneurship Monitor (GEM) data. Other datasets are, however, also in use, either on their own or as a complement to GEM. Examples include data from the World Bank, OECD, WHO, and the IMF.

Patterns related to the parent disciplines

Although a full theoretical review is beyond the scope of this research, Table 6.3 provides a comparison of how IE research has been positioned relative to its parent disciplines since 1989. Given our search parameters, both international business and entrepreneurship theory/concepts are evident in all 551 papers.

McDougall (1989) established the positioning of IE relative to IB by comparing entrepreneurship in an international vs. domestic context. In the following four years, papers included both IB and entrepreneurship concepts but were clearly informed by a dominant or 'lead' discipline – these are indicated

Table 6.2 Nature of empirical studies in IE research (1989–2012)

	Empirical Method						
	Qualitative	Survey	Mixed Method	GEM	Other Database(s)	Other	Total
Type A – Entrepreneurial Internationalization	114	144	29	1	12	7	307 (67%)
Type B – International Comparisons of Entrepreneurship	7	65	6	28	11	7*	124 (27%)
Type C – Comparative Entrepreneurial Internationalization	8	8	6	2	4	0	28 (6%)
Total	129 (28%)	217 (47%)	41 (9%)	31 (7%)	27 (6%)	14 (3%)	**459**

* GEM combined with other databases

Is entrepreneurship research viable? 87

Table 6.3 Patterns of home/informing disciplines, 1989–2012 (n = 551)

Year	International Business	Entrepreneurship	Entrepreneurship in an International Context	International Entrepreneurship
1989			1	
1990	1	1		
1991		4		
1992	1	3		
1993		1		2
1994	1	2	1	2
1995	2			2
1996	2	2	1	3
1997	2	2	3	5
1998	3	2		
1999	4	3		2
2000	4	1	5	8
2001	4	1	4	7
2002	1	2	2	8
2003	2	2	2	15
2004	6	1	5	17
2005	1	8		22
2006	6	3	1	22
2007	3	1	3	33
2008		11	6	33
2009	2	3	8	27
2010	8	2	12	27
2011	9	13	18	41
2012	6	11	12	44
Total	**68 (12%)**	**79 (14%)**	**84 (15%)**	**320 (58%)**

in the first two columns of Table 6.3. This has continued, but column 3 shows a steadily increasing number of entrepreneurship studies with a strong international influence. Most importantly, papers that balance IB and entrepreneurship elements started to emerge in 1993 and have clearly grown in number (see column 4). In 2000, a clear shift in the literature appears, with 8 of 18 studies integrating both international business and entrepreneurship theory. Then, using a yearly average from 2001–2012, approximately two-thirds of the papers are considered to be clearly 'international + entrepreneurship' in terms of how they integrate the literature and develop their arguments. Over all years, this totals 320 articles (58%) positioned at the interface of international business and entrepreneurship. This signals a clear trend in the development of IE as a field of study.

88 *Nicole E. Coviello et al.*

Is IE now a field?

Returning to Hambrick and Chen (2008), the evidence presented thus far suggests that IE has managed to differentiate itself, mobilize, and gain some legitimacy. However, has it? In Table 6.4, we summarize our assessment of IE relative to the criteria used by Hambrick and Chen (2008) in their discussion of new academic fields as admittance-seeking social movements.

Differentiation. In terms of differentiation, Oviatt and McDougall (1994) and McDougall et al. (1994) clearly and strongly made the claim that some important phenomena fell outside the scope of existing disciplines. These and other arguments also recognized that unprecedented change in (e.g.) world markets and technologies were influencing actual firm behaviour. This suggests that one of the reasons IE research was initially well received and then later won various awards, publication opportunities in special issues, and government grants to assist its development was that IE was positioned as having a mission that was socially (as well as economically and intellectually) relevant. Early scholars also seem to have been careful to avoid positioning IE as a "threat or intellectual affront to established fields that were in a position to block its advance" (using the language of Hambrick & Chen, 2008: 36). Explicit calls and efforts were made to integrate extant theory in definitions, constructs, and research designs (e.g. McDougall & Oviatt, 2000; Oviatt & McDougall, 2005; Coviello & Jones, 2004; Jones & Coviello, 2005). Thus, because IE sits (by definition) at the intersection of existing fields, it allows for complementary rather than competing research.

Mobilization. Beneficial to IE mobilization is that its emergence is predicated on supportive environmental conditions. Initially, these included developments in the technology sector, where multitudes of start-up firms found that to compete and survive they needed to reach international markets.

Table 6.4 Assessing IE relative to Hambrick and Chen's (2008) proposed elements of an admittance-seeking social movement

Elements	Criteria	IE
Differentiation	Portrayal of a socially important mission	✓
	Affirmation of worthiness by outside influential parties	✓
	Portrayal of a mission that is complementary to adjacent fields	✓
Mobilization	External demand for community's body of knowledge	✓
	Internal demand (from students)	X
	Bounded set of shared interests	?
	Existence of multiple forums	✓
	Forums pose oblique competition to forums of the establishment	✓
	Socially interconnected core and complementary variety	?
Legitimacy Building	Intellectual persuasion	?
	Emulation of norms and styles of adjacent established fields	X

Thus, there was at least the appearance of external relevance, if not actual evidence of external demand for IE research. More recently, we note that in Europe, national governments are increasingly supportive of entrepreneurship education relative to global markets (e.g. Finland, the UK), and this bodes well for IE.

The situation for internal (student) demand is, however, less evident. Most universities guided by the Association to Advance Collegiate Schools of Business (AACSB) or other accreditation requirements rarely see a strong need for IE courses at the undergraduate or MBA level, and the number of universities offering courses in IE remains limited. Although there have been some exceptions (e.g. the desire of a donor), the most typical situation is that a faculty member with a strong interest in IE successfully lobbies to offer the course. There is some evidence that the faculty-driven internal demand for IE courses is growing in recent years. Beginning in 2007, the University of Colorado Denver began offering an IE workshop targeted to faculty who wished to research IE or who planned to teach an IE course. As of 2014, the workshop has been offered at two US locations and in South Korea and Istanbul. Over 150 faculty members from 40 universities in 23 countries have attended. According to the workshop's Director, Manuel Serapio, about 30 percent of the attendees indicate in their registration materials that their reason for attending is to enable themselves to teach a course in IE that their university plans to offer.

Returning to Hambrick and Chen's (2008) other criteria, do IE scholars have a bounded set of shared interests? This is to some unclear, because of the diverse themes within the domain of IE and the range of methods and theories followed in pursuit of evidence. Furthermore, it is apparent from recent reviews that some view IE differently than we (the current authors) do. However, IE does have a relatively clear definition that has evolved from a narrow focus on international new ventures to one that is more inclusive of different organizational forms, the conceptualization of opportunity and entrepreneurship, and the need to understand behaviour in the process of crossing borders as well as in different national and cultural contexts (Oviatt & McDougall, 2005). Also, although IE research themes may be large in number, they are now more clearly articulated (see Jones et al., 2011).

Another factor important to mobilization is that early discourse was facilitated by a number of social infrastructures. Notably, the Annual McGill Conference (begun in 1998) has been a consistent forum and by rotating that conference in and out of Canada (to Finland, Singapore, Italy, etc.), the international interest in IE research has grown. In recent years, the McGill Conference has also hosted a Doctoral Colloquium, indicating the presence of new scholars in IE. We note too that although IE lacks visibility in the Academy of Management (as of 2014), both the Academy of International Business and Babson Frontiers of Entrepreneurship Research Conferences have consistently included IE research, with IE researchers often attending both. This suggests the existence of a political opportunity structure, i.e. a generally non-hostile

90   *Nicole E. Coviello et al.*

or benign attitude toward IE on the part of established organizations. Furthermore, forums for IE such as the McGill Conference and *ie-scholars.net* provide oblique rather than direct competition.

We also see what Hambrick and Chen (2008: 45) refer to as a "socially interconnected core and complementary variety of scholars." For example, researchers with clear ties to IE sit on numerous review boards. At time of writing in 2014, our count shows that the *Journal of Business Venturing* has sixteen such board members and in 2009 was the first to appoint an editor specific to IE (Nicole Coviello). *Entrepreneurship Theory and Practice* appears to have eighteen IE board members, while *Strategic Entrepreneurship Journal* has seven (with Mike Wright as Editor-Elect). This signals a high level of understanding of IE in the top entrepreneurship journals. Across the various international business and international marketing journals, there is an average of five IE board members per journal, and there are six at the *Academy of Management Journal* (with Gerry George included as Editor).

Finally, IE has benefited from the early commitment and drive of many (now senior) scholars, as well as the many younger scholars who are devoting much of their time to IE research. At the same time, it is important to recognize that to the best of our knowledge, no IE scholars are housed in distinct IE Departments (and we are unaware of any such departments). Rather, IE scholars have homes in other departments. As such, they are under pressure to publish their best work in the top journals in their 'home' discipline. On this issue, one criterion discussed by Hambrick and Chen (2008: 34) is whether or not a "substantial number of major universities designate positions for its members, grant tenure to its members, seek peer tenure evaluations from its members, and allow its members to supervise graduate students". An indirect way of assessing this is to consider professorial titles. In the context of IE, Chairs in International Entrepreneurship are extremely rare. To the best of our knowledge, the earliest were held by Nicole Coviello (University of Auckland) and David Crick (de Montfort University, Birmingham City University). However, these positions were in 'Marketing and International Entrepreneurship'. At time of writing, the only titles specific to IE that we are able to identify are at York University (Moren Levesque), Technische Universität München (Hana Milanov), and Victoria University of Wellington (David Crick). Marian Jones is Professor of International Business and Entrepreneurship at Glasgow, while Robert Hisrich is a named Professor of Global Entrepreneurship at Thunderbird. Notably, although Shaker Zahra held the 3U Professorship of IE at Twente, his title at his home institution is Professor of Entrepreneurship and Strategy. Thus, residing across disciplinary areas is most common, and many senior IE scholars have such an appointment (e.g. Patricia McDougall-Covin is a named Professor of Entrepreneurship and also a Professor of Strategy). In contrast, many of our colleagues reside in a specific discipline. Examples include Marketing (Tage Koed Madsen), Management (Dirk De Clercq), and International Business (Niina Nummela).

Is this problematic? To some extent yes, since as researchers working in (at least) two areas of study, we need to publish in both, and this can dilute the time and effort one devotes to IE. It also means that our training and interests are very diverse. On the other hand, by working across fields, we are informed by (and inform) other types of research and research questions. In our favour is the emerging realization in some universities that economic, social, and technical problems in today's world are complex and require multidisciplinary knowledge and teams to address them. Potentially, the capabilities and knowledge developed through the process of straddling at least two core disciplines may open opportunities for IE scholars.

Legitimatization. Hambrick and Chen (2008) note that legitimacy involves both intellectual persuasion (through arguments and evidence of unique contributions) and emulation of norms in the parent or adjacent fields. Regarding persuasion, we have already noted the various awards for IE research, and Table 6.5 summarizes the journals where IE research is found in the 'top 15' list of articles, based on citations. Notably, this list includes the top journals in both IB and entrepreneurship, as well as others. In certain journals, IE research is ranked particularly well.

Table 6.5 Journals with IE research in 'top 15' list based on citations

Journal	Citation Rank	Authors	Year
Entrepreneurship Theory and Practice	7	Bloodgood, Sapienza, and Almeida	1996
	12	Oviatt and McDougall	2005
International Business Review	1	Madsen and Servais	1997
	3	Coviello and Munro	1997
	5	Rialp, Rialp, and Knight	2005
	9	Sharma and Blomstermo	2003
	11	Yli-Renko, Autio, and Tontti	2002
Journal of Business Venturing	9	McDougall, Shane, and Oviatt	1994
Journal of International Business Studies	4	Oviatt and McDougall	1994
Journal of International Marketing	1	Knight	2000
	2	Jones	1999
	3	Moen and Servais	2002
	4	Chetty and Campbell-Hunt	2004
	5	Burgel and Murray	2000
	6	Crick and Jones	2000
	12	McAuley	1999
Management International Review	1	Coviello and McAuley	1999
	2	Oviatt and McDougall	1997
Small Business Economics	3	Reynolds et al.	2005
	9	Van Stel, Carree, and Thurik	2005

Source: Publish or Perish, October 2013

92　*Nicole E. Coviello et al.*

This is not to say that IE lacks critics in its parent disciplines. For example, a review of fifty years of IB theory (Rugman, Verbeke, & Nguyen, 2011) argues there is (little or) no robust empirical evidence of 'born global' firms. A full discussion on this issue is beyond the scope of this chapter, so we note simply that although national registers and databases may not capture the nature or scope of international new ventures, the IE literature includes comparative evidence from survey and case research regarding various organizational forms. These include not only born globals, but also the born regional firms noted by Rugman et al. (2011) (aka the geographic start-up from Oviatt & McDougall 1994), as well as born-again globals and various other forms of international new venture.

In terms of emulation, which refers to the methodological or paradigmatic conventions of well-established fields, our review suggests that some inroads have been made here (as evidenced by publications in either the top IB or entrepreneurship journals, or outside the parent disciplines). However, much work is yet to be done, since most IE research is not, in fact, published in strong journals. For example, only 38% of IE articles published from 2010 to 2012 were in journals such as the *Journal of Business Venturing, Entrepreneurship Theory and Practice*, and *Journal of International Business Studies*.[5] Even IE's own journal (*Journal of International Entrepreneurship*) has, after a promising start, struggled to maintain its status. It may be that more work needs to be done to respond to Zahra, Korri, and Yu's (2005) call for less mechanical research. Does this mean that IE research must move to a more fully positivistic paradigm? We suggest not, noting that even Hambrick and Chen (2008: 51) criticize the strategic management literature for having moved away from its "interest in deeply textured understanding of strategic decision processes."

Discussion

Based on the previous sections, it appears that although IE has made progress as an emerging field, there is still room to improve. Before discussing the implications of this, we reflect on a number of more philosophical issues. For example, we realize that for survival, some expect a new field to "demonstrate its distinctiveness and assert its worthiness" (Hambrick & Chen, 2008: 36) such that it will not be subsumed over time by one of its antecedent disciplines or claimed by new entrants from other fields. This appears also to be the position of Galkina (2012: 83), who argues that consolidation of IE is necessary in order to overcome its "rather confused and messy body of knowledge." At an operational level, Tranfield, Denyer, and Smart (2003) suggest that a field must develop context-sensitive research and a reliable stock of knowledge to enhance evidence-informed [management] practice and policy. Grégoire et al. (2006: 335) go further to argue that a new field must also establish "a widely shared 'paradigm,' i.e. a set of assumptions about a field's object of study, method of investigation, explanatory model, and overall interpretation scheme".

In part, the Jones et al. (2011) ontology helps clarify the nature and history of IE research but we also wonder: is a widely shared paradigm and demonstrated distinctiveness sensible or even appropriate for IE? In positioning IE at the interface of international business and entrepreneurship, McDougall and Oviatt (2000) note that both antecedent disciplines are becoming less distinct as fields of study (see also Hambrick and Chen's 2008 observations regarding IB). Thus, another question worth considering is: how might a new field sitting at the intersection of two already hybrid and evolving fields claim to be distinctive? If integration is considered to be the new field's distinctiveness, our review shows that IE is not only retaining but increasing in this regard. An additional trend is the integration of IE with theories and perspectives from other domains such as strategic management, institutional theory and cognitive psychology (see Jones et al., 2011). Does this dilute or strengthen IE?

In considering these questions, we return to the phenomena widely attributed as stimulating the emergence of IE. These relate to the early and rapid internationalization of new and small ventures in response to factors such as economic integration, advances in technology and knowledge intensive industries, deregulation, and changes in industry and market structure. Individuals and firms responding to these changes in innovative, proactive, and risk-seeking ways were seen as being entrepreneurial with regard to venturing in a globalizing and increasingly complex world. To us, this complexity suggests a need for multi-theoretical approaches to understand the antecedents, influencing factors, and outcomes of IE (see also Wright & Ricks, 1994). Areas of study like IE that sit at the intersection of parent disciplines reside there because the phenomena under study defy explanation by either one alone. Those working in such an area or space develop means to compare and contrast competing explanations and look for areas of agreement or convergence.[6] They also learn the language, orientation, and structures of each discipline and learn to converse in the language of either. Opportunities for insight and the development of new approaches emerge from researchers' experiential knowledge when coupled with different or new lenses from other fields. Thus, while some call for unifying frameworks and methodological directions in a new field (e.g. Grégoire et al., 2006), as do some of our own early arguments (McDougall & Oviatt, 2000; Coviello & Jones, 2004), a competing but compatible argument is to call for new insights and new entrants to IE from other disciplines to enrich our understanding of the complex phenomena encompassed by IE.

This line of thought views diversity as important. It also provides a counterargument to those such as Hambrick and Chen (2008) who suggest a new field of study requires 'distinctiveness.' Following Schumpeterian reasoning, diversity fuels innovation, opportunity, and sustainable development and is as important in securing IE's survival and position as a field as is the rigorous development of its theories and methods.

Implications for IE

Following from the above, we believe diversity strengthens a research field and should be encouraged. At the same time, we also believe that diversity can fit within definitional parameters such as those provided by Oviatt and McDougall (2005). Thus, our first observation is that scholars must take care to understand what IE research is and what it is not. As noted previously (see Table 6.1), a number of topics are outside of IE because they have their own home (e.g. immigrant entrepreneurship or innovation management) or simply because they provide an organizational context (e.g. SMEs). Second, we recommend careful consideration of, first, what aspects of IE phenomena a theory might help explain and, second, how such theories might be usefully integrated to arrive at more comprehensive explanations or provide new insights. Galkina (2012) draws on Zahra and Newey (2009) to argue that IE is characterized by superficial efforts to borrow and combine concepts without sufficient questioning of their relevance or compatibility. To some extent, our experience leads us to agree with this concern and like Galkina (2012) we would prefer to see more effort to extend and transform borrowed concepts. As identified by Jones et al. (2011), we believe there is clear evidence of increasing sophistication of theoretical integration in IE. We also believe that there will be a stronger interdependence between entrepreneurship and international business because the former explains the behaviour and cognitions of the firm and entrepreneur while the latter explains the context and mechanisms influenced by or influencing that behaviour or those cognitions.

Regarding the arguments of Hambrick and Chen (2008), certain issues need to be addressed. Although IE literature seems to have differentiated itself, ongoing and improved social *mobilization* is a priority. According to McAdam (1982), emergent collectives will advance to the extent that they are effectively organized and able to secure resources. At this time, although IE has an informal network of colleagues and editorial board members, and a virtual community through *ie-scholars.net*, there is no formal membership structure (and no fees) that signify and legitimize "belonging" in comparison to (e.g.) the Strategic Management Society or Academy of International Business. This might lead to IE surviving in a marginal state with limited resources, limited membership, and limited acceptance by the broader academic establishment. In addition, the lack of formal membership may hamper further development of the *Journal of International Entrepreneurship*, either in terms of financial support or providing a clear 'publication home' for IE researchers. The lack of formal structure might also mean that IE researchers will look to established formal organizations (such as the Academy of International Business) to direct their work and thus, IE could be reabsorbed by one of its parent disciplines.

The decision on a formal membership organization for IE is not for us to make. However, we refer to Hambrick and Chen's (2008: 37) observation that a network is critical for "providing cohesion and enhancing the carefully controlled dissemination of the incipient field's purpose, philosophy and agenda."

One available mechanism is *ie-scholars.net* given it has the scope to disseminate both research and teaching materials. On the issue of education, we note with interest that Strategic Management emerged through the classroom; in contrast, IE did not. This needs to be addressed in order to drive internal demand and to this end, and efforts are under way to compile IE education curricula and practices to share through *ie-scholars.net*. Ideally, changes to the *ie-scholars* website could position it as the primary resource for sharing IE research and education, and this might be a sufficient 'home' for IE. A second point is that although there are over 500 IE journal articles and nearly 300 members in *ie-scholars.net*, much of the core network involved with editorial boards, conference leadership, etc. is the same (small) group of researchers. This network needs to be widened.

To improve *legitimacy*, it appears that the issue of emulation (from Hambrick & Chen, 2008) warrants particular attention. This implies a need for a more rigorous approach to IE methods. As a start, a review of methodological fit would be appropriate (as per Edmondson & McManus, 2007). This would help identify where IE and/or specific IE themes fit in the categorization of nascent, intermediate, or mature research. Also, an updated review of methodological patterns (extending Coviello & Jones, 2004) would be welcome, as would in-depth reviews on specific methodological issues.

Given the prevalence of survey data in IE research, scholars must be aware that most leading journals now demand recognition of the potential for common method variance. Thus, if single-informants (e.g. lead entrepreneurs) are studied, additional analysis is likely required to mitigate reviewer concerns regarding bias. IE could also benefit from a compilation of multi-item measures suitable for different types of IE research; measures that can be assessed for cross-national and cultural validity in order to satisfy leading journals. Importantly, IE research has a strong qualitative component and this leads us to make two points. First, because qualitative studies are unable to be assessed with classic meta-analysis, we refer to Walsh and Downe (2005) for guidance on how to conduct a meta-summary of qualitative findings. This could complement the more traditional efforts at meta-analysis that are beginning to emerge. Second, there is much room for improvement in the nature of qualitative design, implementation, and reporting. We encourage IE scholars to learn from those publishing qualitative studies in journals such as *Academy of Management Journal*.

Finally, we note the increased use of secondary databases. In part, this may reflect the lack of quality survey data available (or the difficulty in obtaining it). We also suspect that the increased pressure to publish for tenure-track faculty leads them to use data that are readily available. However, secondary data can be problematic in that firm age is often inaccurate, international dependent variables are often absent, it is difficult to compare databases from different countries, and more often than not, proxy variables have to be used for most measures. Thus, we are somewhat cautious about the use of secondary databases, especially for the study of entrepreneurial internationalization behaviour (Type A and Type C research).

Conclusions

Is IE a field, a viable spin-off from its parent disciplines? Our assessment of IE relative to the criteria established by Hambrick and Chen (2008) suggests that much progress has been made to establish IE as a credible and identifiable field of research. At the same time, we see that additional efforts are required to strengthen the mobilization and legitimization of IE. We also expect that if interest in both entrepreneurship and international business education grow (as we believe they will), there will be a need to ensure that IE is clearly and consistently differentiated from its parent disciplines. IE is unique because of its 'interface' position, one that allows for multi-theoretical and multi-level insights.

Notes

1 See Coviello, McDougall, and Oviatt (2011) for a discussion of the terminology in IE research.
2 The BCERC Index (to 2011) shows that IE research has appeared in various tracks (e.g. Global, 1994; Geographic Expansion, 1996). There was a specified 'International Entrepreneurship Track' from 2005–2009 while in other years 2001–2004 and 2010–2011), it has been labeled 'International'.
3 http://ie-scholars.net
4 See Jones et al. (2011) for a comprehensive breakdown of the primary themes of IE from 1989–2009 inclusive.
5 Journals considered 'strong(er)' for the purposes of this analysis (and where IE articles are found) include *Academy of Management Journal, Strategic Management Journal, Journal of International Business Studies, Journal of Business Venturing, Entrepreneurship Theory and Practice, Strategic Entrepreneurship Journal, Journal of Management Studies, Journal of World Business, Management International Review, International Business Review, Journal of International Marketing, Small Business Economics, International Marketing Review, Journal of Small Business Management.*
6 While a discussion of theory borrowing is beyond the scope of this chapter, we recommend that IE scholars read both Whetten, Felin, and King (2009) and Okhuysen and Bonardi (2011) – the latter being comments from two AMR Editors.

References

Autio, E. (2005). Creative tension: The significance of Ben Oviatt's and Patricia McDougall's article 'Toward a theory of international new ventures'. *Journal of International Business Studies,* 36(1): 9–19.
Burgel, O. & Murray, G. C. (2000). The international market entry choices of start-up companies in high-technology industries. *Journal of International Marketing,* 8(2): 33–62.
Chandra, Y. & Coviello, N. (2010). Broadening the concept of international entrepreneurship: 'consumers as international entrepreneurs'. *Journal of World Business,* 45: 228–236.
Chelekis, J. & Mudambi, S. (2010). MNCs and micro-entrepreneurship in emerging economies: The case of Avon in the Amazon. *Journal of International Management,* 16: 412–424.
Chetty, S. & Campbell-Hunt, C. (2004). A strategic approach to internationalization: A traditional versus a "born-global" approach. *Journal of International Marketing,* 12(1): 57–81.

Choy, C. L. (1990). Sources of business financing and financing practices: A comparison among U.S. and Asian countries. *Journal of Business Venturing*, 5(5): 271–275.

Coombs, J. E., Sadrieh, F., & Annavarjula, M. (2009). Two decades of international entrepreneurship research: What have we learned-where do we go from here? *International Journal of Entrepreneurship*, 13: 23–64.

Coviello, N. E. & Jones, M. V. (2004). Methodological issues in international entrepreneurship research. *Journal of Business Venturing*, 19(4): 485–508.

Coviello, N. E., McDougall, P. P, & Oviatt, B. M. (2011). The emergence, advance and future of international entrepreneurship: An introduction to the special forum. *Journal of Business Venturing*, 26(6): 625–631.

Covin, J. G. & Slevin, D. P. (1990). New venture strategic posture, structure, and performance: An industry life cycle analysis. *Journal of Business Venturing*, 5: 123–135.

De Clercq, D., Meuleman, M., & Wright, M. (2012). A cross-country investigation of micro-angel investment activity: The roles of new business opportunities and institutions. *International Business Review*, 21: 117–129.

Dunning, J. H. & Lundan, S. M. (2008). Institutions and the OLI paradigm of the multinational enterprise. *Asia Pacific Journal of Management*, 25: 573–593.

Edmondson, A. C. & McManus, S. A. (2007). Methodological fit in management field research. *Academy of Management Review*, 32(4): 1155–1179.

Galkina, T. (2012). Broadening the domain of international entrepreneurship: Towards consolidation of the field. In H. Etemad (ed.), *The Process of Internationalization in Emerging SMEs and Emerging Economies* (pp. 68–86). Cheltenham: Edward Elgar.

Giamartino, G. A., McDougall, P. P., & Bird, B. J. (1993). International entrepreneurship: the state of the field. *Entrepreneurship Theory & Practice*, 18(1): 37–42.

Grégoire, D.A., Noël, M. X., Déry, R., & Béchard, J-P. (2006). Is there conceptual convergence in entrepreneurship research? A co-citation analysis of Frontiers in Entrepreneurship Research, 1981–2004. *Entrepreneurship Theory and Practice*, 30(3): 333–357.

Hambrick, D. C. & Chen, M-J. (2008). New academic fields as admittance-seeking social movements: The case of strategic management. *Academy of Management Review*, 33(1): 32–54.

Johnson, P. & Duberley, J. (2000). *Understanding Management Research*. London: Sage Publications.

Jolly, V. K., Alahunta, M., & Jeannet, J-P. (1992). Challenging the incumbents: How high technology start-ups compete globally. *Journal of Strategic Change*, 1(1): 71–82.

Jones, M. V. (1999). The internationalization of small high-technology firms. *Journal of International Marketing*, 7(4): 15–41.

Jones, M. V. & Coviello, N. E. (2005). Internationalization: Conceptualising an entrepreneurial process of behavior in time. *Journal of International Business Studies*, 36(3): 284–303.

Jones, M. V., Coviello, N., & Tang, Y. K. (2011). International entrepreneurship research (1989–2009): A domain ontology and thematic analysis. *Journal of Business Venturing*, 26: 632–659.

Keupp, M. M. & Gassmann, O. (2009). The past and the future of international entrepreneurship: A review and suggestions for developing the field. *Journal of Management*, 35(3): 600–633.

Knight, G. (2000). Entrepreneurship and marketing strategy: The SME under globalization. *Journal of International Marketing*, 8(2): 12–32.

Knight, G. A. & Cavusgil, S. T. (1996). The born global firm: A challenge to traditional internationalization theory. *Advances in International Marketing*, 8: 11–26.

Kohn, T. O. (1988). *International Entrepreneurship: Foreign Direct Investment by Small US-Based Manufacturing Firms*. Doctoral dissertation. Boston, MA: Harvard Business School.

98 *Nicole E. Coviello et al.*

Kuhn, T. S. (1996). *The Structure of Scientific Revolutions*, 3rd ed. Chicago: University of Chicago Press.

Litvak, I. (1990). Instant international: Strategic reality for small high technology firms in Canada. *Multinational Business*, Summer(2): 1–12.

McAdam, D. (1982). *Political Process and the Development of Black Insurgency: 1930–1970.* Chicago: University of Chicago Press.

McDougall, P. P. (1989). International versus domestic entrepreneurship: New venture strategic behavior and industry structure. *Journal of Business Venturing*, 4(6): 387–400.

McDougall, P. P., Shane, S., & Oviatt, B. M. (1994). Explaining the formation of international new ventures: The limits of studies from international business research. *Journal of Business Venturing*, 9(6): 469–487.

McDougall, P. P. & Oviatt, B. M. (2000). International entrepreneurship: The intersection of two research paths. *Academy of Management Journal*, 43(5): 902–906.

McGrath, R. G., MacMillan, I. C., & Scheinberg, S. (1992). Elitists, risk-takers, and rugged individualists? An exploratory analysis of cultural differences between entrepreneurs and non-entrepreneurs. *Journal of Business Venturing*, 7(2): 115–135.

McGrath, R. G., MacMillan, I. C., Yang, E. A.-Y., & Tsai, W. (1992). Does culture endure, or is it malleable? Issues for entrepreneurial economic development. *Journal of Business Venturing*, 7(6): 441–458.

McNaughton, R. B. & Bell, J. (eds.) (2009). *Entrepreneurship and Globalization*, Volumes 1–5. Thousand Oaks, CA: Sage Publications.

Moen, Ø. & Servais, P. (2002). Born global or gradual global? Examining the export behavior of small and medium-sized enterprises. *Journal of International Marketing*, 10(3): 49–72.

Nasra, R. & Dacin, M. T. (2010). Institutional arrangements and international entrepreneurship: The state as international entrepreneur, *Entrepreneurship Theory and Practice*, May: 583–609.

Okhuysen, G. & Bonardi, J-P. (2011). The challenges of building theory by combining lenses. *Academy of Management Review*, 36: 6–11.

Oviatt, B. M. & McDougall, P. P. (1994). Towards a theory of international new ventures. *Journal of International Business Studies*, 25(1): 45–64.

Oviatt, B. M. & McDougall, P. P. (2005). Defining international entrepreneurship and modeling the speed of internationalization. *Entrepreneurship Theory & Practice*, 29(5): 537–553.

Rennie, M. W. (1993). Global competitiveness: Born global. *The McKinsey Quarterly*, 4(4): 45–52.

Rugman, A. M, Verbeke, A., & Nguyen, Q.T.K. (2011). Fifty years of international business theory and beyond. *Management International Review*, 51: 755–786.

Stephan, U. & Uhlaner, L. M. (2010). Performance-based vs socially supportive culture: A cross-national study of descriptive norms and entrepreneurship. *Journal of International Business Studies*, 41: 1347–1364.

Tranfield, D., Denyer, D., & Smart, P. (2003). Towards a methodology for developing evidence informed management knowledge by means of systematic review. *British Journal of Management*, 14(3): 207–222.

Walsh, D. & Downe, S. (2005). Meta-synthesis method for qualitative research: A literature review. *Journal of Advanced Nursing*, 50(2): 204–211.

Whetten, D. A., Felin, T., & King, B. G. (2009). The practice of theory borrowing in organizational studies: Current issues and future directions. *Journal of Management*, 35(3): 537–563.

Wright, R. W. & Ricks, D. A. (1994). Trends in international business research: twenty-five years later. *Journal of International Business Studies*, 25(4): 687–702.

Zahra, S. A. (1993). Environment, corporate entrepreneurship and financial performance: A taxonomic approach. *Journal of Business Venturing*, 8: 319–340.

Zahra, S. A. (2005). A theory of international new ventures: A decade of research. *Journal of International Business Studies*, 36(1): 20–28.

Zahra, S. & George, G. (2002). International entrepreneurship: the current status of the field and future research agenda. In M. A. Hitt, R. D. Ireland, D. Sexton, & M. Camp (eds.), *Strategic Entrepreneurship: Creating an Integrated Mindset*. Malden, MA: Blackwell Publishers.

Zahra, S. A., Ireland, R. D., & Hitt, M. A. (2000). International expansion of new venture firms: International diversity, mode of market entry, technological learning, and performance. *Academy of Management Journal*, 43(5): 925–950.

Zahra, S. A., Korri, J. S., & Yu, J. (2005). Cognition and international entrepreneurship: Implications for research on international opportunity recognition and exploitation. *International Business Review*, 14: 129–146.

Zahra, S. A. & Newey, L. R. (2009). Maximizing the impact of organization science: Theory building at the intersection of disciplines and/or fields. *Journal of Management Studies*, 46(6): 1059–1075.

7 Navigating the growing field of entrepreneurship inquiry
Successionist and relational modes of theory development

Denise Fletcher and Paul Selden
UNIVERSITY OF LUXEMBOURG

Introduction

Reflecting the energy and enthusiasm of a growing multidisciplinary field, entrepreneurship inquiry has generated a profusion of research practices associated with understanding and fostering entrepreneurial attitudes, behaviours, environments, processes, structures, and discourses. Scholarly interest has not only embraced theories from core disciplines, such as economics, psychology, and sociology, it has also expanded into related fields, such as institutional theory, organization studies, strategic management, and international business. The research output that has been generated poses both an opportunity and a challenge. The opportunity concerns the possibility of combining multiple perspectives in new and innovative ways (Pittaway, 2011). The challenge concerns the problem of navigating the complex landscape of entrepreneurship research output (Murphy, 2011).

We concord with those authors who view the 'multi-paradigm' and 'pluralistic' nature of entrepreneurship research as productive in terms of facilitating creative connections, provoking debate, developing conceptual resources, and solving research problems (Grant & Perren, 2002; Jennings et al., 2005; Van de Ven & Poole, 2005; Kyrö, 2006). At the same time, we acknowledge that entrepreneurship research output continues to be regarded as a 'fragmented' and 'heterogeneous' 'multidisciplinary jigsaw' (Harrison & Leitch, 1996; Aldrich & Baker, 1997; Shane & Venkataraman, 2000; Landström, 2001; Busenitz et al., 2003; Reader & Watkins, 2006; Schildt et al., 2006; Moroz & Hindle, 2011; Pittaway, 2011). In spite of the various categorizations that have been proposed and debated within the field, we argue that the problem of navigating entrepreneurship research output is an obstacle to the exploitation of theory development opportunities.

The problem of field navigation persists because the criteria that have been used to differentiate research output, such as ontological and epistemological positions, explanatory foci, levels of analysis and research methods, are elements in the theory development process that are neither mutually exclusive nor intrinsically related. In other words, distinguishing entrepreneurship perspectives in terms of ontological and epistemological positions does not preclude that those perspectives are related in terms of methodological approach, forms of explanation, or theory outcomes. For example, while the evolutionary realism of complexity science and the relativism of social constructionist/post-positivist perspectives are philosophically incommensurable, these research traditions both develop theory in terms of dynamic principles and explanatory mechanisms that explain localized and emergent processes (McKelvey, 2004). Extant categorizations, therefore, do not explain how apparently divergent entrepreneurship perspectives can share important similarities with respect to theory development.

In this article, we propose that the challenge of field navigation can be addressed by grouping and comparing entrepreneurship perspectives in terms of *modes of theory development.*

We define a *mode of theory development* as a holistic characterization of a *type* of theory development process that encompasses a range of apparently divergent research perspectives. In other words, a mode of theory development connects research perspectives despite the fact that they differ in relation to an element, or some elements, of the theory development process, such as meta-theoretical assumptions, unit of analysis, research foci, level of analysis, or methodological practice.

A holistic characterization of any process is rooted in the specification of an *outcome*, which distinguishes that type of process. For example, in relation to the issue of what defines the domain of entrepreneurship inquiry, McMullen and Dimov (2013) point out, "precisely defining the outcome that concludes the entrepreneurial journey is important because this definition determines the nature of the prerequisite elements and assessment of whether they are present" (pp. 1497–1498). In other words, the characterization of a generic outcome sets the parameters for a range of possible prior events.

We propose that the outcome of a theory development process that characterizes a mode of theory development is *the temporal organization of causal relationships between units of theory building in a theoretical generalization.* Units of theory building are constructs, variables, factors, and concepts (Dubin, 1978; Whetten, 1989) that are used to organize empirical material into theoretical generalizations. We propose that *actions, contexts* and *outcomes* are *universal* units of theory building and that causal relationships between actions, contexts, and outcomes are organized *temporally* in the sense that they are related either *successively* or *contemporaneously.* We also propose that theory outcomes in an *entrepreneurship* mode of theory development describe and explain *novel artefacts,* such as new market and social ventures, organizations, opportunities, and commodities (Gartner, 1985; Sarasvathy, 2003; Venkataraman et al., 2012). The theory outcome that characterizes an *entrepreneurship* mode of theory development is, therefore, *the temporal organization of causal relationships between actions, contexts, and outcomes in an explanation of novel artefacts* (Wiklund et al., 2011; Venkataraman et al., 2012).

In what is to follow, we first describe the complexity of entrepreneurship as an emerging field and explain the limitations of extant categorizations. We then

102 Denise Fletcher and Paul Selden

explain that entrepreneurship perspectives can be grouped in terms of modes of theory development according to the principle that theory development processes are characterized by the temporal organization of causal relationships between units of theory building. We explain why actions, contexts, and outcomes should be regarded as universally comparable units of theory building. We also explain why temporality should be regarded as the universal criterion for distinguishing the organization of causal relationships. A fundamental distinction is then made between a *successionist* mode of theory development that organizes causal relationships in terms of *successive* (intertemporal) relationships and a *relational* mode of theory development that organizes causal relationships in terms of *interdependent and contemporaneous* relationships (Harré, 1972; Gottlieb & Halpern, 2002). We discuss the implications of the distinction between *successionist* and *relational* modes of theory development for navigating the emerging field of entrepreneurship inquiry. In particular, we explain how modes of theory development enable us to group apparently divergent perspectives according to underlying assumptions about causality. We conclude that the identification of modes of entrepreneurship theory development is an important step towards a holistic and integrated understanding of a complex and emergent field.

Unbounded by context: the emergence and migration of a field

The story of entrepreneurship inquiry so far, is one in which the increasing social, economic, and cultural significance of entrepreneurship has fuelled the diversification of the field (Landström, 2005). In recent times this process has accelerated as the problematization of entrepreneurial phenomena has migrated across extant boundaries and into new spaces of inquiry. Entrepreneurship inquiry first emerged, in the context of economic theory, and developed through a focus on the functional role of the entrepreneur in the transformation of market processes (Schumpeter, 1911/61; Knight, 1921; Kirzner, 1973; Lachmann, 1977; Casson, 1982). In the post-war period, as the significance of entrepreneurship began to be recognized more widely, entrepreneurship inquiry migrated into management and organizational contexts, and the focus shifted towards psychological, social psychological, and sociological theory. Entrepreneurship researchers drew on psychological theories to explain entrepreneurial action in terms of personality traits and cognitive dispositions (McClelland, 1961; Cole, 1969; Shapero, 1975), while a greater emphasis was also placed on entrepreneurship as a social, historical, and cultural phenomenon (Cole, 1959; Greiner, 1972).

With a dramatic increase in the social, economic and cultural significance of entrepreneurship in the 1980s, there was a shift away from the individual entrepreneur towards viewing entrepreneurship as a type of *behavioural process* (Gartner, 1985; Low & MacMillan, 1988). This new focus on what entrepreneurs actually 'do', rather than 'who' they are (Gartner, 1988), opened up entrepreneurship research as a growing multidisciplinary field of inquiry. Academics were now able to theorize the multicontextual and multidimensional aspects of the entrepreneurial process from a range of disciplinary perspectives, such as population ecology and evolutionary perspectives (Aldrich, 2001b), cognitive bias and heuristics research (Baron, 2000), resource-based theory (Alvarez & Busenitz, 2001), complexity theory (McKelvey, 2004), social theory (Sarason et al., 2006), constructivism (Woods & McKinley, 2010), phenomenology (Berglund, 2007), as well as language-based and discourse-oriented approaches (Steyaert & Hjorth, 2004; Fletcher, 2006).

The concept of entrepreneurship not only migrated into new disciplinary contexts but also into neighbouring fields, such as institutional theory, organization studies, strategic management, and international business. As a result, subfields began to emerge, such as strategic entrepreneurship, institutional entrepreneurship, technological entrepreneurship, social entrepreneurship, international entrepreneurship, organizational/corporate entrepreneurship, and family entrepreneurship. In the case of strategic entrepreneurship, the domain of strategy was linked to or interfaced with entrepreneurship to create a subfield, which now has its own journal, conference, and academic community. The subfield of international entrepreneurship was created when international business intersected with topics and concepts from entrepreneurship. As seen in Chapter 5, international entrepreneurship has now grown and developed to the extent that certain field parameters (such as citations, core definitions, academic chairs, journals, and domain specific conferences) legitimize the relevance and autonomy of the new subfield. Other subfields include institutional entrepreneurship, which was created from the intersection of institutional theory and entrepreneurship; organizational entrepreneurship, which was created at the interface of organization studies and entrepreneurship; and family entrepreneurship, which combines the topic of family business and entrepreneurship. Finally, there is social entrepreneurship, which involves the merging of the domain of social enterprise with entrepreneurship.

As the field of entrepreneurship inquiry has grown it has become progressively more formalized and institutionalized (Aldrich, 2012), which in turn has reinforced perceptions not only of the social, economic, and cultural significance of entrepreneurship, but also its academic value. This process incentivizes the exploitation of academic opportunities by *entrepreneurial* researchers and drives the growth and diversification of the field. Passionate *carriers* 'translate' entrepreneurship ideas and discourse into new contexts (Czarniawska & Sevon, 1996; Powell et al., 2005). In the same way that entrepreneurial business ideas are imitated in equilibrating markets and recontextualized as innovations in new market contexts, so entrepreneurial theories and concepts are actively recontextualized in new academic contexts with institutionalizing and normalizing effects. The story of the emergence of the field of entrepreneurship can, therefore, be regarded as one of 'unfinished discursiveness' (Bourriaud, 2002) in which ideas 'travel' from satiated contexts to non-satiated contexts (Czarniawska & Sevon, 1996; Powell et al., 2005; Fletcher, 2006).

The diversification of the field coincides with the view that entrepreneurship is a 'phenomenon' or 'process' associated with the creation of new ventures, organizations, opportunities, commodities, and markets, rather than a type of 'context' or 'setting', such as small business or owner-managed business (Shane & Venkataraman, 2000; Wiklund et al., 2011; McMullen & Dimov, 2013). If entrepreneurship is context-specific, time-specific, and multidimensional in time and space, then researchers are free to problematize an array of entrepreneurial phenomena in terms of different levels of analysis, units of analysis, and theoretical perspectives (see McMullen & Dimov, 2013: 1497).

The diversification of the field across extant boundaries is also associated with the view that entrepreneurship is a general societal force that permeates everyday life, rather than a context-bound business decision (Steyaert & Katz, 2004). Saravathy & Venkataraman (2011), for example, propose that entrepreneurship is a general social and economic problem-solving 'method', in much the same way that scientific method is a general form of academic inquiry. Similarly, Hjorth & Bjerke (2006) suggest that "everyday living is made possible through entrepreneurship as forms of social creativity" (p. 119). From this perspective, entrepreneurship is a social embodiment of the universal principles that a "thing moved from one place to another cannot emerge unchanged" and "to set something in a new place is to construct it anew" (Czarniawska & Sevon, 1996: 8).

Entrepreneurship is, therefore, a "rather diffuse concept, one not tied to a specific content or meaning" (Powell et al., 2005: 237, quoting Sahlin-Andersson & Engwall, 2002). Entrepreneurship can occur anywhere and at any time – unbounded by context. It can occur in the process of creating a new venture, the process of innovating within an established high growth venture or in the process of spinning out a venture from a university department. It can occur in a financial or non-financial domain; in an institutional context or a market context; as a technological innovation or the innovation of any form of socio-cultural artefact; and through team formation or individual endeavour. It can even occur at any point in the life cycle of a business, emergence of an organization or the development of an opportunity.

The problem of field navigation

Various categorizations, analytical distinctions, and typologies have been proposed and debated in the field to help us make sense of the diversity of entrepreneurship research output. Categorizations include 'design specifications' of the research process, such as research purpose, theoretical perspective, focus, level of analysis, time frame, and methodology (Low & MacMillan, 1988). Methodological distinctions include induction vs. deduction (Bygrave, 1989), cross-sectional vs. longitudinal (Van de Ven & Engleman, 2004), quantitative vs. qualitative (West III, 1997), and macro vs. micro (West III, 1997). At the same time, many different criteria have been used to differentiate theoretical perspectives, such as unidisciplinary and multidisciplinary approaches (Murphy, 2011), behavioural process theory vs. trait theory (Gartner, 1988; Moroz & Hindle, 2011), and paradigms, such as positivism/functionalism vs.

complexity, evolutionary, and post-positivist theory (Grant & Perren, 2002; Downing, 2005; Jennings et al., 2005; McKelvey, 2004).

At the level of meta-theory, distinctions have been made between epistemological positions, such as objectivist vs. subjectivist opportunities (Klein, 2008; Shane, 2012) and pragmatism/realism vs. positivism (Watson, 2013). Meta-theoretical distinctions have also been made between ontological positions, such as causal antecedence vs. emergence/becoming (Sarason et al., 2010; Mole & Mole, 2010; Steyaert, 2007), realism vs. evolutionary realism/constructionism (Alvarez & Barney, 2007), and entitative vs. relational thinking (Fletcher, 2006). Furthermore, entrepreneurship researchers have distinguished explanatory frameworks, such as the individual-opportunity nexus (Shane & Venkataraman, 2000) and the action-interaction nexus (Venkataman et al., 2012), forms of explanation, such as outcome-driven vs. event-driven explanation (Van de Ven & Engleman, 2004), and types of entrepreneurial phenomena, such as discovered vs. created opportunities (Alvarez & Barney, 2007) and causal vs. contingent decision making (Sarasvathy, 2008).

These categories, however, do not explain how context-specific studies can speak to each other when they are based on different assumptions and involve different research choices (Bull & Willard, 1993; Murphy, 2011). How does an economic perspective that uses functionalist explanation speak to a psychological perspective that uses causal variance, or how does a realist sociological perspective speak to a pragmatist psycho-social perspective. Some theorists suggest that this problem concerns the lack of a 'conceptual foundation' that distinguishes entrepreneurship inquiry and which would allow researchers to speak to each other despite a 'labyrinth of assumptions' (Murphy, 2011: 362).

A consensually agreed conceptual foundation for entrepreneurship, however, would not explain *how* some perspectives are complementary despite being incommensurable in relation to one or more aspect of the theory development process. How does one explain that perspectives with distinct epistemologies, ontologies, explanatory frameworks, and research methodologies also can generate complementary research outcomes? The answer we propose is to categorize research output in terms of modes of theory development. Each mode of theory development encompasses a range of meta-theoretical assumptions, explanatory frameworks, levels of analysis, research foci, and research practices. This approach to the navigation of the field enables us to cut across not only disciplinary boundaries, but also emergent subfield boundaries in order to explain how apparently divergent perspectives are related. In the next section, we explain what characterizes and distinguishes a mode of theory development.

Modes of theory development

The first step in characterizing and distinguishing a mode of theory development is to identify those aspects of a theory outcome that are generalizable to all research perspectives. A theory outcome is a simplified and generalizable representation of a real-world phenomenon (Bacharach, 1989: 496). It is generally considered that there are four essential elements of a theory outcome (Dubin, 1978; Whetten, 1989). These elements are, firstly, the specification of 'what' (Whetten, 1989) aspects of a phenomenon are being represented in the theory, in terms of units of theory building, factors, constructs, concepts, and variables (cf. Dubin's notion of 'units of the theory', 1978). Secondly, a conceptualization of 'how' (Whetten, 1989) the units of a theory are causally related (cf. Dubin's notion of 'laws of interaction', 1978). Thirdly, a justification of 'why' the units of theory are causally related in the way being proposed (Whetten, 1989). Lastly, a specification of the generalizability of the theory in terms of 'who, where, when', or the temporal and contextual boundary conditions (Whetten, 1989).

Elements three and four are research project specific. Elements one and two, however, are generalizable to all research projects. We, therefore, propose that a mode of theory development is characterized in terms of *how* the units of theory building are causally related in a theory outcome (Whetten, 1989; Bacharach, 1989). In the following discussion, we specify *universal* units of theory building that can be used to characterize causal relationships in any theory outcome and explain that *temporality* should be used as the criterion to differentiate causal relationships associated with different modes of theory development.

Various analytic distinctions have been used in entrepreneurship inquiry to differentiate units of theory building in theoretical explanations. Many of these distinctions have been based on a subject-object dichotomy or *inner-outer* distinction between the individual and environment. For example, the 'individual-opportunity nexus' (Shane & Venkataraman, 2000) and the 'action–interaction nexus' (Venkataraman et al., 2012) have been used to frame theoretical discussions by making a distinction between explanatory elements that are 'internal' to the individual, such as cognitive structures and forms of decision making, and elements that are 'external' to the individual, such as social interactions, firm processes, and market opportunities (Venkataraman et al., 2012). The limitation of this approach is that there are dynamics within the individual, such as relationships between cognitive structures and actions, as well as within the environment, such as social interactions, which are not explained by an inner-outer distinction.

Instead, we propose that a universally applicable distinction is that between *actions, contexts,* and *outcomes.* The rationale for this distinction is that social events are contingent upon *actions*, and that the *outcomes* of these actions then become the *contexts* for subsequent actions. This *time-relative* understanding of the relationship between action, context, and outcome flows from the generally acknowledged principle that social phenomena are 'action-dependent' (Giddens, 1984; Archer, 1995; Shane, 2003; Sarasvathy, 2008). All social phenomena are either directly contingent on actions in the *present* or indirectly contingent on actions in the *past* (whether in the historical past or the immediate past) that have become contextual to the present. From this perspective, the notion of action incorporates any *present* event, whether purposeful or serendipitous or whether a thought event or a social communication event. A context, on the other hand, is an *outcome* of *prior* actions, which can be experienced cognitively in the form of a cognitive schema, prior knowledge, contingent event, material artefact, social practice, or social structure.

All theory outcomes in entrepreneurship inquiry can be characterized in terms of action, context, and outcome relationships. Consider, for example, a theory outcome which states that there is co-variation between a variable moderating entrepreneurial action (such as the moderating effect of information on creativity) and an entrepreneurial outcome (such as opportunity identification) (Gielnik et al., 2012). In this case the moderating variable is a context for action, and both the context and action are causally related to the outcome. Consider, also, a theory outcome which states that entrepreneurs take non-predictive control over uncertain situations by modifying means-end relationships in the light of contingent stakeholder interaction (Sarasvathy, 2008). In this case, stakeholder interaction is contextual to entrepreneurial action which creates the outcome of means-end modification.

What distinguishes the causal organization of actions, contexts and outcomes in these explanations is the *temporal* organization of the causal relationships. In the first example, the theorist assumes a sequential or intertemporal perspective in which contexts are antecedent to actions, and actions are antecedent to outcomes. In the second example, the theorist assumes that actions and contexts are interdependent and mutually constitute an emergent outcome over a duration of time.

This temporal characterization of causal explanations correlates with the distinction that has been made between 'linear causality' and 'relational causality' (Gottlieb & Halpern, 2002) or what has also been termed 'successionist theory' and 'generative theory' (Harré, 1972). We will refer to this distinction as successionist causality vs. relational causality. In successionist causality, "cause can be described perfectly and completely without reference to what effect it has, and the effect of a cause is an independently specifiable event or happening or state" (Harré, 1972: 116). Successionist explanations, therefore, organize cause (action and/or context) and effect (outcome) in successive relationships so that the cause comes 'first in time' (Harré, 1972:115) before the effect (outcome). In relational causality there is an interdependence between causal processes that produces an effect in the moment of this interdependence (Gottlieb & Halpern, 2002). In relational explanations the causal interrelationship of processes (actions and contexts), therefore, runs 'contemporaneously' with an emergent outcome (Harré, 1972: 116). In other words, outcomes emerge at the same time as action-context interactions.

We use the distinction between successionist and relational theory outcomes to make a distinction between successionist and relational modes of entrepreneurship theory development. Any entrepreneurship research project that explains an entrepreneurial artefact in terms of connections between temporally separated cause and effect relationships falls within the successionist mode of entrepreneurship theory development. Any entrepreneurship research project that explains an entrepreneurial artefact as emergent in the moment of action-context relationships falls within the relational mode of entrepreneurship theory development.

The distinction between successionist and relational modes of theory development should not be confused with Van de Ven & Engleman's (2004) distinction between 'variance theory' ('outcome-driven explanation') and 'process theory' ('event-driven explanation') (see also Mohr, 1982, and Dimov, 2011). While a variance theory explanation is 'built backwards' from a problematized outcome to 'prior causally significant events' (Aldrich, 2001a: 118), a process theory explanation is 'built forwards' from 'observed or recorded events to outcomes' (Aldrich, 2001a: 119). In both cases, units of theory building are organized *successively* either in terms of causal antecedence in the case of variance theory or in terms of 'sequences of events' in the case of process theory. The successionist-relational dichotomy, therefore, involves a temporal distinction between successive and contemporaneous relationships which is not implicated in the distinction between variance and process theory.

In the next two sections, we examine how successionist and relational conceptions of causality are involved in the development of entrepreneurship theory outcomes. We also discuss how apparently divergent entrepreneurship perspectives are interrelated in successionist and relational modes of entrepreneurship theory development.

The successionist mode of entrepreneurship theory development

In the successionist mode of entrepreneurship theory development, theory is developed in terms of identifying causal regularities between intertemporally related market conditions, moderating contexts, individual entrepreneurial qualities, the characteristics of entrepreneurial decision-making processes, behavioural actions and process outcomes. How these variables are successively related as action, contexts and outcomes in specific research projects is not always clear. We do not have the space here to examine this issue in detail. Instead, we will give an indication of the sorts of variables that can be understood as actions, contexts and outcomes, and give some examples of how they are causally related.

In the successionist literature, action and context are distinct entities that are causally related in the subject-object dualism between the individual entrepreneurial decision maker and environmental (contextual) information. A context is, therefore, an objectified *boundary condition* for entrepreneurial action, which can *moderate* the causal effects of individual action on entrepreneurial outcomes or function as the source of an opportunity or an obstacle to entrepreneurial action. Welter (2011) explains that, "context simultaneously provides individuals with entrepreneurial opportunities and sets boundaries for their actions; in other words, individuals may experience it as asset or liability"

Navigating entrepreneurship inquiry 109

(pp. 165–166). From a successionist perspective, the notion of context is, therefore, usually equated with aspects of a changing firm/market environment or the wider social environment (such as cultural, institutional, technological, regulatory, economic, and political artefacts).

We extend the term 'context' to include entrepreneurial qualities, such as traits, mental states and cognitive capabilities, on the basis that these qualities are prior aggregated actions and causal antecedents to present decision-making and behavioural actions. From this perspective, contextual variables include (1) *market conditions,* i.e. objectified sources of opportunities in market relationships (Shane & Venkataraman, 2000); (2) *moderating contexts* (or 'information context', Simon & Houghton, 2002), such as environmental information relating to firm characteristics, demographic characteristics, social institutions, and social networks (Gielnik & Frese, 2013); (3) *entrepreneurial qualities,* such as traits, mental states (intention, affect, and motivation), and cognitive capabilities (knowledge, cognitive bias, and heuristics) which are *mediating* contexts for entrepreneurial actions (Baron, 2008); and (4) *decision contexts* (Simon & Houghton, 2002), such as the decision task or the information search process, which form the context for subsequent decision-making actions.

In contrast, entrepreneurial actions can be categorized as: (1) *decision-making events,* such as a choice, perception, or belief; (2) *decision-making processes,* such as information search, opportunity identification, problem-solving, and discovery; (3) *characteristics of decision making,* such as 'entrepreneurial orientation', 'proactiveness', 'risk-taking', 'innovativeness', 'self-starting', and 'persistence' (Frese, 2009); and (4) *behavioural processes,* such as resource acquisition and business legitimization. Entrepreneurial outcomes are the artefactual outcomes of decision-making processes, such as a perception, decision, choice, or business idea, and the artefactual outcomes of behavioural processes at different levels of analysis and stages in the entrepreneurial process, such as a business plan, resource acquisition, new venture, new product, and firm growth.

In terms of the causal relationships between actions, contexts and outcomes in successionist theory: (1) actions are viewed as having direct causal effects on entrepreneurial outcomes, which can be *mediated* by subsequent action processes; (2) contexts are viewed as having indirect effects in the sense of conditions for the possibility of action or as a variable that moderates the causal effects of action on an outcome; and (3) an outcome is explained in terms of the prior independent causal effects of actions and contexts.

An example of the temporal organization of actions, contexts and outcomes at the level of entrepreneurial decision making is Simon & Houghton's (2002) model of causal relationships in the process of 'pioneering product introduction'. In the model, Simon & Houghton (2002) hypothesize a succession of causally related variables which are antecedent to the 'decision to pioneer'. The initial causal connection concerns the effect of two 'information contexts', firm age (*moderating context*) and 'pioneering decision context', on whether a subsequent information search process is 'active', 'personal' or 'external' (*decision-making process*). The model then posits that the information gathered by the search process functions as a condition that makes certain cognitive biases (*entrepreneurial qualities*) more or less probable. The ensuing cognitive bias, such as illusion of control, is then associated with a misperception or misjudgement (*decision-making event*) of an uncertain environment, such as overestimating market demand. Finally, the misperception makes a decision to pioneer more or less probable (*outcome*). This succession of causal connections can be schematized as a context (decision context and firm age), which is causally linked to an action (information search process), which is then causally linked to a mental context (cognitive bias), which is then linked to an action (misperception), and finally an outcome (decision to pioneer).

Having discussed how a successionist theory outcome can be conceptualized as successively related actions, contexts and outcomes, we will now discuss the complementarity of apparently diverse perspectives contained by the successionist mode of theory development. We focus on the disciplinary perspectives of economic functionalism and cognitivism, and the multidisciplinary perspectives of psychological rationalism and variance theory.

Economic entrepreneurship perspectives (Schumpeter, 1911/1961; Kirzner, 1973; Casson, 1982) use functionalist explanation to organize causal relationships in terms of the function of entrepreneurial action within a market system. In neoclassical economic theory, entrepreneurial decisions function to realize the capacity of a market system to generate equilibrium states. In the context of the successionist mode of entrepreneurship theory development, economic functionalism identifies the initial market conditions of the market system as an *overarching context* for entrepreneurial action. The overarching context is an *entrepreneurial opportunity* that pre-exists entrepreneurial action in the form of initial market conditions or exogenous market inefficiencies, and is then 'discovered and mitigated' by entrepreneurial action (Shane & Venkataraman, 2000: 219). Market conditions are, therefore, a *condition of possibility for entrepreneurial action* in the sense of both a context for entrepreneurial action and a possible outcome built into the market system. Whether entrepreneurial action is successful or not in actualizing the possibility of the future market depends on the entrepreneur's perception of market conditions (context).

The economic functionalist notion that entrepreneurial outcomes are explained by the relationship between entrepreneurial action and antecedent opportunities (context) connects with other successionist perspectives through the principle of opportunity discovery and the veridical perception of the market environment (Drucker, 1985; Gaglio & Katz, 2001). Cognitivist research, for example, concerns the veridical perception or 'fit' of cognitive schema (action) with environmental information (context) (Gaglio & Katz, 2001; Baum et al., 2007), while the 'individual-opportunity nexus' (Shane, 2003; Murphy, 2011) is concerned with the discovery of antecedent opportunities (context) by entrepreneurial cognition and decision-making processes (action) (Shane & Venkataraman, 2000).

Psychological rationalism is a multidisciplinary perspective which stresses the centrality of entrepreneurial action as an efficient cause of entrepreneurial outcomes (McMullen & Shepherd, 2006; Frese, 2009; Gielnik & Frese, 2013). In entrepreneurship 'action theory', for example, an entrepreneur's actions and 'action strategies' are 'central determinants of entrepreneurial success' (Frese, 2009). These actions and 'action strategies' include 'forming a goal', 'seeking information', 'planning', 'monitoring the execution', and 'feedback processing' (Frese, 2009). Contextual factors have an effect on the outcome of success in so far as they moderate entrepreneurial action (Frese, 2009). The focus of psychological rationalist research is, therefore, on: (1) the entrepreneurial qualities that are antecedents to behavioural actions, such as intention/motivation, means-end (belief-desire) relationships, prior knowledge, and alertness (Shane, 2000); (2) the characteristics of behavioural actions, such as risk-taking, innovativeness, and proactiveness, which are causal antecedents to firm-level outcomes, such as growth; and (3) the structure of the entrepreneurial process in terms of phases and steps in decision making and behavioural processes, such as the identification, elaboration, and exploitation of entrepreneurial opportunities, searching for and selecting information, developing a new product, organizing resources, and fulfilling legal requirements.

In the successionist mode of theory development, psychological rationalist assumptions complement cognitivist and functionalist perspectives because they focus at the level of relationships between behavioural actions, rather than mental contexts and market conditions. Moreover, psychological rationalist principles are combined with cognitivist and functionalist approaches in a range of disciplinary areas and perspectives, such as economic theory (Casson, 1982), discovery theory (Shane, 2003), rational decision making (Fiet, 2006), action theory (Frese, 2009), and biases and heuristics research (Baron, 2000). For example, discovery theory emphasizes phases of behavioural actions in the process of identifying, evaluating, and exploiting opportunities (psychological rationalism), at the same time as explaining individual entrepreneurial actions in terms of the relationship between individual perception (cognitivism) and antecedent opportunities in the market system (functionalism).

Multivariable, or variance, theory development is a multidisciplinary methodology and form of explanation, which measures causal connections between antecedent variables and outcomes (Mohr, 1982; Van de Ven & Engleman, 2004). In variance theory (outcome-driven explanation), theoretical generalizations are 'built backwards' from a problematized outcome to 'prior causally significant events' (Aldrich, 2001: 118). Methodologically, variance theory is *empiricist* in the sense that statistical and probabilistic correlations are made between independent, moderating and intervening (mediating) variables, and dependent outcomes. Change or variation in an outcome (dependent) variable is explained by the measurement of cross-sectional correlations with antecedent (independent) variables. It does not matter how variables are ordered, it is the antecedence of a variable to an outcome that is causally significant (Van de Ven & Engleman, 2004).

The principle of empirical co-variance can be applied to a variety of action, context, and outcome relationships in the successionist mode of entrepreneurship

112 *Denise Fletcher and Paul Selden*

theory development. It can apply to functionalist and positivist forms of explanation, realist and objectivist assumptions, and different disciplinary units and levels of analysis. For example, it can apply to cognitivist research, such as the effects of cognitive biases and heuristics on entrepreneurial action (Simon & Houghton, 2002); to psychological rationalist decision-making research, such as the moderating effects of information on creativity (Gielnik et al., 2012); and economic firm-level research, such as causal effects between firm resources and firm outcomes (Wiklund & Shepherd, 2003).

The relational mode of entrepreneurship theory development

In the *relational* mode of theory development, actions, contexts, and outcomes are not separate causal entities, but rather interrelated in the same moment of time. In the *successionist* mode of theory development, the general assumption that context is prior to action is associated with the separation of action and context as causal entities. In the relational mode of theory development, however, the notion that context is prior to action concerns how prior contexts *become* a part of a present moment of action and create emergent outcomes in that moment. The focus of the relational mode of theory development is, therefore, the 'moving present' (Dimov, 2011) or moment in which an entrepreneurial process emerges and is transformed through the relational interdependence of action and context (Dewey & Bentley, 1949; Emirbayer, 1997). A context is not a *situation* or *condition* in which an action happens, but something that is *created* as past actions become present action.

This viewpoint has been termed an 'activity as context' approach (van Oers, 1998), and is associated with non-entitative and non-individualistic traditions in education science (Vygotsky, 1994; Bakhtin, 1981), philosophy (Heidegger, 1962; Ricouer, 1984), and forms of social inquiry (Shotter, 1993; Emirbayer, 1997). From an 'activity as context' perspective, context emerges as it becomes clear, through self-reflexive mental activities and social interaction activities, what kind of activity is being practised. In relation to social activity, for example, Shotter (1993) states, "It is the joint activity between [people] and their socially (and linguistically) constituted situation that 'structures' what they do and say" (Shotter, 1993: 8, quoted in Oers, 1998: 480).

In the relational mode of entrepreneurship theory development, the emergence of entrepreneurial outcomes (artefacts) is explained in terms of the identification of dynamic relationships (or explanatory mechanisms) between actions and contexts. These explanatory mechanisms include notions of 'process emergence' (McKelvey, 2004), 'dynamic creation' (Chiles et al., 2010), entrepreneurial 'opportunity creation' (Alvarez & Barney, 2007), 'entrepreneurial becoming' (Fletcher, 2006; Steyaert, 2007), 'effectual logic' (Sarasvathy, 2008), 'action-interaction nexus' (Venkataraman et al., 2012), 'adaptive tension' (McKelvey, 2004), and 'opportunity tension' (Lichtenstein, 2009). The range of theory development processes that fall within the relational mode of entrepreneurship

Navigating entrepreneurship inquiry 113

theory development, therefore, concerns the variety of ways in which outcomes are conceptualized as emerging through a relationship between action and context. We identify three types of action-context relationships:

1 *action-as-self-contextualization*, which concerns self-organizing and self-reflexive thought processes;
2 *action-as-transactional-contextualization*, which concerns dialogical social interaction; and
3 *action-as-embedded-contextualization*, which concerns the relationship between action and aggregated actions at different levels of analysis, such as technological paths, market systems, firm structures, social practices, discourses, networks, and institutions.

In 'action-as-self-contextualization', context is created by purposeful sense-making actions in order to contextualize subsequent actions undertaken within a self-regulating sense-making process (see van Oers, 1998). In 'action-as-transactional-contextualization', social communications function as 'contextualization cues' (Gumperz, 1982), which are intended contexts within a process of dialogical interaction. In 'action-as-embedded-contextualization' both self-contextualizing and transactional-contextualizing actions are embedded in actions that have been aggregated as distinct entities, such as networks, technological media and organizational structures. We now discuss how these action-context relationships are implicated in a range of perspectives.

Self-contextualization is associated with perspectives that focus on the transformational effects of prior visions, goals, and strategies on self-reflexive sense-making actions. The tension between prior contextualization and action in the present moment is the dynamic principle or mechanism that explains the emergence of mental artefacts, such as business ideas and decisions. 'Opportunity development' research (Ardichvili et al., 2003; Sanz-Velasco, 2006; Dimov, 2007), for example, emphasizes an action-centred 'shaping process' (Ardichvili et al., 2003; Sanz-Velasco, 2006; Dimov, 2007) in which present action is contextualized by an open-ended telos that leaves room for individual endeavour and circumstantial adaptation (Sanz-Velasco, 2006). Similarly, radical subjectivists and constructivists (Lachmann, 1977; Shackle, 1979; Chiles et al., 2010; Sarason et al., 2006; Woods & McKinley, 2010) focus on the relationship between purposeful goal-oriented states and present action. Lachmann (1977), for example, focuses on how unfettered imagination contextualizes present action by envisioning new combinations of capital resources, which bridges the gap to an uncertain future. Sarason et al. (2006) use a constructivist interpretation of structuration theory to argue that entrepreneurial action is a "reflexive" process in which the entrepreneur reflects on and responds to the consequences of their own actions. In other words, the entrepreneurs' past actions contextualize their present actions within a self-reflexive thought process.

Transactional contextualization is associated with perspectives which focus on the transformational effects of social interaction on entrepreneurial actions.

114 *Denise Fletcher and Paul Selden*

Asymmetries between contingent social interactions and entrepreneurial actions are the mechanisms that explain how present actions are contextualized by past events and contextualizing of future events. For example, in effectuation theory (Sarasvarthy, 2008) asymmetries between the entrepreneur's and stakeholder's commitments to particular strategies and resources enable and constrain entrepreneurial action. The context of social interaction continually redefines the possibilities of entrepreneurial action by redrawing problem spaces and enabling the entrepreneur to take 'non-predictive' control over uncertain situations by exploiting contingent events as they arise.

Gartner et al.'s (1992 and 2003) 'opportunity enactment' perspective assumes a similar psycho-social approach in emphasizing the dynamic action-context relationship between sense-making action (enactment) and the contingent experience of stakeholder interaction. Initially, the entrepreneur 'enacts' (actively makes sense of) the environment with the expectation of creating an 'unequivocal' future, i.e. the successful venture. The concrete process of opportunity emergence, however, is driven by the contingent stakeholder responses to these actions. The stakeholder's response is a context in which the entrepreneur carries out subsequent actions. The entrepreneur, therefore, learns to create the emerging venture through contradictions between personal and stakeholder understandings.

Transactional contextualization perspectives can also focus on how entrepreneurial processes emerge through a process in which context migrates ('stretching away') through 'spatial' relationships in "dialogue, exchanges, conversations, relations, joint acts and co-ordinations" (Fletcher, 2007: 657). In other words, the fluid nature of the relational interdependence between action and context creates opportunities for making creative connections:

> . . . cultural and social practices, ideas or images don't 'stay' in one place, they travel and migrate across boundaries. As they do so, they sometimes bring about change or transformation.
>
> (Fletcher, 2006: 435)

Embedded contextualization is associated with structural contexts, such as higher level market systems, social networks, and firm structures (Aldrich & Kenworthy, 1999; McKelvey, 2004; Mole & Mole, 2010; Chiles et al., 2010), and material contexts, such as technologies and resources (Garud & Karnøe, 2003; Baker & Nelson, 2005). In other words, structural contexts and material contexts are viewed as having properties that are mutually constituted with action, but endure separately and, therefore, have their own dynamic with entrepreneurial action. The nature of this mediating relationship depends on the ontological and epistemological commitments of the perspective in question.

In entrepreneurship 'complexity' research, for example, entrepreneurial creativity is explained in terms of the spatio-temporal differential between 'tangible' entrepreneurial actions and the context of market-level opportunities

Navigating entrepreneurship inquiry 115

(Lichtenstein & Kurjanowicz, 2010). This differential engenders an 'adaptive tension' (McKelvey, 2004) or 'opportunity tension' (Lichtenstein, 2009), which can be exploited by entrepreneurial creativity. In other words, the spatio-temporal differences between market-level contexts and entrepreneurial actions engender contradictions that are opportunities for creating market heterogeneity.

In bricolage theory, the medium of 'technology' is a material context that structures the actions of entrepreneur and stakeholders (cf. the social construction of technological systems, Bijker et al., 1987, and actor network theory, Latour, 1991). For example, Garud and Karnøe (2003) argue that an entrepreneurial opportunity is created by a process of 'bricolage', in which "an accumulation of inputs [e.g. knowledge, artefacts, learning and information] from multiple actors generates a momentum . . . [that] begins enabling and constraining the activities of the involved actors" (p. 278). Knowledge and resources accumulate in the 'structure' of the technological path because the actors' agency is embedded and embodied in the artefacts, tools, practices, rules, knowledge, and learning associated with the technology. Entrepreneurial action then exploits the 'intersection' of, and 'interpretive asymmetry' between, the actions of different actors relative to the context of the emergent technological path.

Navigating the field of entrepreneurship

The distinction between successionist and relational modes of entrepreneurship theory development has important implications for how we understand the linkages, relative significance, and complementarity between unidisciplinary, multidisciplinary, and subfield perspectives. In the case of the successionist mode of entrepreneurship theory development, the principle that actions, contexts, and outcomes are causally organized in successive relationships is associated with a range of theoretical, explanatory, and methodological positions which cut across entrepreneurship perspective boundaries. These positions can be listed as follows:

1   objectivist assumptions about the veridical perception of opportunities, conditions, and contexts which are antecedent and exogenous to entrepreneurial action;
2   objectivist assumptions about the context-relativity and contingency of individual actions;
3   subjectivist assumptions about bounded rationality, cognitive bias, heuristics, prior knowledge, risk-taking, intention, uncertainty, etc.
4   choice of research foci, unit of analysis and level of analysis based on ontological realist assumptions about the independent causal effects of discrete entities;
5   functionalist and psychological rationalist forms of explanation based on ontological realist assumptions about the independent causal effects of discrete entities;

116 *Denise Fletcher and Paul Selden*

6　empiricist methodological assumptions about the probabilistic nature of causal relationships and covariance between successive variables;

7　research design practices concerning the development of testable propositions from exploratory qualitative research and the testing of propositions through measurement of covariant relationships.

8　theory developed in terms of analytical frameworks, deductive hypothesis generation, predictive generalizations, schematic models of successive causal relationships, and inductive generalized typologies.

The above positions are potentially compatible and complementary because they all involve organizing actions, contexts, and outcomes in successive causal relationships.

The cohesiveness of the successionist mode of theory development is partly explained by the centrality of neoclassical economics to successionist theory development. Neoclassical economics has a dual explanatory structure which combines the subjective freedom and 'rationalist teleology' of the entrepreneur with the 'formative teleology' (Stacey, 2001) of a closed equilibrium–oriented market system. In other words, neoclassical theory combines a subjectivist understanding of contingent entrepreneurial actions with the ontologically realist view that the entrepreneur is objectively constrained and enabled by entities at different levels of analysis, such as firms, networks, and markets. The discovery perspective (Shane & Venkataraman, 2000; Shane, 2003), for example, is compatible with all the elements in the above list because it is strongly influenced by Kirznerian economic theory. Shane and Venkataraman (2000) view "entrepreneurship as the mechanism through which temporal and spatial inefficiencies in an economy are discovered and mitigated [by entrepreneurial action]" (Shane & Venkataraman, 2000: 219). This economic functionalist position enables Shane and Venkataraman (2000) to recognize that subjective entrepreneurial action is constrained by objective market conditions. Ultimately, however, successionist perspectives are complementary because intertemporal causal relationships between actions, contexts and outcomes can be schematically arranged and causally integrated in a temporally ordered sequence (see earlier Simon & Houghton model, 2002).

In the relational mode of entrepreneurship theory development, the principle that actions, contexts, and outcomes are emergent in the *moving present* is associated with various transformative action-context mechanisms. These mechanisms are developed from a range of apparently incommensurable disciplinary and subdisciplinary perspectives associated with distinctive epistemological and ontological assumptions. There are self-reflexive mechanisms developed from subjectivist epistemologies (Sarason et al., 2006); there are transactional mechanisms developed from pragmatist epistemologies (Sarasvathy, 2008) and social constructionist ontologies (Fletcher, 2006); and there are embedded mechanisms developed from realist ontologies (Garud & Karnøe, 2003; Mole & Mole, 2010).

While these viewpoints are incommensurable at an epistemological and ontological level, they identify complementary explanatory mechanisms because each viewpoint focuses on different forms of contextualization in the entrepreneurial process. For example, self-reflexive and transactional mechanisms are complementary because self-contextualization and transactional contextualization processes run contemporaneously and in parallel as sensemaking and behavioural dimensions of an entrepreneurial process. Explanatory mechanisms are also complementary if they explain different moments in the emergence of a process and so can be used to piece together sequences of events in the story of emergence. Furthermore, embedded mechanisms can contribute to multilevel explanations because they explain how actions are contextualized by artefacts that have already emerged at higher levels of analysis, such as technological paths, tangible artefacts, venture formation, and even institutional and international contexts. Embedded mechanisms can also explain how entrepreneurial actions are related to *distal* contexts in wider society, such as discourse, narratives and social practices, and to the dynamics within these contexts.

In conclusion, the distinction between a successionist and relational mode of entrepreneurship theory development contributes to solving the task of how to navigate the multiple perspectives of an emerging field. We have explained how the successionist and relational modes of entrepreneurship theory development reconnect an apparently fragmented field of inquiry caused by the multicontextual migration of the entrepreneurship concept. The successionist mode of entrepreneurship theory development explains how apparently incommensurable perspectives cohere around a set of assumptions about the nature of successionist causality. We have also explained how perspectives in the relational mode of entrepreneurship theory development are complementary because they focus on action-context relationships in different time frames of emergence, at different stages in emergence and across different levels of emergence.

References

Aldrich, H. E. (2001). Who wants to be an evolutionary theorist: Remarks on the occasion of the Year 2000 OMT Distinguished Scholarly Career Award Presentation. *Journal of Management Inquiry*, 10(2): 115–127.

Aldrich, H. E. (2001b). Many are called, but few are chosen: An evolutionary perspective for the study of entrepreneurship. *Entrepreneurship Theory and Practice*, 25, Summer: 41–55.

Aldrich, H. E. (2012). The emergence of entrepreneurship as an academic field: A personal essay on institutional entrepreneurship. *Research Policy*, 41(7): 1240–1248.

Aldrich, H. E. & Baker, T. (1997). Blinded by the cities? Has there been progress in entrepreneurship research? In D. L. Sexton, R. W. Smilor (eds.) *Entrepreneurship 2000*. Chicago: Upstart Publishing.

Aldrich H. E. & Kenworthy A. (1999). The accidental entrepreneur: Campbellian antinomies and organizational foundings. In J.A.C. Baum, B. McKelvey (eds.), *Variations in Organization Science: In Honor of Donald T. Campbell* (pp. 19–33). Newbury Park, CA: Sage.

118 *Denise Fletcher and Paul Selden*

Alvarez, S. A. & Barney, S. A. (2007). Discovery and creation: Alternative theories of entrepreneurial action. *Strategic Entrepreneurship Journal*, 1: 11–26.

Alvarez, S. A. & Busenitz, L. W. (2001). The entrepreneurship of resource-based theory. *Journal of Management*, 27(6): 755–775.

Archer, M. S. (1995). *Realist Social Theory: A Morphogenetic Approach*. Cambridge: Cambridge University Press.

Ardichvili, A., Cardozo, R., & Ray, S. (2003). A theory of entrepreneurial opportunity identification and development. *Journal of Business Venturing*, 18: 105–123.

Bacharach, S. B. (1989). Organizational theories: Some criteria for evaluation. *Academy of Management Review*, 14(4): 496–515.

Baker, T. & Nelson, R. E. (2005). Creating something from nothing: Resource construction through entrepreneurial bricolage. *Administrative Science Quarterly*, 50: 329–66.

Bakhtin, M. M. (1981). *The Dialogic Imagination*. Austin: University of Texas Press.

Baron, R. A. (2000). Psychological perspectives on entrepreneurship: Cognitive and social factors in entrepreneur's success. *Current Directions in Psychological Science*, 9: 15–18.

Baron R. A. (2008). The role of effect in the entrepreneurial process. *Academy of Management Review*, 33: 328–340.

Baum, J. R., Frese, M., & Baron, R. A. (2007). *The Psychology of Entrepreneurship*. Mahwah NJ: Lawrence Erlbaum.

Berglund, H. (2007). Opportunities as existing and created: A study of entrepreneurs in the Swedish mobile internet industry. *Journal of Enterprising Culture*, 15: 243–273.

Bijker, W., Hughes, T., & Pinch, T. (eds.) (1987). *The Social Construction of Technological Systems*. Cambridge, MA: The MIT Press.

Bourriaud, N. (2002). *Relational Aesthetics*. Paris: Presses du Réel.

Bull, I. & Willard, G. E. (1993). Towards a theory of entrepreneurship. *Journal of Business Venturing*, 8: 183–195.

Busenitz, L. W., West, G. P. III, Shepherd, D., Nelson, T., Chandler, G. N., & Zacharakis, A. (2003). Entrepreneurship research in emergence: Past trends and future directions. *Journal of Management*, 29(3): 285–308.

Bygrave, W. D. (1989). The entrepreneurship paradigm (1): A philosophical look at its research methodologies. *Entrepreneurship Theory and Practice*, 14(1): 7–26.

Casson, M. (1982). *The Entrepreneur: An Economic Theory* (2nd ed.). Oxford: Edward Elgar.

Chiles, T. H., Tuggle, C. S., McMullan, J. S., Bierman, L., & Greening, D. W. (2010). Dynamic creation: Extending the radical Austrian approach to entrepreneurship. *Organization Studies*, 31(7): 7–46.

Cole, A. (1959). *Business Enterprise in its Social Setting*. Boston: Harvard University Press.

Cole, A. (1969). Definition of entrepreneurship. In J. C. Komives & K. A. Bostrum (eds.), *Seminar in the Study of Enterprise* (pp. 10–22). Milwaukee Center for Venture Management.

Czarniawska, B., & Sevón, G. (eds.). (1996). *Translating organizational change* (Vol. 56). New York: Gruyter.

Dewey, J. & Bentley, A. F. (1949). *Knowing and the Known*. Boston: Beacon.

Dimov, D. (2007). Beyond the single-person, single-insight attribution of understanding entrepreneurial opportunities. *Entrepreneurship Theory and Practice*, 31(5): 713–731.

Dimov, D. (2011). Grappling with the unbearable elusiveness of entrepreneurial opportunities. *Entrepreneurship Theory and Practice*, 35, 1: 57–81.

Downing, S. (2005). The social construction of entrepreneurship: Narrative and dramatic processes in the coproduction of organizations and identities. *Entrepreneurship Theory and Practice*, 29(2): 185–204.

Drucker, P. (1985). *Innovation and Entrepreneurship*. New York: Harper and Row.

Navigating entrepreneurship inquiry 119

Dubin, R. (1978). *Theory Development*. New York: Free Press.

Emirbayer, M. (1997). Manifesto for a relational sociology. *American Journal of Sociology*, 103(2): 281–317.

Fiet, J.O. (2006). A prescriptive analysis of search and discovery. *Journal of Management Studies*, 44: 592–611.

Fletcher, D. E. (2006). Entrepreneurial processes and the social construction of opportunity. *Entrepreneurship and Regional Development*, 18: 421–440.

Fletcher, D. E. (2007). Toy story: The narrative world of entrepreneurship and the creation of interpretive communities. *Journal of Business Venturing*, 22: 649–672.

Frese, M. (2009). Toward a psychology of entrepreneurship – an action theory perspective. *Foundations and Trends in Entrepreneurship*, 5(6): 435–494.

Gaglio, C.M. & Katz, J.A. (2001). The psychological basis of opportunity identification: Entrepreneurial alertness. *Journal of Small Business Economics*, 16: 95–111.

Gartner, W. B. (1985). A conceptual framework for describing the phenomenon of new venture creation. *Academy of management review*, 10(4): 696–706.

Gartner, W. B. (1988) "Who is an entrepreneur?" is the wrong question. *American Journal of Small Business*, 12 (4): 11–32.

Gartner, W.B., Bird, B., & Starr, J. (1992). Acting as if: Differentiating entrepreneurial from organizational behaviour. *Entrepreneurship: Theory and Practice*, 16(3): 13–30.

Gartner, W. B., Carter, N. M. & Hills, G. E. (2003). The language of opportunity. In C. Steyaert, & D. Hjorth, (eds.), *New Movements in Entrepreneurship*, (pp. 103–124). Cheltenham: Edward Elgar.

Garud, R. & Karnøe, P. (2003). Bricolage versus breakthrough: Distributed and embedded agency in technology entrepreneurship. *Research Policy*, 32(2): 277–300.

Gielnik, M.M., Frese, M., Graf, J.M., & Kampschulte, A. (2012). Creativity in the opportunity identification process and the moderating effect of diversity of information. *Journal of Business Venturing*, 27(5): 559–576.

Gielnik, M.M. & Frese, M. (2013). Entrepreneurship and poverty reduction: Applying I-O psychology to microbusiness and entrepreneurship in developing countries. In J. Olson-Buchanan, L. Koppes Bryan, & L. Foster Thompson (eds.), *Using I-O Psychology for the Greater Good: Helping Those Who Help Others* (pp. 394–438). New York: Routledge, Taylor and Francis.

Giddens, A. (1984). *The Constitution of Society*. Berkeley: University of California Press.

Gottlieb, G. & Halpern, C.T. (2002). A relational view of causality in normal and abnormal development. *Development and Psychopathology*, 14: 421–435.

Grant, P. & Perren, L. (2002). Small business and entrepreneurial research: Meta-theories, paradigms and prejudices. *International Small Business Journal*, 20(2): 185–211.

Greiner, L.E. (1972). Evolution and revolution as organizations grow. *Harvard Business Review*, 4: 37–46.

Gumperz, J.J. (1982). *Discourse Strategies*. Cambridge: Cambridge University Press.

Harrison, R.T. & Leitch, C.M. (1996). Discipline emergence in entrepreneurship: Accumulative fragmentalism or paradigmatic science? *Entrepreneurship, Innovation, and Change*, 5(2): 65–83.

Harré, R. (1972). *The Philosophies of Science*. Oxford: Oxford University Press.

Heidegger, M. (1962). *Being and Time*. New York: Harper & Row.

Hjorth, D. & Bjerke, B. (2006). Public entrepreneurship; creating sociality. In C. Steyaert, D. Hjorth (eds.), *Entrepreneurship as Social Change*. Cheltenham: Edward Elgar.

Jennings, P.L., Perren, L., & Carter, S. (2005). Alternative perspectives on entrepreneurship research. *Entrepreneurship Theory and Practice*, 29(2): 145–152.

120 Denise Fletcher and Paul Selden

Kirzner, I. M. (1973). *Competition and Entrepreneurship*. Chicago: University of Chicago Press.

Klein, P. G. (2008). Opportunity discovery, entrepreneurial action and economic organization. *Strategic Entrepreneurship Journal*, 2(3): 175–190.

Knight, F. (1921). *Risk, Uncertainty and Profit*. New York: Augustus Kelley.

Lachmann, L. (1977). *Capital, Expectations and the Market Process*. Kansas City, MO: Sheed Andrews and McMeel.

Kyrö, P. (2006). The dynamics of scientific inquiry in entrepreneurship research: From revolutionary development to transitional dialogue. *Liiketaloudellinen Aikakausikirja*, 4: 539–564.

Landström, H. (2001). *Who Love Entrepreneurship Research: Knowledge Accumulation within a Transient Field of Research*. RENT XV Conference, Turku, Finland, 22–23 November.

Landström, H. (2005). The emergence of an academic field. In H. Landström (ed.), *Pioneers in Entrepreneurship and Small Business Research. International Studies in Entrepreneurship*, 8: 55–93.

Latour, B. (1991). Technology is society made durable. In J. Law (ed.), *A Sociology of Monsters? Essays on Power, Technology and Domination*. Sociological Review Monograph. Routledge, London. 38: 103–131.

Lichtenstein, B. B. (2009). Moving far from far-from-equilibrium: Opportunity tension as the catalyst of emergence. *Emergence*, 11(4): 15–25.

Lichtenstein, B. B., & Kurjanowicz, B. (2010). Tangibility, momentum and emergence in the Republic of Tea. *Entrepreneurial Narrative Theory Ethnomethodology and Reflexivity – An Issue about The Republic of Tea*: 75–96.

Low, M. B. & MacMillan, I. C. (1988). Entrepreneurship: past research and future challenges. *Journal of Management*, 14(2): 139–161.

McClelland, D. C. (1961). *The Achieving Society*. Princeton, NJ: D. Van Nostrand.

McKelvey, B. (2004). Towards a complexity science of entrepreneurship. *Journal of Business Venturing*, 19: 313–342.

McMullen, J. S. & Shepherd, D. A. (2006). Entrepreneurial action and the role of uncertainty in the theory of the entrepreneur. *Academy of Management Review*, 31(1): 132–152.

McMullen, J. S. & Dimov, D. (2013). Time and the entrepreneurship journey: The problems and promise of studying entrepreneurship as a process. *Journal of Management Studies*, 50(8): 1481–1512.

Mole, K. F. & Mole, M. (2010). Entrepreneurship as the structuration of individual and opportunity: A response using a critical realist perspective. *Journal of Business Venturing*, 25(2): 230–237.

Mohr, L. (1982). *Explaining Organizational Behaviour*. San Francisco: Jossey-Bass.

Moroz, P. W. & Hindle, K. (2011). Entrepreneurship as process: Toward harmonizing multiple perspectives. *Entrepreneurship Theory and Practice*, 36(4): 781–818.

Murphy, P. J. (2011). A 2×2 conceptual foundation for entrepreneurial discovery theory. *Entrepreneurship Theory and Practice*, March: 359–374.

Pittaway, L. (2011). The evolution of entrepreneurship theory. In S. Carter, Jones-Evans, D. (Eds.), Enterprise and Small Business, 3rd ed. (pp. 9–26). Harlow: Pearson Education.

Powell, W. W., Gammal, D. L., Simard, C. (2005). Close Encounters: The Circulation and Reception of Managerial Practices in the San Francisco Bay Area Non-Profit Community. In B. Czarniawska, N. G. Sevon (eds.), *Global Ideas: How Ideas, Objects and Practices Travel in the Global Economy* (pp. 233–258). Malmo, Sweden: Liber A. G.

Reader, D. & Watkins, D. (2006). The social and collaborative nature of entrepreneurship scholarship: A co-citation and perceptual analysis. *Entrepreneurship Theory and Practice*, 30(3): 417–441.

Ricoeur, P. (1984). *Time and Narrative* Vol. 1. Chicago: The University of Chicago Press.

Sanz-Velasco, S. A. (2006). Opportunity development as a learning process for entrepreneurs. *International Journal of Entrepreneurial Behaviour and Research*, 12(5): 251–271.

Sarason, Y., Dean, T., & Dillard, J. F. (2006). Entrepreneurship as the nexus of individual and opportunity: A structuration view. *Journal of Business Venturing*, 21: 286–305.

Sarason, Y., J. F. Dillard, et al. (2010). How can we know the dancer from the dance?: Reply to "Entrepreneurship as the structuration of individual and opportunity: A response using a critical realist perspective." *Journal of Business Venturing* 25(2): 238–243.

Sarasvathy, S. D. (2003). Entrepreneurship as a science of the artificial. *Journal of Economic Psychology*, 24: 203–220.

Sarasvathy, S. D. (2008). *Effectuation: Elements of Entrepreneurial Expertise.* Cheltenham: Edward Elgar.

Sarasvathy, S. D. & Venkataraman, S. (2011). Entrepreneurship as method: Open questions for an entrepreneurial future. *Entrepreneurship Theory and Practice*, 35(1): 113–135.

Schildt, H. A., Zahra, S.A., & Sillanpaa, A. (2006). Scholarly communities in entrepreneurship research: A co-citation analysis. *Entrepreneurship Theory and Practice*, 30(3): 399–415.

Schumpeter, J. A. (1911/1961). *The Theory of Economic Development.* Oxford: Oxford University Press.

Shackle, G.L.S. (1961). *Decision, Order and Time in Human Affairs.* London: Cambridge University Press.

Shane, S. (2000). Prior knowledge and the discovery of entrepreneurial opportunities. *Organization Science*, 11(4): 448–469.

Shane, S. (2003). *A General Theory of Entrepreneurship: The Individual-Opportunity Nexus.* Cheltenham: Edward Elgar.

Shane, S. (2012). Reflections of the 2010 AMR Decade Award: Delivering on the promise of entrepreneurship as a field of research. *Academy of Management Review*, 37(1): 10–20.

Shane, S. & Venkataraman, S. (2000). The promise of entrepreneurship as a field of research. *Academy of Management Review*, 25(1): 217–226.

Shapero, A. (1975). The displaced, uncomfortable entrepreneur. *Psychology Today*, November: 83–88.

Shotter, J. (1993). *Conversational Realities: Constructing Life through Language.* London: Sage Publications.

Simon, M. & Houghton, S. M. (2002). The relationship among biases, misperceptions, and the introduction of pioneering products: Examining differences in venture decision contexts. *Entrepreneurship Theory and Practice*, 27(2): 105–124.

Stacey, R. D. (2001). *Complex Responsive Processes in Organizations.* New York: Routledge.

Steyaert, C. & Hjorth, D. (2004). *Narrative and Discursive Approaches to Entrepreneurship: A Second Movements in Entrepreneurship Book.* Cheltenham: Edward Elgar.

Steyaert, C. & Katz, J. (2004). Reclaiming the space of entrepreneurship in society: Geographical, discursive and social dimensions. *Entrepreneurship and Regional Development*, 16(3): 179–196.

Steyaert, C. (2007). 'Entrepreneuring' as a conceptual attractor? A review of process theories in 20 years of entrepreneurship studies. *Entrepreneurship and Regional Development*, 19(6): 453–477.

Van Oers, B. (1998). From context to contextualizing. In E. Forman & B. van Oers (eds.), *Mathematics Learning in Socio-Cultural Contexts.* Special Issue of *Learning and Instruction*, 8(6): 473–488.

Van de Ven, A. H. & Engleman, R. M. (2004). Event- and outcome-driven explanations of entrepreneurship. *Journal of Business Venturing*, 19: 343–358.

Van de Ven, A. H. & Poole, M. S. (2005). Alternative approaches for studying organizational change. *Organization Studies*, 26(9): 1377–1404.

Vygotsky, L. S. (1994). *Thought and Language*. Cambridge, MA: MIT Press.

Watson, T. J. (2013). Entrepreneurial action and the Euro-American social science tradition: Pragmatism, realism and looking beyond 'the entrepreneur'. *Entrepreneurship and Regional Development*, 25(1–2): 16–33.

Venkataraman, S., Sarasvathy, S. D., Dew, N., & Forster, W. R. (2012). Reflections on the 2010 AMR decade award: Whither the promise? Moving forward with entrepreneurship as a science of the artificial. *Academy of Management Review*, 37(1): 21–33.

Welter, F. (2011). Contextualizing entrepreneurship: Conceptual challenges and ways forward. *Entrepreneurship Theory and Practice*, 35(1): 165–184.

West, G. P. III. (1997). Frameworks for research and theory development in entrepreneurship. *Academy of Management Proceedings*, August: 113–117.

Whetten, D. A. (1989). What constitutes a theoretical contribution? *Academy of Management Review*, 14(4): 490–495.

Wiklund, J., Davidsson, P., Audretsch, D., & Karlsson, C. (2011). The future of entrepreneurship research. *Entrepreneurship Theory And Practice*, 35(1): 1–9.

Wiklund, J. & Shepherd, D. (2003). Knowledge-based resources, entrepreneurial orientation and the performance of small and medium-sized businesses. *Strategic Management Journal* 24(13): 1307–1314.

Wood, M. S. & McKinley, W. (2010). The production of entrepreneurial opportunity: A constructivist perspective. *Strategic Entrepreneurship Journal*, 4: 66–83.

8 Institutionalization of the field and its impact on both the ethics and the quality of entrepreneurship research in the coming decades

*Benson Honig**

Institutionalization of the entrepreneurship field

The scholarship of entrepreneurship has been a rather successful enterprise, in terms of numbers of faculty, chaired professorships, students, courses, University, community, and national interest (Katz, 2003). The most recent evidence of the growing esteem for the 'heroic' value of entrepreneurship can be seen in the increasing popularity and diffusion of the "Shark Tank", "Dragon's Den", or "Tiger Money", reality shows that now take place in over 22 countries (including Israel, Finland, USA, Canada, Japan, Afghanistan, Nigeria, and Saudi Arabia). In fact, these entertainment shows have already been the subject of two major journal articles in the field (Maxwell, Jeffrey, & Lévesque, 2011; Maxwell & Lévesque, 2011). Business plan competitions and public business idea competitions are increasingly normative worldwide. In and of themselves, the growing popularity of entrepreneurship for public consumption demonstrates the considerable growth of the field's worldwide institutionalization. The research and teaching of entrepreneurship, irrespective of its outcomes, is an increasingly well-entrenched social norm in wealthy as well as emergent economies. As a result, it has taken on its own 'myths and ceremonies' (Meyer & Rowan, 1977).

What is particularly interesting regarding the institutionalization of the field of entrepreneurship is its global attraction. A sociologist observing popular culture might want to contrast entrepreneurship today with the diffusion of the Horatio Alger stories widely read in the USA in the late 19th century (the so-called gilded age). Alger's 'rags to riches' books (over 100 titles) were essentially replications of the same theme. A very poor young man, by virtue of his integrity or hard work (e.g. he returns a huge some of found money, or shows his virtue some other way) is introduced to a very wealthy gentleman, who changes his life – he becomes a successful member of the middle/upper class as a result, sometimes even marrying the 'bosses daughter'. Alger's publications, reaching over 20,000,000, peaked in the 1920s, after which they soon became obscure, out of print, and unread. Although out of print, his message carries on with the Horatio Alger Society in the USA, which

> "has strived to further the philosophy of Horatio Alger, Jr. and to encourage the spirit of Strive & Succeed that for half a century guided Alger's

124 *Benson Honig*

undaunted heroes. Our members conduct research and provide scholarship on the life of Horatio Alger, Jr., his works and influence on the culture of America.

(Horatio Alger Society homepage)

Yet, unlike the shark tank derivatives, Alger's books failed to cross the seas, there was no comparable internationalization of a theme that must have appeared quintessentially American, as well as absurdly unlikely. Multiple causes might account for the ubiquitous diffusion of one 'myth' and not another. Globalization, the internet, neoliberalism, the ending of the Cold War, the dominance of one superpower, Hollywood, and mass media all come to mind as advancing the global drive toward entrepreneurial research and promotion. Evidently, entrepreneurship seems to have followed in the global wake of Facebook and the iPhone.

Given that this paper is meant to reflect 'out of the box' thinking, I am going to present a somewhat novel explanation for the global diffusion of the entrepreneurship 'myth'. I refer to it as a myth, at the risk of being castigated by my entrepreneurial scholarly colleagues, because, in reality, there are so very few who truly achieve the 'star status' of the Richard Bransons, Larry Ellisons, Steve Jobses, and Bill Gateses of the world, the aspirations of so many entrepreneurial entrants (none of whom, it should be noted, completed a university degree or had formal entrepreneurship training). Of the 7 million firms started in the USA each year, fewer than a few thousand will ever get venture capital, fewer than a few hundred will become publically listed – both typical requirements for the star-like wealth so many viewers, students, and government officials yearn for. Forty percent will fail in the first five years, and the vast majority will remain solo-self employed 'lifestyle' firms, working long hours for only mediocre compensation. Thus, the odds are fairly slim of becoming a millionaire from self-employment in the USA, where resources still abound, and markets are relatively competitive and open. The chances of 'making it big' are even more remote in environments characterized by resource constraints, heavy competition, and emerging markets. However, just as lotteries are popular in all parts of the world – seemingly the poorer the country, the more popular the lottery system – so, too, does entrepreneurship offer hope to individuals facing a bleak future framed by an increasing Gini coefficient, the loss of manufacturing jobs (in the developed world), and the increasing probabilities that this next generation will, for the first time in a long time, be significantly less wealthy than the previous generation. I am not saying that there is anything wrong with starting a business that nets 60% of the annual wages of a unionized factory worker in 1965. My only concern is the size and shape of the carrot we collectively wave in front of increasingly desperate individuals, along with the associated expectations. Our business cases, our textbooks, our visiting classroom entrepreneurs – these are too often framed by a relatively rare and select group – while we collectively fail to inform our audience of their precise odds. Like the lottery billboards or the advertisements for Las Vegas, we show only the happy winners, and gloss over the losers of the entrepreneurial 'game'. As academics attempting to represent a research informed perspective on the world, our cases, textbooks, and visitors should more accurately reflect the empirical reality that we study.

Evidently, growth in entrepreneurship has been considerable, particularly during the most recent economically troubled times. For example, GEM reported that in 2011, the USA appreciated a 60% growth rate in entrepreneurial startups over the previous two years (GEM, 2011). This, following the worst economic decline since the depression, can be no coincidence. Lottery sales, in 2011, broke all-time records in 17 states (US News and World Report, 2011). Entrepreneurship, simply put, represents the Horatio Alger of the new millennia. It also presents an aspirational option for the unemployed and under-employed. Policy experts, politicians, mayors promote and develop our normative cultural scripts (Barley, 1986) such that hope is around the corner, success simply a matter of 'tightening one's boot straps, taking risks, and being clever'. Markets are presented as a fair and transparent route to reward the diligent and punish the slothful. What accounts for the exceptional driving of this entrepreneurial myth? Further, what are the actual consequences of the diffusion of this myth?

Allow me to present a thought experiment. Imagine I find myself as a prime minister or benevolent dictator of a middle income country. The economy I am asked to manage is undergoing hard times. Global competition, weak institutions, loss of human capital – all are summing up to an increasingly bifurcated labor market, whereby the wealthiest 1% are enjoying 40% of the GDP, with an income inequality gap only growing as the economy worsens. Consequently, our national tax revenues are being reduced, limiting my ability to ameliorate the conditions of an increasingly large (potentially hostile) working poor, underemployed, and unemployed population. Fortunately, my minister of finance is a very astute Wharton MBA. He explains a very simple proposal to me. If we can get 1000 more individuals to try their hand at entrepreneurial endeavors, at least one of them will succeed, yielding a tax-paying firm employing 500 people. Our tax revenues can grow! If only we can convince 100,000 individuals to try and start up a new firm, the odds are they would eventually yield 100 new firms paying taxes – as well as 50,000 new taxpayers. Indeed, the cabinet decides we should market this idea extensively, and so we develop a campaign to encourage as many people as possible to risk everything they have, and enter the entrepreneurial marketplace. Of course, as with all entrepreneurial ventures, there is risk. It might be the case that in order to produce one 500-person company, 900 people need to mortgage their home and life savings, quit their jobs, eventually losing everything to the marketplace. In such a circumstance, it is entirely probable that the misery of the 900 is far outweighed by the tax revenues generated by the fortunate 500 newly employed. Perhaps the social costs eventually exceed the economic benefits. There are recognized problems regarding agency and divided incentives between investors and entrepreneurs (Sorenson & Stuart, 2008). However,

126 *Benson Honig*

political expediency often trumps social or economic efficiency. Should any reader doubt this logic, she need only turn to the prevalence of government lotteries for confirmation. People act in decidedly stupid ways, often against their own economic interests. Hope springs eternal, and taxes need to be collected.

What this suggests is that in addition to responsibly teaching and researching the characteristics of successful entrepreneurs, we should be obliged to fully disclose the costs of failure, the actual chances of success, and the full social and economic costs and benefits in addition to the implications for any individual's future life chances. Just as every investment fund comes with the footnote "past performance is not an indicator of future success", so, too, our textbooks, our syllabi and research journals, and our public discourse should reflect both the 'down side' as well as the 'up side' of entrepreneurial activities, inclusive of the social and psychological costs. Our failure to do this suggests that our collective scholarly wisdom is limited to providing leverage for the committed, rather than facts for the undecided. While perusing entrepreneurship textbooks, and even many of our scholarly journals, I sometimes get the impression we are Madison Avenue advertisers working for the tobacco industry.

As scholars, we owe our constituency – consisting of our students, our tax-paying neighbors, and our public policy actors – a full disclosure regarding not only what entrepreneurship may or may not deliver, but also, the full costs and benefits of our own contributions to the field. As scholars, we should be asking each other "to what extent does our entrepreneurship education or research benefit our community?" We need more studies that compare and contrast different entrepreneurial teaching and learning strategies (e.g. Fayolle, Lassas-Clerc, & Tounés, 2009). Our research should be replete with studies examining the efficiency of our theories and how they are used in entrepreneurship training, evaluating our course materials, and our lectures, as well as our own capability as educators to impact individuals.

I will add one additional perspective to the institutionalization of entrepreneurship education, an evaluation issue that is rarely considered but has the potential to yield considerable returns. Much entrepreneurship education occurs when individuals are still quite young, relatively malleable, and reasonably open minded regarding their future life course. For this reason, I view entrepreneurship education as a wonderful entry point to help individuals examine their own place in the world, the philosophical and existential qualities they wish to develop, and to identify and experiment with various possible alternative career trajectories that may or may not have been considered previously. Because entrepreneurship is essentially a wide-open construct, our courses can serve as important opportunities for young people to begin experimenting with what they want to accomplish in their lives. Do they want to be leader followers, or solo-self employed? Do they want to work ambitiously for material benefits, for psychological returns, or for social rewards? Do they wish to 'rush to the front of the line', or are they more comfortable experimenting and taking their time to make life course decisions? I have found that students, in particular graduate students from all majors and disciplines, appreciate a course that helps them to identify possible alternative career options – with entrepreneurship being only one of many others. As our institutions of higher education become increasingly more vocationally oriented (whether or not we, as academics, agree with this emphasis), I believe entrepreneurship education can play an important but as yet underrecognized role in assisting individuals regarding life and career decision making. Further, as we live longer, healthier lives, many of us will be in a position to reconsider how to invest our later years. When retirement ages were set at 65, most males averaged only 67 years of life. In many countries, the figure now exceeds 80. How might individuals best occupy themselves for an additional 15 years? What kind of insight can entrepreneurial education provide a mature and longer-living population?

The ethical implications of the institutionalization of the entrepreneurship field

The considerable rapid growth of entrepreneurship as a field has consequential implications for the development of scholarly research. A growing number of endowed chairs, tenure-track positions, and centre directorships have been created in the wake of our global enthusiasm (Katz, 2003). The lucrative remuneration associated with these positions has both increased competition for the positions themselves, as well as for the very limited scholarly outlets deemed sufficiently legitimate to support these considerable salaries and perquisites. While there seems to be an ever-enlarging number of journals that embrace entrepreneurship – well over 60 – there are only 2 listed in the FT45, and only 5 or 6 that have reasonable impact factors. Publication exclusively in only the leading entrepreneurship journals would fail to qualify a candidate at a top 10 university for tenure – although this may represent an entirely different set of institutional norms unrelated to the field of entrepreneurship (I am not advocating these standards, only pointing them out).

Rapid growth of any field, however, has significant consequences. One unintended outcome is that our field has considerable interdisciplinary dimensions. This has both positive and negative outcomes. On the positive side, entrepreneurship has become a wonderful arena for scholars of different interests to converge regarding overlapping empirical interest. On the negative side, it has simultaneously encouraged shortcuts with dubious ethical dimensions. I have recently completed a critical chapter examining some of the methodological weaknesses of contemporary entrepreneurship research, including issues related to resource allocation, network relationships, journal rejection rates, salaries, cross citation practices, and collaborative scholarship (Honig, 2014). I shall not entirely repeat myself in this article, but suffice it to say that from a methodological perspective, we typically follow in the wake of others, and appear mesmerized by new modeling techniques that few of us have the statistical competence to truly understand. Rather, I will focus in this chapter on more general ethical issues related to our scholarly research.

128 *Benson Honig*

One of our most seemingly obsessive and demonstrably youthful field-level characteristics is our near ubiquitous insistence that all entrepreneurship research incorporate new theory. It remains unclear exactly why entrepreneurship requires a distinctive theory – most worrisome, however, is the evident failure of entrepreneurship to produce theories usable by others in different disciplines. Our incessant need for new theory highlights an important outcome of the institutionalization of our emergent field, and also underscores one of our most apparent weaknesses. As Hambrick (2007) points out, *"the requirement that every paper must contribute to theory is not very sensible; it is probably a sign of our academic insecurity; and it is costing us in multiple ways"* (2007: 1346).

Our search in entrepreneurship for overarching generalizable theories may, in fact, be a pointless 'holy grail' effort (Sorenson & Stuart, 2008). The subfields that already take an ambitious look at entrepreneurship – particularly sociology, psychology, and economics, provide extensive theoretical tool kits easy applied to the domain of entrepreneurship, that do not necessitate unique or specialized field level modifications in order to be useful. By isolating ourselves into a separate field, we run the risk of erecting barriers that prevent an easy flow of information between the disciplines and ourselves. This could negatively impact our field, as we fail to keep pace with current discipline based developments. Another aspect of this apparent insecurity is our splitting into ever smaller subdivisions of interest, few of which keep well informed about other subdivisions. Thus, we have seemingly odd configurations of an ever-growing subfield of 'specialties', including nascent entrepreneurship, cognition and entrepreneurship, gender and entrepreneurship, international entrepreneurship, entrepreneurial opportunity (EO), entrepreneurial growth, venture capital, social entrepreneurship, strategic entrepreneurship, corporate entrepreneurship, and family business, the latter two arguably well served in the domain of general management or strategy.

In any case, the role of research should not be limited to generating new theory but should also carefully examine existing theory and existing empirical evidence. How do we know that what was published 10 years ago was accurate and conducted correctly? Verification is normally done through replication.[1] My experience in discussing replication with both editors and my colleagues is they seem to have only the weakest notion of what replication is. Some confine scholarly replication to repeating the same experiment with a different population. While this is also replication, it is not the only method, and fails to verify previously published results. Repeating the same experiment, even using the same data and rerunning the same analysis for confirmation, is replication worthy of our attention (Freese, 2007; King, 1995). Extending such a study provides an important longitudinal focus. Identifying that previously published material is erroneous is worthy of scholarly discourse. It should not be limited to retraction – rather, it should be embraced, discussed, and debated as strongly as any theoretical contribution. Yet, in my experience, senior editors in the entrepreneurship field fail to see either replication or extension as a scholarly contribution, and avoid publishing controversial results that might undermine previously published material. I am sometimes reminded of Galileo

Institutionalization of the field   129

insisting on the accuracy of geocentrism and, facing reams of contradicting 'research', being declared a heretic, and forced to recant.

Given the recent proliferation of plagiarism and journal retractions, our field should develop systems and procedures to encourage scholars to verify each other's scholarly work. We have recently seen clear examples of plagiarism and fraudulent data manipulation (Carey, 2011; Honig & Bedi, 2012; Bouyssour, Martello, & Plastria, 2006, 2009; Bakker & Wicherts, 2011). One professor of the University of Mannheim was forced to resign after retracing sixteen articles from top management journals (Retraction Watch, 2014) after readers noticed statistical irregularities (Storbeck, 2012). Diederik Stapel, a Dutch psychologist, has admitted to considerable scientific fraud published in high impact journals (Vogel, 2011), there are now over 50 retractions associated with him (Retraction Watch, 2012). As Stapel himself stated, when explaining his 'addition' to manufacturing data:

"Nobody ever checked my work. They trusted me . . . I did everything myself, and next to me was a big jar of cookies. No mother, no lock, not even a lid . . . Every day, I would be working and there would be this big jar of cookies, filled with sweets, within reach, right next to me – with nobody even near. All I had to do was take it"

(Boorsboom & Wagenmakers, 2012, citing a translation of Stapel, 2012: 164)

Yet, despite evidence of possible fraud and error, our field continues to validate 'A' journal articles with a kind of ideological reverence. This is not so surprising – the established echelon of senior scholars inhabit positions of significant influence. Few would be happy to condone research that questioned the accuracy or quality of their previous contributions. This, too, is a result of our rapid institutionalization, for we have failed to incorporate adequate checks and balances for the development of a sound scientific foundation.

Knowledge in entrepreneurship must continually be verified and tested, lest our theories become canonized. We need to incorporate better mechanisms for substantiating our research and better methods of identifying fraudulent or erroneous research in order for our field to develop. As Hambrick asserts, the only way to ensure evidence based knowledge is "*to allow ample testing and replication*" (2007:1350).

In sum, our field needs to begin grappling with authenticity, verification, and replication, in order to advance and make a substantial contribution to social science, as well as to entrepreneurship.

Recommendations regarding how to improve entrepreneurship research in the face of institutional pressures

Entrepreneurship, and management, are not alone regarding the need to verify and validate published material. The National Science Foundation, in the USA, now requires all grantees to provide access to data publically, in order to

130 Benson Honig

encourage validation of analysis and to authenticate data. Psychologists have launched a major validation project regarding published material. The Reproducibility Initiative is a partnership between Science Exchange, PLoS ONE, figshare, and Mendeley, designed to verify reproducible scientific research (Reproducibility Initiative). Sociologists, as well, have called for a more rigorous approach to data dissemination for published works (Freese, 2007). What follows are my own recommendations for improving the accuracy and quality of published materials, along with short explanations regarding why I believe these are important goals for us to strive for in our field:

1   *All entrepreneurship journals should insist that authors of any published article upload anonymous data published in the article on a complimentary website.*

Leading journals in both economics and finance already have this policy. Editors might not even have to be directly involved – authors could simply download their material to a jointly managed consortium database available to the public. Standards could be in place to ensure that the data would not be taken and used for publication purposes without permission. Alternatively, authors of well-used databases might be cited for the use – offering an incentive to share data. This should include both qualitative and quantitative data, available to any scholar or student who wishes to examine the accuracy of the analysis or interpretation. The case of qualitative data is somewhat unique – but the problem in certainly solvable. Some aspects of anonymous or coded qualitative data could be made available, such as transcripts, or NVIVO coding routines and findings. Perhaps users of the public data would be required to sign confidentiality agreements.

2   *All entrepreneurship journals should reserve dedicated space for publishing replication studies. These studies might include extension of previously published work or discovery that previously published work was incorrectly analyzed, presented, or misinterpreted.*

Replication is a critical component of scientific discovery. If we fail to replicate, we fail to identify whether or not our research is truly generalizable. Replication studies that question the accuracy or methodology of previously published material, including those that use the same data sets, should be actively encouraged. Studies that replicate and extend material should also be supported.

3   *All entrepreneurship journals should insist that data scripts (statistical routines, subprocesses, and intermediate work conducted for published results) be publicly available on a downloadable website.*

While coding does take considerable time, the statistical 'scripts' that operate much of our quantitative work should be open to scrutiny and verification. Simple mistakes – honest mistakes – can easily result in huge variations of

Institutionalization of the field 131

outcomes. Providing other scholars with the technical 'logic' followed in any particular analysis is as important a component of the research design as the sampling frame or the instrument utilized. In short, this information is very pertinent to validate the outcome of the research, and should be made transparent for editors, reviewers, readers, and future scholars.

4   *Entrepreneurship journals need to be established that allow a more open dialogue with fewer gatekeepers and more discussion, debate, and controversy.*

I believe that our collective field level failure to precipitate active debate and discussion of alternative points of view highlights both our newness and our relative insecurity as a field of study. Too many of our conference fail to inspire, rather, they simply tell and retell the same information that will eventually appear in our scholarly journals. Authors should be reminded of their responsibility to earnestly and honestly assist emergent scholarship in this way.

One obvious and emergent solution is to develop high quality open source publications that provide some measure of evidence of the quality of scholarly work, in a more open platform. I believe it important that we develop ways of measuring the impact of such contributions (much as impact factor is evaluated with citations), but inclusive of both the qualitative contribution, and the creative contribution, to the development of entrepreneurial scholarship. Citation impact scores suffer from the problems of coercive citations and self-citations. Neither represent a healthy dialogue in the field. The absence of public controversy in the field of entrepreneurship is lamentable – and represents another visible outcome of our newness. Mature fields maintain healthy debate and controversy. Mature fields encourage scholars to challenge each other's basic assumptions, opinions, and research. Entrepreneurship should strive to develop multiple locations where debate and disagreement take place.

5   *All entrepreneurship journals should henceforth discourage self-citation. Further, those that specifically encourage authors to 'over cite' their own journal, in order to advance their own citation impact, should immediately desist from doing so.*

Coercive citation is a very harmful outcome of our institutional environment. I have been told that certain editors of entrepreneurship journals insist on increasing the journal's citation rate in their letters to the author. While every scholar and every editor anxiously examines his citation counts, forcing others to cite our work in order to get published is a major ethical violation and serves only to encourage triviality and insider thinking. We already have too many 'micro communities' in entrepreneurship where each subfield discovers the necessity of citing certain 'sacred texts', usually those of the subfield founders, editors, and first-comers to the field. While recognizing that intellectual ancestry is important, doing so as a result of overt pressure or normative demands causes inward thinking and impedes innovation and creativity. We should develop citation measures to examine field-level impact, as well

132　*Benson Honig*

as impact for the general social sciences. Impact factor for all journals should eliminate both author self citation and same journal citation to eliminate these sources of undue pressure.

6　*All authors should be required to disclose any financial or other support, consulting fees, ownership, memberships, relationships between themselves and the subject of their respondent/scholarly papers.*

Many of our colleagues are consultants, and frequently data examined in major articles are outcomes of this paid consultancy. As readers, we should be informed of these relationships, lest there be a perceived conflict of interest on the part of the scholar. Such relationships, if undisclosed, could easily bias research results. For examples of two such policies, see (www.nber.org/researchdisclosurepolicy.html; www.aeaweb.org/aea_journals/AEA_Disclosure_Policy.pdf).

7　*All entrepreneurship journals should provide a venue linking published authors with emergent scholarship (scholars) to communicate, obtain clarification, instruments, and verification after publication takes place.*

As published authors we have responsibilities that transcend the authorship of peer review research papers. While many actively participate in inculcating the next generation of scholars, there are those that simply lock themselves away, insulate themselves from others, and produce article after article. Unfortunately, our field will fail to develop with such norms and habits. We have a collective responsibility to educate, train, and advise the next generation of scholars. Each time we are published, we enjoy both a measure of publicity and a measure of responsibility to ensure that future research tests confirm or invalidate our own work. Journals should begin to provide a public dialog/blog space for published authors to carry out these activities.

Finally, our academic journals have become all too complacent, as demonstrated by the increasing necessity of retractions. Too much of what is done by journals occurs 'below the surface', as tacit knowledge provided to a select group of insider scholars. To what extent does familiarity with the editor and editorial board impact publication probabilities? How much distance occurs between the reviewer and editor, and how are special issues monitored? A recent editorial in the journal *The Scientist* calls for a transparency in index for journals, predicated on the following recommended policies (Marcus & Oransky, 2012):

- The journal's review protocol, including whether or not its articles are peer-reviewed, the typical number of reviewers, time for review, manuscript acceptance rate, and details of the appeals process
- Names and expertise of editorial board members, including whether or not they know they're on the board. (That last part shouldn't be controversial, but we've spoken to a number of alleged editorial board members who

are surprised to hear about such appointments. The publishers of many of those journals show up on University of Colorado Denver librarian Jeffrey Beall's List of Predatory, Open-Access Publishers. Read his Critic at Large, "Predatory Publishing".[2])

- How authors are asked to disclose conflicts of interest, and the threshold for sharing those conflicts with readers
- Contact information for the journal's editor-in-chief, including an e-mail account that someone actually reads
- Costs, not only for authors, but for readers. How much does it cost someone without a subscription (personal or institutional) to read a paper?
- Whether the journal requires that underlying data are made available
- Whether the journal uses plagiarism detection software and reviews figures for evidence of image manipulation
- The journal's mechanism for dealing with allegations of errors or misconduct, including whether it investigates such allegations from anonymous whistle-blowers
- Whether corrections and retraction notices are as clear as possible, conforming to accepted publishing ethics guidelines such as those from the Committee on Publication Ethics (COPE) or the International Committee of Medical Journal Editors (ICMJE).

My understanding is that few if any of our entrepreneurship journals have transparent mechanisms for managing the aforementioned ethical norms. Some journals, for example, now incorporate plagiarism checking, but by no means do the majority. A few entrepreneurship journals have had to deal with retraction issues, but the mechanisms used are far from transparent. Even basic review turnaround and acceptance rate data are not always available on entrepreneurship journal websites. In short, our field can substantially improve our credibility and scholarly quality by implementing some of the relatively minor suggestions made for this index.

Institutionalization: the past and the future

The very drivers of entrepreneurship institutionalization – the massive public and student interest, the many resources, the exciting new developments – these represent hopes and requests placed upon our field's collective shoulders that many other fields can only dream of. As scholars in entrepreneurship, we must actively learn the art and science of field-level skepticism and self-criticism in order to begin delivering on some of the many hopes and requests that are made of our field. Unfortunately, the flip side of our newfound popularity lends a kind of hubris to our own conceptual view of the field. We think of ourselves as critically important, as taking the correct measures to improve the field, as leading scholars in an increasingly influential arena. To provide some historical comparison regarding our perceived or real centrality, I offer the following two historical vignettes for the reader's consideration.

134 *Benson Honig*

In the early 19th century, medicine, something we now consider a 'hard' science, was steeped in mystery, superstition, and unproven quackery. The theories of the day included miasma – that illness was transmitted through scent – and typical solutions involved altering that olfactory relationship by wearing sweet smelling herbs (posies – as in 'a pocket full of posies, we all fall down') and burning pitch. Blood letting was the widely accepted medical practice against disease used to rebalance the 'four humours' of the body. Women giving birth in the hospital were much likelier to die in childbirth, as were their babies, due to a complete lack of basic hygiene, or an understanding of germs, infection, and contagion. Doctors would move from dissecting cadavers to delivering babies without so much as washing their hands. In this environment, one creative Austrian researcher, Ignaz Semmelweis, deduced a theory of contagion and microbiology through careful measurement and observation (Wyklicky & Skopec, 1983). Poor Ignaz was laughed out of Austria, as the idea that a bourgeois medical doctor could carry something unhealthy and invisible to a poor patient was simply out of the question – not worth replicating – or investigating. Ignaz Semmelweis, genius scientist that he was, died from beatings he received in an insane asylum at the age of 47.

Some years later, the noted statistician William Farr began statistically studying human health and disease (Eyler, 1979; Burke, 1985). Farr most notably deduced the cause of cholera through a combination of statistical empirical examination, hypotheses testing, and replication. Because Farr decided to replicate his own earlier work, he discovered his own errors, leading to his major findings. Further, because his science was taken seriously by his colleagues of the day, particularly those in Britain, Farr's research saved countless lives, before Louis Pasteur was able to systematically confirm his work.

While entrepreneurship scholars are not in the business of saving lives, we are in the business of spending public money, and hopefully delivering useful and accurate information to the benefit of the societies that support our activities. In this chapter I have outlined a number of weaknesses that I believe constrain our ability to advance and prosper as a scientific field of inquiry. These weaknesses include institutionalized normative activities related to our publishing systems, the way we conduct and verify our research, and the normative practices that constitute our teaching in the field. While I do not believe we are alone in our lack of accountability and our somewhat questionable ethical norms, I strongly believe that we must learn to vigilantly guard our intellectual integrity in order to advance our knowledge. Doing so requires a spirit of transparency and integrity and, above all, an openness to both inquiry and debate.

As a field, we do have alternatives. We can act as the Austrian medical establishment, and laugh away our innovators. Alternatively, we can embrace new ideas, including outcomes based on replication, and create an environment more willing to question normative theory, as the British did regarding Farr. Our continued growth and evolution as a field depends on our ability to be open and supportive of new 'out of the box' theory and debate, as well as to learn to better engage in more transparent processes. I trust that our evolution will reflect such innovation, and wish to thank organizers and editors of conferences for taking us one step further in the direction of the way Farr was received, and numerous steps opposite the reception provided to Semmelweis.

Notes

* I wish to thank the staff and faculty of the Halpert Center at the Hebrew University, Jerusalem, for providing a fellowship allowing me to conduct this research.
1 Note – meta-analysis is NOT replication. In fact, I maintain that there is an abuse and overuse of meta-analysis in our field. The assumptions most meta-analytic papers in entrepreneurship make would fail even the most basic scientific measures of validity.
2 www.the-scientist.com/?articles.view/articleNo/32426/title/Predatory-Publishing/

References

Bakker, M. & Wicherts, J. M. (2011). The (mis)reporting of statistical results in psychology. *Behavior Research Methods*, 43: 666–678.

Barley, S. R. (1986). Technology as an occasion for structuring: Evidence from observations of CT scanners and the social order of radiology departments. *Administrative Science Quarterly*, 31(1): 78–108.

Boorsboom, D. & Wagenmakers, E. (2012). *The Observer, Book Review: The Rise and Fall of Diederick Stapel.* www.psychologicalscience.org/index.php/publications/observer/2013/january-13/derailed-the-rise-and-fall-of-diederik-stapel.html [accessed 15/4/2012].

Bouyssou, D., Martello, S., & Plastria, F. (2006). A case of plagiarism: Dănuţ Marcu. *4OR: A Quarterly Journal of Operations Research*, 4(1): 11–13.

Bouyssou, D., Martello, S., & Plastria, F. (2009). Plagiarism again: Sreenivas and Srinivas, with an update on Marcu. *4OR*, 7(1): 17–20. Burke, W. (1985). *The Day the Universe Changed.* Boston: Little Brown and Co.

Cary, B. (2011). Fraud case seen as red flag for psychology research. *New York Times*, 2 November 2011. http://www.nytimes.com/2011/11/03/health/research/noted-dutch-psychologist-stapel-accused-of-research-fraud.html?_r=0

Eyler, J. (1979). *Victorian Social Medicine: The Ideas and Methods of William Farr.* Baltimore: Johns Hopkins University Press.

Fayolle, A., Lassas-Clerc, N., & Tounés, A. (2009). *The Effects of Real Versus Virtual Business Planning as Learning Process.* Paper presented at Babson College Entrepreneurship Research Conference, Babson Park, MA.

Freese, J. (2007). Replication standards for quantitative social science. *Sociological Methods and Research*, 36(2): 153–172.

Maxwell, A. L., Jeffrey, S. A., & Lévesque, M. (2011). Business angel early stage decision making. *Journal of Business Venturing*, 26(2): 212–225.

Maxwell, A. L. & Lévesque, M. (2011). Trustworthiness: A critical ingredient for entrepreneurs seeking investors. *Entrepreneurship Theory and Practice*, 38(5): 1057–1080.

Global Entrepreneurship Monitor (2011). National Entrepreneurial Assessment for the United States of America. www.babson.edu/Academics/centers/blank-center/global-research/gem/Documents/GEM%20US%202012%20Report%20FINAL.pdf [accessed 10/6/2015].

Hambrick, D. (2007). The field of management's devotion to theory: Too much of a good thing? *Academy of Management Journal*, 50(6): 1346–1352.

136 *Benson Honig*

Horatio Alger Society, home page. www.horatioalgersociety.net/200_history.html [accessed 10/4/2013]. The Horatio Alger Society, 2011.

Honig, B. (2014). Salesmen or scholars: A critical examination of research scholarship in the field of entrepreneurship. In Frederike Welter & Ted Baker (eds). *Routledge Companion on Entrepreneurship*, 467–480.

Honig, B. & Bedi, A. (2012). The fox in the hen house: A critical examination of plagiarism among members of the Academy of Management. *Academy of Management Learning and Education*, 11(1): 101–123.

Katz, Jerry (2003). The chronology and intellectual trajectory of American entrepreneurship education 1876–1999. *Journal of Business Venturing*, 18: 283–300.

King, G. (1995). Replication, replication. *PS: Political Science and Politics*, 28: 444–452.

Meyer, J. W. & Rowan, B. (1977). Institutionalized organizations: Formal structure as myth and ceremony. *American Journal of Sociology*, 83(2): 340–363.

Marcus, A. & Oransky, I. (2012). Bring on the transparency index. *The Scientist,* 1 August 2012.

Reproducibility Initiative. www.scienceexchange.com/reproducibility [accessed 12/4/2013].

Retraction Watch. http://retractionwatch.com/2014/10/10/after-16-retractions-management-professor-lichtenthaler-resigns-post/ [accessed Dec. 12, 2014] published Oct. 10, 2014.

Sorenson, O. & Stuart, T. E. (2008). 12 Entrepreneurship: A field of dreams? *Academy of Management Annals*, 2(1): 517–543.

Stapel, D. (2012). *Ontsporing* [Derailment]. Amsterdam: Prometeus. [in Dutch]

Storbeck, O. (2012). Top-flight German business prof faces severe accusations of academic misconduct. *Economics Intelligence*, 19 July 2012. http://economicsintelligence.com/2012/07/19/top-flight-german-business-prof-faces-severe-accusations-of-academic-misconduct [accessed 15/8/2012]. Additional sources: http://retractionwatch.wordpress.com; www.elsevier.com/wps/find/intro.cws_home/article_withdrawal

US News and World Report (2011). Lottery sales increase across the country. 1 September 2011.

Vogel, G. (2011). Psychologist accused of fraud on 'astonishing scale'. *Science*, 334(6056): 579.

Wyklicky, H. & Skopec, M. (1983). Ignaz Philipp Semmelweis, the prophet of bacteriology. *Infection Control*, 4(5): 367–370.

9 Legitimacy or relevance – that is the question

Bengt Johannisson

A commentary on Benson Honig's paper 'Institutionalization of the Field, and Its Impact on both the Ethics and the Quality of Entrepreneurship Research in the Coming Decades'[1]

A triple review

Benson Honig puts his finger on a very important issue when he makes visible the dangers of prematurely closing our understanding of entrepreneurship and concerning ourselves mainly with its bright and heroic aspects. However, elaborating upon what measures should be taken in order to construct a more solid scientific foundation for entrepreneurship studies, Honig remains within the academic box. This means that his (only) concern is for increased legitimacy of entrepreneurship studies in the global research community. Honig's choice to focus on increasing reliability by repeated empirical studies is, though, not the only way to increase the relevance of entrepreneurship research in society. Nevertheless I really enjoyed reading his paper and I am especially happy with his statement at the end: "we must learn to vigilantly guard our intellectual integrity in order to advance our knowledge. Doing so requires a spirit of transparency and integrity and, above all, an openness to both inquiry and debate." I share this view and in the spirit that it communicates I have written this commentary that obviously begins where Benson Honig's discourse ends.

Reviewing in the context of scholarly work means reflecting upon documented research and proposing ways of dealing with the weaknesses and expanding upon the strengths of the text. Such reflections may adopt three different modes. One means taking the text and the reported research for granted and scrutinizing its strengths and shortcomings in terms of, for example, creative moves and enlightenments as well as inconsistencies and incompleteness. This kind of reviewing thus concerns what is explicitly being proposed in the article. Such reviews we unusually expected to be administered by editors of scholarly journals.

A second mode of review is to practice a 'reflexive' inquiry. This means systematically searching for hidden assumptions and interests among those who speak through the text, from secondary sources to subjects being researched

138 *Bengt Johannisson*

to the researchers themselves; compare Alvesson and Sköldberg (2000). Then the inquiry also includes what is silenced, what is not being said and why. This means that the (academic) box remains while its contents are being questioned and alternative ways of refinement are proposed.

A third mode of review that I propose here implies exploring aspects of the inquiry and asking the question: Opening the box and moving where and by what means? How to enact the consequences of a disclosure? The two first-mentioned modes take it for granted that the context is the academic community. But there may be good reasons for inviting other communities of practice to become part of a reformed knowledge-creating process in the field of entrepreneurship. Reflecting upon Honig's article I will allocate a section to each of these three modes of review. I close my contribution here with some comments on the implications of my argument for how we may/should teach entrepreneurship at our universities and make them as organizations and their students more entrepreneurial.

Honig's contribution as a piece of research in its own right

Honig's paper tells a story about how the field of entrepreneurship has become institutionalized as reflected in an increasing number of professional associations, scientific journals, and conferences. His focus is upon the contents of this institutionalization, as is also done, for example, by Landström and Huse (1996). Honig, however, also reflects upon what images of entrepreneurship are being objectified through this institutionalization. These interpretations, for example, include the image of entrepreneurship as being always beneficial to mankind and its focus on the strong-willed and capable man as the subject that epitomizes entrepreneurship. Honig's major concern is, however, the constant search for new conceptualizations that ultimately will reveal *the* theory. He argues that a more thorough underpinning of existing proposed conceptual frameworks by replication studies is more urgent. He thus proposes public access to databases being used in published research, which in addition to providing a basis for comparative research also has a potential to reveal fraud in research.

These and other measures provided by Honig mainly concern controlling for quality by increasing reliability in empirical research. This means that however considerate these suggestions may be, they refine the contents of the box rather than open it for new perspectives on inquiries into entrepreneurship. Honig's argument seems to be that the fast growth of our field of research and the frequent financing of new chairs by donations by successful entrepreneurs have produced sloppy research. If this is the case I think it is more important to pay attention to the validity of the models that provide the basis for empirical research. Appropriating a vocabulary from the field of management studies, Honig seems to be more concerned with efficiency (do proper measuring) in entrepreneurship research than with its effectiveness (measuring the right things).

Honig's paper reveals the author's strong belief in objectivist research, explicitly giving priority to a nomothetic methodology. This also reveals his conviction that the field of entrepreneurship will only get legitimacy if it submits to natural-science standards. This paradigmatic positioning makes his arguments for the need for quality improvement and the ways to achieve that sound awkward in the context of entrepreneurship and how it may be researched. Already the slightest belief in the social reality as interactively constructed by actors and agents and not another kind of natural system makes such assumptions misleading. It becomes even paradoxical if entrepreneurship is recognized as the enactment of something that is unique and different, ultimately creating new worlds carried by will and commitment. Compare Spinosa et al. (1997).

Honig's concern for ethical issues, mainly the risk for fraud, and the examples he brings up, are also based on experiences that are directly imported from research outside the social field. Intentional fraud of course may appear also in social-science research. However, those persons being studied may themselves oppose researchers' interpretations. Also, in entrepreneurship research it seems to be far more important to consider unconscious misinterpretations of definitions in comparative studies, such as the global GEM project.

Honig seems to be convinced that repeated comparative-static quantitative research is the best way to produce solid research about entrepreneurship. But what if entrepreneurship is a genuinely processual phenomenon and best studied accordingly? Compare for example Steyaert (2007). Adopting a process view has several implications for Honig's argumentation. Thus, for example, the major problem is not that he argues that our research may inspire people to launch ventures that may fail. A much larger mistake in my mind is that we do not enough point out that 'entrepreneuring' is a learning process that must be enacted experimentally, preferably in small steps; compare Weick (1984). Honig seems to be stuck in the conviction that the proper way to do research is to test a limited number of candidates for the best model to use in order to accomplish viable ventures. But there is no road to entrepreneurship, entrepreneuring is the road.

Honig's box is made in America

Understandings of entrepreneurship are, as much as images of organizations as another field of study within the social sciences, a product of a specific culture, here the American one. See Hofstede (1980). Due to the dominance of the American culture, in general and in (entrepreneurship) research in particular, it has seduced researchers from all over the world to overlook the role of context in any (social) research. This means that researchers deny their own cultural identity and choke their reflexivity. The social and cultural context of what is being researched and by whom influences the whole research process from how the phenomenon, here entrepreneurship, is defined to how it is being researched. Although Honig questions the (American) image of entrepreneurship as enacted by a rationally calculating male guided by greed, he

140   *Bengt Johannisson*

does not discuss alternative understandings of entrepreneurship. Such are for example provided by European research, presenting entrepreneurship as collective and concerned with everyday life rather than individualistic and associated with dramas in the market place; see for example Hjorth et al. (2003), Johannisson (2003), and Steyaert (2004).

Obviously the contextuality of both the conceptual frameworks used and empirical findings made implies that replication as well as double-checking becomes more difficult and less meaningful than what Honig proposes. How entrepreneurship is conceptualized is historically and culturally dependent. Say's image of the entrepreneur as an organizer reflected a time at, or even before, the dawn of the industrial revolution when societal change was relatively slow. Schumpeter's image of the entrepreneur as a revolutionary appearing in *The Theory of Economical Development,* originally published in German in 1912, codified the intense technological development that peaked at turn of the century. Thus we have to accept that how we conceptualize entrepreneurship varies according to context and in addition moves with changes in society. This is self-evident to many European scholars but less so to American researchers. Accordingly many Europeans stay with the broad basic statement that entrepreneurship is about accepting change as a natural state, a mode of relating to the world that we all adopt as children. European research also more often reveals the dark side of entrepreneurship; compare for example Berglund and Johansson (2012). But it also points out the difficulties in defining entrepreneurship as good or bad; see Rehn and Taalaas (2004).

Further important issues in the field of entrepreneurship research that are silenced or misinterpreted probably due to Honig's American cultural bias include his argument that corporate entrepreneurship and family business – but not strategic entrepreneurship! – may be "well served in the domain of general management or strategy". Many Europeans, including myself, would argue that management and entrepreneurship represent different ideologies; cf. Hjorth et al. (2003). Entrepreneurship then rather should be associated with tactical moves according to what situations emerge than with the systematic implementation of long-term plans. Corporate entrepreneurship as an organizing challenge certainly contributes to the core of entrepreneurship (see Hjorth, 2012). Considering that family businesses are charged with emotions, dreams, and hopes, they carry the same 'muscles' that are called for when entrepreneurship is enacted.

As in any other research field, in the natural as well as in the social sciences, academic journals play a significant role in the institutionalization of the research field. Benson Honig's mistrust of journal editors who remind submitting authors to read and cite previous research reported in the journal is difficult to understand. After all, he presents a 'model' for improving the quality of entrepreneurship research through replication of earlier studiers. As a former journal editor in the field, I saw/see two main reasons why 'intra-journal' references should be encouraged. First, this should be considered as part of needed homework and contribution to knowledge accumulation whether it is about refining an emerging conceptual framework or presenting replication studies (sic!). Also, with the increasing number of journals in the field of entrepreneurship, specialization is called for and journals' self-citation then becomes instrumental in a self-organizing process in that direction.

Need for non-academic tools in order to open the box

Benson Honig's ambitious attempt to envision the implications of an opening of the box fettering entrepreneurship research by using instruments that submit to academic orthodoxy is honourable. However, I argue that breaking out of existing research practices is almost an impossible mission if the attempted escape, such as Honig's, is organized from inside the field of entrepreneurship or even the academic community in general. Such attempts run the risk of only offering centripetal solutions and enforce the box. As much as most escapes from prisons rely on support form the outside, entrepreneurship researchers presumably are dependent on powerful allies in their attempt to advance the field. However, Honig seems to be suspicious of external allies such as consultants. He may be right in the specific case considering that many consultants associate with academia mainly in order to gain legitimacy when communicating their normative advice to practicing entrepreneurs. But the fact that entrepreneurs seem to be more prone to listen to consultants who are expected to be paid than to researchers who long for an audience should be seriously considered by members of the academic community. I am, however, even more concerned about Honig's negligence of the insights of 'genuine practitioners in the field of entrepreneurship, in our case obviously living entrepreneurs. The same natural-sciences research community that he uses as a role model in his plea for more replication research after all save no effort to get as close as possible to the phenomena that they study.

The stories told by invited entrepreneurs (and sponsors!) at the opening or closing dinner table at research conferences usually provide the most distinct memories we as scholars bring home. Adopting an objectivist approach makes it all too easy to brush aside such insights as 'anecdotal evidence'. I rather argue that the cognitive and emotional imprint that such storytelling makes signals how an escape out of the box may be organized. When Honig and other researchers silence the doings of entrepreneurship, they certainly brush aside the advice by Peter Drucker (1985) to consider entrepreneurship as a practice. If we accept that view, we have to encounter the entrepreneurs in their practising of their trade. Considering that "[a] 'practice' . . . is a routinized type of behaviour which consists of several elements, interconnected to one another: forms of bodily activities, forms of mental activities, 'things' and their use, a background knowledge of understanding, know-how, states of emotion and motivational knowledge" (Reckwitz, 2002: 249), we cannot just enjoy what entrepreneurs tell us in formal research settings. We must communicate even more intensely with these practitioners by dwelling in their everyday setting.

142 *Bengt Johannisson*

Only then will it be possible to open the box and fill it with new insights of entrepreneurship.

Doing research on entrepreneurship as a practice means that the traditional set of scientific instruments used in social research must be replaced. Submission to the natural-science standards that Honig proposes will only widen the gap between academics and practitioners with respect to how they make sense of entrepreneurship. Inspired by Chia and Holt (2009), I elsewhere (Johannisson, 2014a) argue that entrepreneurship research can only free itself and do itself justice as scientific work if it acknowledges as its leading stars two Aristotelian knowledge interests that are denied by the powers that keep entrepreneurship research inside the box. The tacit and situated knowledge that practitioners use combine phronesis and mētis. Phronesis then "is the tacit form of prudent practical intelligence and wisdom, acquired through experience, that accounts for the ability to perform expediently and appropriately in defined social circumstances" (Chia & Rasche, 2010: 39).

While there are previous calls for phronesis in social science research (see for example Flyvbjerg, 2001), mētis is so far seldom referred to in social science research. Mētis represents an internalized disposition that "is characterized by agility, suppleness, swiftness of action and the art of dissimulation (seeing without being seen or acting without being seen to act)" (Chia & Rasche, 2010: 40). Bringing in phronesis and mētis helps us to make intelligible not only that entrepreneurship ultimately is about an attentive attitude to the world and an urge to enact imagined potentialities. This perspective on knowledge guides us when we try to understand why entrepreneurship is a genuinely hands-on, paperless activity. This view provides an alternative to the 'linguistic turn' that has set the tone in much European research into entrepreneurship; see the Movement series edited by Hjorth and Steyaert. The phronesis/mētis concepts also bridge between knowledge creation in the field of entrepreneurship and the broader theorizing on tacit knowledge by Nonaka and Takeuchi (1995). What is more, phronesis and mētis also complete the epistemological foundation of the different logics associated with the enactment of entrepreneurship according to Sarasvathy (2001).

Proposing phronesis and mētis as the forms of knowledge used to enact entrepreneurship means that the overall paradigm for entrepreneurship research has to be reconsidered. Obviously scientific inquiry in that field then calls for a different metaphor/theory and another puzzle-solving device, that is methodology; compare Morgan (1980). Over the last decades there has been an increasing interest in practice theory; see for example Schatzki (1996, 2001) and Chia and Holt (2009). The practice framework conceptualizes and (thus) legitimizes what we intuitively have associated with entrepreneurial (inter)action, namely spontaneity and improvisation, and how that is achieved becomes in a phronesis/mētis knowledge framework rationalized. This view generically presents entrepreneurship as creative organizing and as an emerging bricolage and means that focus is on embodied (inter)action, in itself and as a road to understanding. This practice approach and the form of knowledge it allies with

Legitimacy or relevance 143

in my mind can help us to make sense of the entrepreneurial phenomenon in a way that pays due respect to the insights of those who enact entrepreneurship outside the academic box.

European researchers in general and Scandinavian scholars in particular have contributed with appropriate methodology for studying social phenomena, such as entrepreneurship, as practice. In so far as practices are created in inter-action, dialogue should also guide the interface between academia and visited settings for entrepreneurship. Then we have to move beyond action research because this is concerned with creating change together with the marginal-ized actors who are targeted. See for example Reason and Bradbury (2001). Joint knowledge-creation thus is not the main concern. 'Collaborative research' (Adler et al., 2004) and 'engaged scholarship' (Van de Ven, 2007), though, aim at co-producing knowledge out of dialogues between researchers and practi-tioners in their professional roles. I, however, argue that the researcher has to immerse even deeper into the situated crafting of the entrepreneurial project. Accordingly I propose 'interactive research' where the researcher personally is involved in the entrepreneurial processes being studied. See Johannisson (2014). The ultimate road to insight is 'enactive research', which means that the researcher by her/himself launches a venture and practises auto-ethnography as a basis for learning and reflection.

Interactive approaches provide different routes and are more ambitious when it comes to increasing quality and ethical conduct in entrepreneurship research than is proposed by Benson Honig. His road is bordered with techni-cal control mechanisms that may be a faster and safer way to gain legitimacy within the contemporary academic community. But again it is a centripetal advice that will not help us to move outside the box that like an iron cage restricts contemporary research. Only an approach that theoretically elaborates on the practice of entrepreneurship and uses dialogue that includes phronesis and mētis as forms of knowledge will make sense both inside and outside the academic box. Interactive approach for sure makes the research more depen-dent on the researcher as a person and the researcher more responsible for the findings. But as much as no believer in entrepreneurship/-ing as processual and collective can deny the role of a person/entrepreneur in initiating the process, no inquiry into social realities, whatever the quality criteria used, can deny the impact of the researcher as a complete human in translating field accounts into academic reporting.

Education as a road to more open-minded entrepreneurship research

I fully agree with Benson Honig that we as established entrepreneurship scholars have a responsibility towards future generations of researchers. I also think that his suggestions with respect to how those responsibilities should be practiced are consistent with Honig's image of high-quality entrepreneurship research. But I think that his image of our doctoral students foredoomed to

144   *Bengt Johannisson*

stay docile victims of both established institutional orders and the egocentricity of senior faculty members can and should be changed. Thus I argue that our primary responsibilities are, on the one hand, to increase the students' self-confidence and, on the other hand, to empower them to take own responsibility as becoming academic professionals.

Helping the students to craft an own entrepreneurial identity is rather a matter of how our teaching and their learning are designed than about what (scientific) facts about entrepreneurship are communicated. The students must be invited to mobilize their own capabilities in their learning process. Elsewhere we propose the use of blogging as a generic way of both furnishing students with capabilities needed for different modes of reflexivity and creating their entrepreneurial selves (Achtenhagen & Johannisson, 2013). Correspondingly how we teach entrepreneurship is much more important than what we teach them. If we are able to turn our students into critical, yet creative, subjects, they will themselves become able to identify their needs and how we as scholars may satisfy them. This is the way to encourage the students to acknowledge their entrepreneurial selves.

My own experience from academic teaching in and for entrepreneurship for four decades has taught me that students are not passive recipients of what knowledge we may be able to transmit. They are easily activated in their own learning process and subsequently they will help us to move outside the box when it comes to making sense of entrepreneurial phenomena. This can be achieved by organizing internships in entrepreneurial firms and providing appropriate assignments that involve the entrepreneurs themselves. The students then become close to the entrepreneurial setting and can experience the everydayness of such knowledge-creating processes. Thereby the students are turned into translators of the phronesis and mētis forms of knowledge that energize venturing processes into scholarly work.

Since the turn of the millennium it has become fashionable to transform universities from bureaucratic to entrepreneurial organizations. I however doubt that their staffs can enact such an identity on their own. A formal-explicit knowledge ideal, episteme, is dominating the universities, which presumably impedes the 'bricolaging' that is called for in order to make them live up to their own espoused vision. The 2012 OECD review of Sweden's innovation policy (OECD, 2013) on the one hand recognizes that some knowledge centres in the country are constructed to promote academic intelligence, and on the other hand identifies competence centres that are user oriented. Nevertheless the reviewers recommend *"[s]trengthen[ing] links between HEIs and the business sector on teaching and curriculum design . . ."* (italics in original) (2013: 36). Even if the report does not elaborate on the reasons for creating such direct links between academia and the world of business, the quoted statement signals an increasing awareness of the importance of an ongoing dialogue between representatives of academic and practical knowledge, between episteme and mētis. If the former knowledge ideal is the only one promoted at our universities, for example along the lines suggested by Honig, neither will the university staff become able to practice entrepreneurship in its own setting nor will society get a fair return on its investment in higher education.

Note

1 I am grateful to the Kamprad Research Foundation for making it possible for me to participate in the conference.

References

Achtenhagen, L. & Johannisson, B. (2013). *Fostering Reflexive Entrepreneurs in Business Schools – Blogging as the Core of an Adequate Pedagogy.* Working Paper. Jönköping: JIBS.

Adler, N., Shani, A. B., & Styhre, A. (eds.) (2004). *Collaborative Research in Organizations: Foundations for Learning, Change and Theoretical Development.* Thousand Oaks, CA: Sage.

Alvesson, M. & Sköldberg, K (2000). *Reflexive Methodology. New Vistas for Qualitative Research.* London: Sage.

Berglund, K. & Johansson, A. W (2012). Dark and bright effects of a polarized entrepreneurship discourse . . . and the prospects of transformation. In K. Berglund, B. Johannisson, & B. Schwartz (eds.), *Societal Entrepreneurship* (pp. 163–186). Cheltenham: Edward Elgar.

Chia, R.C.H. & Holt, R. (2009). *Strategy without Design. The Silent Efficacy of Indirect Action.* Cambridge: Cambridge University Press.

Chia, R.C.H. & Rasche, A. (2010). Epistemological alternatives for researching strategy as practice: building and dwelling worldviews. In D. Golsorkhi, L. Rouleau, D. Seidl, & E. Vaara (eds.), *Cambridge Handbook of Strategy as Practice* (pp. 34–46). Cambridge: Cambridge University Press.

Drucker, P. (1985). *Innovation and Entrepreneurship.* New York: Harper & Row.

Flyvbjerg, B. (2001). *Making Social Science Matter. Why Social Inquiry Fails and How It Can Succeed Again.* Cambridge: Cambridge University Press.

Hjorth, D. (ed.) (2012). *Handbook of Organizational Entrepreneurship.* Cheltenham: Edward Elgar.

Hjorth, D., Johannisson, B., & Steyaert, C. (2003). Entrepreneurship as discourse and life style. In B. Czarniawska & G. Sevón (eds.), *Northern Light – Organization Theory in Scandinavia* (pp. 91–110). Malmö: Liber.

Hofstede, G. (1980). Motivation, leadership and organization: Do American theories apply abroad? *Organizational Dynamics,* Summer: 42–63.

Johannisson, B. (2003). Entrepreneurship as a Collective Phenomenon. In E. Genescà, D. Urbano, J. Capelleras, C. Guallarte, & J. Vergès (eds.), *Creación de Empresas – Entrepreneurship* (pp. 87–109). Barcelona, Spain: Servei de Publicacions de la Universitat Autònoma de Barcelona.

Johannisson, B. (2014). The practice approach and interactive research in entrepreneurship and small-scale venturing. In Alan Carsrud & Malin Brännback (eds.), *Handbook of Research Methods and Applications in Entrepreneurship and Small Business* (pp. 228–258). Cheltenham, UK and Northampton, MA: Edward Elgar Publishing.

Johannisson, B. (2014a). Entrepreneurship: the practice of cunning intelligence. In Braunerhjelm, P (ed.), *20 Years of Entrepreneurship Research – From Small Business Dynamics to Entrepreneurial Growth and Societal Prosperity* (pp. 109–119). Stockholm: Swedish Entrepreneurship Forum.

Landström, H. & Huse, M. (1996). *Trends in European Entrepreneurship and Small-Business Research. A Comparison between Europe and the U.S.* SIRE-Working Paper 1996:3, Halmstad and Växjö University.

146 *Bengt Johannisson*

Morgan, G. (1980). Paradigms, metaphors and puzzle solving in organization theory. *Administrative Science Quarterly*, 25: 605–622.

Nonaka, I. & Takeuchi, H. (1995). *The Knowledge-Creating Company*. Oxford: Oxford University Press.

OECD (2013). *Reviews of Innovation Policy: Sweden 2012*.

Reason, P. & Bradbury, H. (2001). Introduction. In P. Reason & H. Bradbury (eds.), *Handbook of Action Research. Participative Inquiry and Practice* (pp. 1–14). Thousands Oaks, CA: Sage.

Reckwitz, A. (2002). Toward a theory of social practices. A development in culturalist theorizing. *European Journal of Social Theory*, 5(2): 243–263.

Rehn, A. & Taalaas, S. (2004). Znakomstva I Svyazi' [Acquaintances and Connections] – *Blat*, the Soviet Union and mundane entrepreneurship. *Entrepreneurship & Regional Development*, 16(3): 235–250.

Sarasvathy, S. D. (2001). Causation and effectuation: Toward a theoretical shift from economic inevitability to entrepreneurial contingency. *Academy of Management Review*, 26(2): 243–263.

Schatzki, T. R. (1996). *Social Practices: A Wittgensteinian Approach to Human Activity and the Social*. Cambridge: Cambridge University Press.

Schatzki, T. R. (2001). Introduction: Practice theory. In T. R. Schatzki, K. Knorr Cetina, & E. von Savigny (eds.), *The Practice Turn in Contemporary Theory* (pp. 1–14). London: Routledge.

Spinosa, C., Flores, F., & Dreyfus, H. (1997). *Disclosing New Worlds – Entrepreneurship, Democratic Action and Cultivation of Solidarity*. Cambridge, MA: MIT Press.

Steyaert, C. (2004). The prosaics of entrepreneurship. In D. Hjorth & C. Steyaert (eds.), *Narrative and Discursive Approaches in Entrepreneurship* (pp. 8–21). Cheltenham: Edward Elgar.

Steyaert, C. (2007). Entrepreneuring as a conceptual attractor? A review of process theories in 20 years of entrepreneurship studies. *Entrepreneurship & Regional Development*, 19(6): 453–477.

Van de Ven, A. H. (2007). *Engaged Scholarship. A Guide to Organizational and Social Research*. New York: Oxford University Press.

Weick, K. E. (1984). Small wins. Redefining the scale of social problems. *American Psychologist*, January: 40–49.

10 What makes scholarly works "interesting" in entrepreneurship research?

Learning from the past

Hans Landström

Introduction

What makes music interesting?

Some things draw you in, touch you in different ways, expanding and stretching your senses, that is, you experience them as "interesting". The point of departure of this chapter was a conversation over dinner that I had with my daughter some time ago about one such thing, namely music. The conversation concerned our interest in different genres of music and the question that emerged was: What makes music interesting?

I grew up in the 1960s with English guitar pop music and idols such as The Kinks and, not least, The Who, but also a strong folk tradition represented by, for example, Bob Dylan, Donovan, and Joan Baez. By the end of the 1960s I was listening to Led Zeppelin – an English rock band that had a major influence on early hard rock bands such as Deep Purple and Black Sabbath, something that I considered "interesting". My daughter grew up in the 1990s – a decade of fairly accessible pop music with stars such as Mariah Carey, Spice Girls, and boy-bands such as Backstreet Boys. However, she was early attracted by Indie-pop music, and especially bands such as The Smiths captured her attention. The Smiths with their lead-singer Morrissey started in the UK in the 1980s and played accessible music that fitted the charts but with lyrics that articulated strong social criticism.

From our discussion it was obvious that what I considered interesting did not necessarily appeal to my daughter – what we find interesting is a matter of taste, something personal, and subjective. However, we came to the conclusion that there might be some aspects that make music interesting. For example, we found Led Zeppelin and The Smiths interesting as both groups created new sounds that caught our attention, while at the same time their music was inspired by earlier music traditions – Led Zeppelin by blues and folk and The Smiths by punk-rock. It was also obvious that music we find interesting evokes emotions leading to an intrinsically motivated behaviour that fuels our interest over time, for example, my first experience of Led Zeppelin led me to a two decade long fascination with (hard) rock music.

148   *Hans Landström*

Having been involved in entrepreneurship research for over three decades and conducted three research projects in the course of the last ten years on the core contributions to entrepreneurship research,[1] it seemed obvious to draw some analogies between my interests in music and research. Despite the fact that there are clear differences between research and music, especially in terms of the focus on the work as opposed to the individual and the personality cult that in many cases surrounds musicians, the conversation with my daughter made me reflect on what I found interesting in these core entrepreneurship works. In order to provide some suggestions to new scholars within the field in order to help them conduct interesting research, in this chapter I will (1) elaborate on works and scholars that I have found interesting over the last 30 years and that have challenged my assumptions about entrepreneurship, (2) propose a more general construct of what can be regarded as interesting in entrepreneurship research in terms of challenging the assumptions within the field, (3) elaborate on the concept "interesting" in the context of entrepreneurship studies, and (4) propose some recommendations for the future in an effort to keep the field vibrant and "interesting".

The chapter comprises four sections. In the next section I will briefly describe the evolution of entrepreneurship as a research field and explain the background to my view of what is interesting in such research. Then I will discuss some contributions that have challenged my assumptions about entrepreneurship and that I regard as interesting. The section ends with a general construct of what makes entrepreneurship research "interesting" in the sense of challenging my assumptions about entrepreneurship. The following section contains reflections on "interesting" as a concept and a discussion on what makes entrepreneurship research interesting. Finally, I will discuss how the field can remain "interesting" and continue to challenge our view of entrepreneurship.

The need to sustain "interesting" in entrepreneurship research

In recent decades, scientific knowledge has grown significantly and many research fields have witnessed extensive growth in the number of scholars, conferences, published articles, and journals. Entrepreneurship is no exception and it could even be argued that, compared with many other research fields, entrepreneurship has been tremendously successful.

The main explanation for the popularity and success of entrepreneurship research is that entrepreneurship is important for societal dynamics and growth. Entrepreneurship has been a relevant issue for politicians and policymakers in many countries around the world and a great deal of resources have been made available for entrepreneurship research and education. However, in this chapter I will argue that not only is entrepreneurship research important and relevant, but also that entrepreneurship scholars have been very successful in formulating interesting research questions and conducting interesting research. Entrepreneurship scholars have always been very open-minded when it comes to recognizing changes in society as well as experimental in their use

What makes works "interesting"   149

of methods and not afraid to challenge the assumptions of mainstream disciplines as well as in practice. Thus, entrepreneurship scholars have attracted new researchers who migrated into the field (Landström & Benner, 2010), making entrepreneurship a fast growing research area in recent decades (Landström, Harirchi, & Åström, 2012).

However, the question of what makes entrepreneurship research interesting is seldom raised – despite the fact that it is critical for a dynamic research field. It is necessary that our research is regarded as "interesting". On a more general level, it is fundamental to all research fields that scholars are able to formulate interesting research questions and conduct interesting research that will "open up" new research areas, resolve long-standing controversies, thereby allowing the integration of different approaches and conventional beliefs to be challenged (Sandberg & Alvesson, 2011). If scholars fail to present interesting research, the field will become less attractive and over time few will pay attention to it. Therefore, interesting research is necessary for the survival and progress of entrepreneurship as a research field.

On an individual level, there is increased pressure on entrepreneurship scholars to be published and cited. However, in the same way as in other fields, entrepreneurship scholars are faced with an information overload – the number of articles on entrepreneurship is growing more or less exponentially and the range of published articles greatly exceeds any one person's ability to read or keep track of them all. At a time when influence (citations) is becoming more and more important for an academic career (Rynes, 2007) and an ever-increasing volume of research is produced within the field, individual research achievements must be interesting to become influential.

Entrepreneurship as an evolving field of research

Sociology of science scholars have addressed a wide range of issues related to the establishment of new academic fields (e.g. Cole, 1983; Pfeffer, 1993). A few years ago, Hambrick and Chen (2008) presented a model to explain the emergence and growth of new academic fields, which comprises three overlapping phases: (1) differentiation from existing fields; (2) resource mobilization in order to attract a critical mass of scholars; and (3) legitimacy building in the eyes of the academic establishment.

Having been a fairly marginal topic in some mainstream disciplines such as economics, economic history, and psychology, entrepreneurship gradually became a field in its own right in the 1970s and 1980s – mainly triggered by the "creative destruction" prevalent in many Western societies at that time (Landström, 2005b). The 1980s was the era of "academic entrepreneurs" characterized by an enthusiastic but small and fragmented research community, whose members accomplished many pioneering achievements both in terms of new knowledge and in terms of many different initiatives in order to build a research community within the field (Landström, 2005a). These early achievements contributed to successful differentiation of the field from other disciplines, making it more visible not only to researchers but also, and not least, to policymakers and politicians, providing it with external legitimacy.

The 1990s was a decade characterized by strong resource mobilization, including extensive growth and the building of a strong infrastructure – new publication opportunities, social networks (conferences and professional organizations), and more sources of funding, what Aldrich (2012) called "institutional entrepreneurship" involving collective action by many scholars, groups, and associations that were instrumental in the building of an infrastructure within the field. I find the 1990s extremely interesting in the sense that the field – although becoming highly fragmented – was a "melting pot" for scholars from various fields, a range of new research issues emerged, and different methodological approaches and concepts/theories were imported.

To some extent a divergence of the field continued during the 2000s. It was partly "internal", brought about by entrepreneurship scholars who were critical of the perceived lack of creativity and imposition of rigid norms in entrepreneurship research approaches and suggested alternative paradigmatic assumptions within the field (Steyaert & Hjorth, 2003), but also from scholars who wanted a broader view on entrepreneurship, not only as an economic achievement but also a social phenomenon, for example in the form of social and societal entrepreneurship. The other reason for the divergence is "external", as entrepreneurship has attracted the interest of scholars anchored in many different disciplines, creating a rather scattered and loosely connected group of researchers who occasionally conduct studies on entrepreneurship (Landström & Persson, 2010).

In addition, I have identified a contrasting trend towards increased convergence and institutionalization in the field. In order to become a legitimate field of research, entrepreneurship research has in many ways begun to conform to the norms and standards of established fields by adopting a "normal science" approach. Over time there has been a stronger focus on robustness in entrepreneurship studies, reflected in the use of larger samples, pre-tested variables, sophisticated statistical analyses, etc. In addition, to some extent entrepreneurship has become "mainstream" – thousands around the world regard themselves as entrepreneurship scholars and teachers and in many countries entrepreneurship is considered an integral part of the academic system. This means that it is evaluated on the basis of traditional measures, and in this sense it will have conservative consequences for the field.

However, we have to bear in mind that this "normal science" approach in entrepreneurship research has produced a great deal of high quality and interesting research that has deepened our knowledge of entrepreneurship today in comparison with a couple of decades ago as well as inspiring many scholars in their own research, teaching, and practice (Davidsson, 2013). It could also be argued that the approach has provided a strong infrastructure for research, for example, with regard PhD programmes, co-production of research, role models, etc. Even within mainstream entrepreneurship research there is great variation in terms of research and methodologies as well as scholars with different backgrounds and research traditions.

Having said that, this institutionalization process carries a risk that individual scholars will become embedded in a culture and incentive system that places greater emphasis on the more incremental research questions addressed. Studies will contribute less and less, merely creating nuances of what we already know, thus reducing the incentive for individual scholars to conduct challenging, long-term research. Robust studies are of course important, but we also need to stimulate entrepreneurship scholars, especially PhD candidates, to formulate interesting research questions and conduct interesting research.

Some "interesting" entrepreneurship research contributions that challenged my assumptions about entrepreneurship in scientific studies

When scholars are asked what they regard as high quality research (Astley, 1985; Bartunek, Rynes, & Ireland, 2006; Craig, 2010; Das & Long, 2010) they often mention the importance of the research question, that the study is "well-crafted" in line with accepted scientific practice, the validity and relevance of the conclusions, and that the work is well written. For example, in the field of management, Bartunek et al. (2006) presented aspects that determine what is considered interesting: studies that are counterintuitive and novel in terms of assumptions, ideas and methodologies, well-crafted in relation to theory, methods, and analysis, well written with a logical argumentation, that make the readers feel involved and generate usable knowledge in the "real" world.

Authors such as Astley (1985), Bartunek et al. (2006), and not least Davis (1971) argued that while valid and well-crafted works are important, this is often not enough for them to be considered "interesting" – something more is required. In his 1971 seminal article Murray Davis asked: How do theories that are generally considered "interesting" differ from those that are considered "non-interesting"? His answer was that scholars are regarded as "great" not because their theories are true but because their theories are "interesting" in the sense that they challenge certain assumptions, while non-interesting theories affirm the assumptions of their audience. When theories challenge certain assumptions they stand out and capture the attention of their audience. In a similar vein, Garfinkel (1967) characterized the state of low attention as "the routinized taken-for-granted world of everyday life." This implies that a theory will be regarded as interesting if it challenges accepted truths and represent an attack on the taken-for-granted world of the audience. If it does not challenge but merely confirms taken-for-granted beliefs the members of the audience will reject its value and the response will be: "Of course!", "That's obvious!", or "Everybody knows that!"

Davis' (1971) reasoning has been empirically tested in a number of studies. For example, Johnson (2003) revealed that "interesting" is often used in scientific articles as a rhetorical framing device in the Introduction and Concluding sections. However, rhetoric alone will not make the article more influential or innovative, i.e. it is difficult to "cheat" the readers. It has also been found that scholars rarely antagonize their peers by challenging their theories. For

152 *Hans Landström*

example, negative citations are seldom used in research articles (Murugesan & Moravcsik, 1978; Spiegel-Rosing, 1977), and in many cases challenging an opponent is regarded as impolite, as well as making it more difficult to get the work published (Landström & Åström, 2011).

I have been involved in entrepreneurship and small business research since the early 1980s and wrote my thesis on the financing of new technology-based ventures in Sweden in 1987. It is usually these formative years as a PhD student and postdoc that to a large degree shape the rest of one's career – a form of "imprinting" that will have a persistent impact on behaviour and the perception of what is interesting in research (Stinchcombe, 1965; Marquis & Tilcsik, 2013). Over the years I have read many works that I found interesting in the sense that they were well written with an interesting and detailed story to be told, studies that were well-crafted with robust results, studies that appeared to be applicable to my own research or relevant for practice, but also studies that confirmed or articulated doubts that I have felt with earlier knowledge or studies within the field. However, few works challenged my thinking or assumptions about entrepreneurship. In this section, I will provide examples of entrepreneurship research contributions that I found interesting, including scholars as well as works that have influenced me, with a focus on those that challenged my assumptions about entrepreneurship.

According to Barley (2006), interesting works – in the sense of challenging existing assumptions – can be divided into three categories:

1   Interesting subjects: Some works are regarded as interesting because they address subjects that depart from the mainstream and challenge our view of entrepreneurship.
2   Interesting methodologies: In many cases we consider works interesting because the methodologies used challenge the traditional methodologies of entrepreneurship research.
3   Interesting concepts/theories: Works interest us because they challenge prevailing knowledge and propose concepts and/or theories that differ from the familiar yet make sense in our understanding of entrepreneurship.

I will follow this categorization in my presentation of works that I have found interesting over the years. Obviously, some scholars and works challenged my thinking in many different ways. For example, Arnold Cooper was highly influential for my thesis, not only because of his contributions to our knowledge of technology-based ventures but also because of his methodological insights, while Saras Sarasvathy's "effectuation" article (2001) was both interesting conceptually and attracted the attention of researchers as well as practitioners.

Interesting subjects

In entrepreneurship research, as in many other social sciences, there is a close relationship between the development of society and the evolution of the research field. This was particularly the case in the early stages of entrepreneurship research. In the 1970s and 1980s we could identify significant social and economic changes in western societies. Scholars interested in entrepreneurship were sensitive to and identified these changes. Among the pioneering studies in entrepreneurship, many interesting contributions significantly influenced my research interest as a young PhD student. For example, I was greatly inspired by the *Encyclopedia of Entrepreneurship* (Kent, Sexton, & Vesper, 1982), the first "state-of-the-art book" edited by Donald Sexton, which was included in the reference list of my first PhD course on entrepreneurship headed by Professor Bengt Johannisson, Växjö University in Sweden. I was also influenced by some early studies conducted in the UK, such as the Bolton Report (1971), despite the fact that it took a fairly pessimistic view of the future of small businesses, and not least the study by John Stanworth and James Curran "Growth and the Small Firm: An Alternative View" (1976). In addition, based on the changes that I could identify myself, following the establishment of a science park (IDEON) more or less outside my office window at Lund Institute of Technology (LTH) in the southern part of Sweden, I became interested in the studies by Arnold Cooper on technology-based firms in Silicon Valley revealing that firms tend to cluster around science parks (Cooper, 1971, 1973; Cooper & Komives, 1972). Other studies that fascinated me were those by Ed Roberts on the individuals who created new ventures around Route 128 in Boston (Roberts, 1968; Roberts & Weiner, 1968, 1971) and a large survey on new technology-based ventures conducted in Sweden by James Utterback and Göran Reitberger (1982).

A main characteristic of these pioneering studies was an enthusiastic and ideological view of entrepreneurship. When anchored in a neoliberal capitalistic political ideology represented, for example, by Margaret Thatcher in the UK and Ronald Reagan in the US, entrepreneurship was regarded as something positive for society as a generator of economic growth and prosperity. As a consequence, entrepreneurship research was anchored for many years in assumptions about how society works and the importance of entrepreneurship in society with focus on the individual entrepreneurial as well as growth and success of companies and individuals. Over the years, I have been relieved when reading works that, in different ways, have challenged these ideological assumptions. One example is Chris Steyaert and Daniel Hjorth's "Movements in Entrepreneurship Series" (Steyaert & Hjorth, 2001, 2004, 2007, 2009) in which they introduced a different political agenda and broadened the scope of entrepreneurship to include the creation of social value in society. Another example is William Baumol's article "Entrepreneurship: Productive, Unproductive and Destructive" (1990), which challenges the "good for society" view, arguing that entrepreneurship can be "productive" as well as "unproductive" and that the incentive system in place in different contexts influences its direction.

Thus, over time entrepreneurship scholars have been sensitive to changes in society. However, they have also been close to practice, which enables them to challenge part of the ongoing practice and policy activities. In this respect there are many examples of interesting works. Early in my PhD studies I read

154 *Hans Landström*

Richard Normann's thesis *Skapande företagsledning* [Creative Management], published in 1976 in which he introduced the concept "business idea", which can be regarded as a forerunner of today's popular concept "business model" (e.g. Osterwalder, Pigneur, & Tucci, 2005). In his discussion of business renewal, Normann made extensive use of the insights he gained as a management consultant – creating an interesting story and a strong linkage between research and practice. Another major contribution that challenged current practice was Amarnath Bhidé's article in the *Harvard Business Review* (1992) on "Bootstrap Finance: The Art of Start-ups" in which he challenged the "big money assumption" among entrepreneurs and argued for the use of bootstrapping finance. In a later work (Bhide, 2000) he showed that most entrepreneurs who started a venture that appeared on the Inc500 list – the fastest-growing businesses in the US – did not have a written business plan, and in cases where they did, the business changed significantly compared to the original plan. A further example is Saras Sarasvathy's article in the *Academy of Management Review* (2001) "Causation and Effectuation: Toward a Theoretical Shift from Economic Inevitability to Entrepreneurial Contingency" that challenged the rational view of the entrepreneurial process and has become one of few works to successfully attract interest among entrepreneurship researchers as well as practitioners.

Entrepreneurship scholars have not only focused on entrepreneurial practices, as policy has also played a crucial role in research, especially among European scholars. For example, policymakers assume that new ventures are good because they create new jobs. It was therefore interesting to read David Storey's excellent book *Understanding the Small Business Sector* (1994), in which he demonstrated that growth is not predominant in the small business sector and that very few new ventures grow and create jobs. Finally, during many years of research into venture capital, I found it difficult to accept policymakers' overconfidence in the venture capital market as a means of stimulating entrepreneurship and growth in society. Josh Lerner's critical review of venture capital policies around the world, *Boulevard of Broken Dreams* (2009), really challenged these beliefs.

Interesting methodologies

Historically, entrepreneurship research has been characterized as a multidisciplinary field with a high migration of scholars from many different fields, leading to the application of various methodological traditions and approaches. Despite this fact and in line with the increased institutionalization of the field, entrepreneurship research has developed into a more or less mono-methodological research field (Aldrich & Baker, 1997; Edelman, Manolova, & Brush, 2009), heavily relying on quantitative approaches based on surveys and archival data that are analyzed using sophisticated statistical techniques. Against this background I have found several research achievements interesting due to their attempts to challenge the dominant positivist/realist research paradigm (Grant & Perren, 2002) and methodological approaches. Examples are Chris

What makes works "interesting" 155

Steyaert and Daniel Hjorth's bid to challenge the ontological and epistemological conceptions within the field by introducing a social constructionist position (e.g. Steyaert & Hjorth, 2001) in which they stressed the importance of developing a closer relationship with "the real world" as well as the social and cultural context in which entrepreneurship operates.

I was also impressed by some studies that have challenged the dominating methodological approaches in entrepreneurship research, not least studies by Arnold Cooper and his research on the entrepreneurial process and new firm performance (e.g. Cooper, Folta, & Woo, 1995; Cooper, Woo, & Dunkelberg, 1988; Gimeno et al., 1997). Cooper was one of the first to conduct longitudinal studies in entrepreneurship research and reflected on the measures employed in entrepreneurship research. Another example is a study by Cliff, Jenning, & Greenwood (2006) in which they addressed the question of whether industry insiders or outsiders are more innovative, using a sample from one industry (law firms) in the Greater Vancouver area between 1990 and 1998. By employing a focused one-industry sample, they challenged the traditional multi-industry sample frames within the field.

In general, qualitative studies are regarded as more interesting than quantitative ones. As an examination question James March once asked a student at Stanford to "name one paper that has made a substantial theoretical contribution to our knowledge that also contained a regression equation" (Barley, 2006: 19). Rynes (2005) came to a similar conclusion when analyzing the "best article" winner at the *Academy of Management Journal* and found that qualitative studies were honoured disproportionately to their representation in the journal. There are reasons for the overrepresentation of qualitative studies that we regard as "interesting". If rigorously conducted, such studies often discover something new because the methodology seldom decides beforehand what they will found.

In entrepreneurship research I have found many examples of qualitative research that includes detailed process descriptions and makes interesting reading. A few examples are Giacomo Becattini's extensive case study of the Prato region as an industrial district (1989) is an impressive piece of work in the same way as the Van de Ven, Angle, and Poole innovation studies (the Minnesota Study) in 1989 and Andrew Pettigrew's (1987, 1990) in-depth qualitative process studies in different organizational settings that make theory "come to life". In addition, I have gradually started to appreciate analyses by economic historians. Historical methods allow the study to be event-driven, where explanations are built forward from observed events to outcomes, whereas many entrepreneurship studies are outcome-driven, building the explanations backwards from an observed outcome to previous significant events. Karl Gratzer's historical analysis of the automated restaurant industry in Sweden during the early years of the 20th century is an excellent example (Gratzer, 1996). Finally, some of my former doctoral students wrote theses that represent interesting qualitative research in the sense that they tried new avenues. For example, Jaqueline Bergendahl (2009) used diaries to follow the creation

156 *Hans Landström*

of new ventures among student entrepreneurs and Diamanto Politis (2005) employed narratives to understand the careers of business angels.

Interesting concepts/theories

For a long time, entrepreneurship research has been empirical in character and few (if any) genuine concepts and theories emerged. The concepts and theories were mainly borrowed from mainstream disciplines – but not always applied in a "rigorous" way (Landström & Lohrke, 2010). One reason for the lack of theories in entrepreneurship research might be that before we can theorize the phenomenon we need a detailed empirical understanding of it (Eisenhardt, 1989). Such understanding also strengthens the validity and power of the concepts and theories developed (Ghoshal, 2005). However, over the last decade we have seen an emerging interest in theory-based studies (Davidsson, 2008; Brush, Manolova, & Edelman, 2008; Landström et al., 2012) as well as some conceptual and theoretical attempts to understand entrepreneurship, albeit often rooted in earlier mainstream disciplines, for example, "the evolutionary perspective" (Aldrich, 1999), "nascent entrepreneurs" (Reynolds, 2000), "effectuation" (Sarasvathy, 2001) and "bricolage" (Baker & Nelson, 2005).

Over the years we have seen major changes in the direction of the research field, often initiated by scholars who have challenged the basic assumptions underlying the field in general and accepted as unproblematic by its advocates. William Gartner's contributions in 1985 and 1988 are examples in which he emphasized the heterogeneity of entrepreneurship as a phenomenon and argued that entrepreneurs are defined by their behaviour rather than by their traits, thus challenging the prevailing assumptions within the field and changing the direction of entrepreneurship research. Another early contribution to the conceptual development of the field was that of Howard Stevenson, who put forward an opportunity-based view of entrepreneurship, which he defined as a process by which individuals pursue and exploit opportunities irrespective of the resources they currently control (Stevenson & Gumpert, 1985; Stevenson & Jarillo, 1986). In addition, the article by Shane and Venkataraman (2000) (see also Venkataraman, 1997) significantly changed the direction of the domain and triggered several developments; a renewed interest in the Austrian school of economics, focus on "business opportunity recognition", and intense debate regarding the definition of the domain of entrepreneurship research.

There are other works that have been interesting to me in the sense that they challenged the assumptions or the conceptions underlying a specific theme within entrepreneurship research. For many years, scholars interested in entrepreneurs focused strongly on identifying the characteristics of the individual entrepreneur and entrepreneurship was more or less seen as a "one-man-show". However, in the 1980s several researchers demonstrated that entrepreneurship is a "social achievement" in which the entrepreneurs' social network plays an influential role in the creation and success of new ventures (e.g. Birley, 1985;

Aldrich & Zimmer, 1986; Johannisson, 1987; Larson, 1992) – thus challenging the individual focus within this research theme. Another example concerns research on the entrepreneurial process. Ever since I wrote my thesis in the mid-1980s I have been unhappy with the assumptions underlying our knowledge about the entrepreneurial process – often viewed as logical and rational and reinforced by a large number of entrepreneurship textbooks that focused on market analysis and business planning. In my thesis I made some trivial attempts to challenge this view by talking about "decision events" as an alternative to the "rational process view" but without any real success. Therefore, my readings of Howard Aldrich's contributions and his "evolutionary perspective" on the entrepreneurial process (e.g. summarized in his book *Organization Evolving* in 1999) in addition to his elegant way of analyzing the process by means of four concepts – variation, selection, retention, and struggle – impressed and made me understand the entrepreneurial process in a new way. However, the contribution that influenced me most was Saras Sarasvathy's "effectuation" article (2001). The article became a turning point for me, as it made me realize that my original idea was fairly valid. In the article, Sarasvathy outlined an "effectuation process" of venture creation based on the entrepreneur's available resources and competence.

Finally, a range of interesting studies have challenged the assumptions underlying the empirical descriptions within the field. In my thesis I was for example particularly intrigued by the financial aspects of new technology-based firms, and there were a lot of empirical contributions mainly with regard the formal venture capital market in the US (e.g. studies by MacMillan and Bygrave). I have always been interested in studies that challenge these descriptions and the assumptions underlying the success of the US venture capital market. These studies are often based on methodologically more robust studies, for example, with regard to concepts, variables, sample, and/or analysis, which create a knowledge that is more nuanced and precise. Some studies that have influenced me more than others are those by William Sahlman (1990) in which he tried to explain the behaviour of venture capitalists and the studies by Paul Gompers and Josh Lerner on the same subject (e.g. Gompers & Lerner, 1999). I have also frequently referred to a study by Sapienza, Manigart, and Vermeir (1996), in which they demonstrated that the explanatory value of agency theory, which has been the dominant theoretical framework in venture capital research, diminishes away from the US, indicating the questionable influence of US research when studying venture capital.

Construct of what makes entrepreneurship research interesting: challenging assumptions within the field

The main conclusion to be made is that there are many researchers within the field of entrepreneurship who challenged my assumptions about entrepreneurship. Inspired by Alvesson and Sandberg's article in the *Academy of Management*

158 *Hans Landström*

Review (2011), I have summarized my arguments in the form of a general construct of what makes entrepreneurship research interesting in the sense of challenging our assumptions, see Table 10.1. I am aware that this attempt may be pointless – as what is interesting is individual and highly subjective, making it difficult to find a general construct. Nevertheless, it could stimulate discussion and raise awareness about what constitutes interesting research within the field.

Table 10.1 A general construct of what makes studies "interesting" in entrepreneurship research: challenging our assumptions

Interesting subjects		
Challenging the ideological assumptions within the field	Political, moral and gender-related assumptions underlying existing views about the phenomenon	Steyaert & Hjorth (2001, 2004, 2007, 2009) Baumol (1990)
Challenging the assumptions about society	Underlying structures in a society and the changes in these structures over time	Bolton Report (1971), Stanworth & Curran (1976), Kent et al. (1982), Cooper (1973), Roberts (1968)
Challenging myths and common sense in practice and policy	Underlying assumptions of the way practice is managed and policy measures formulated	Normann (1976), Bhidé (1992; 2000), Sarasvathy (2001) Storey (1994), Lerner (2009)
Interesting methodologies		
Challenging paradigmatic assumptions	Ontological and epistemological assumptions underlying existing research	Steyaert & Hjorth (2001)
Challenging existing methodologies	Underlying methodological approaches and data collection methods within the field	Becattini (1989), Van de Ven et al. (1989), Pettigrew (1987; 1990) Cooper (1993), Cliff et al. (2006) Gratzer (1996)
Interesting concepts/theories		
Challenging the domain assumptions within the field	Basic assumptions underlying the research field in general	Gartner (1985, 1988), Stevenson & Gumpert (1985) Shane & Venkataraman (2000)
Challenging research theme assumptions	Assumptions that exist within a specific topic or theme of research and accepted as unproblematic by its advocates	Aldrich & Zimmer (1986), Birley (1986), Johannisson (1987) Aldrich (1999), Sarasvathy (2001)
Challenging the assumptions in empirical studies	Assumptions that are shared in empirical studies within the field	Sahlman (1990), Gompers & Lerner (1999)

That's interesting: some general thoughts

What characterizes these contributions which, in different ways, have challenged my assumptions about entrepreneurship? I have already emphasized that what is regarded as "interesting" is something subjective and a question of individual taste – what one scholar regards as interesting in entrepreneurship research does not necessarily attract another scholar – which means that no research finding is inherently interesting. However, "interestingness" is not only a matter of idiosyncratic opinions – there are collectively held assessments of what is regarded as interesting. Following this line of argumentation, research findings are only interesting in relation to an audience. The reason they are considered interesting can vary – results can attract the attention of one audience but not necessarily another, but the same results can also be regarded as interesting for different reasons by different audiences.

There are many potential audiences for entrepreneurship research, from a set of fellow researchers conducting research on the same topic, to researchers in a broad range of disciplines, educators, students, textbook writers, as well as external audiences of entrepreneurs, consultants, investors, and funding agencies, media, policymakers, and politicians. To be interesting, entrepreneurship research needs to attract at least one of these audiences – the wider the audience that finds the research interesting the more impact it will have (Shugan, 2003). The heterogeneity of audiences in entrepreneurship research creates great potential for entrepreneurship research to be regarded as "interesting" by at least one audience but is also challenging due to the intermediaries we use to disseminate our findings.

Interesting research motivates us to explore the issue and learn more, leading to a higher level of learning (Bartunek et al., 2006). For example, a scientific article perceived as interesting will probably be read to the end, in addition to generating a positive feeling that enhances and maintains interest, thus enabling continued learning. Interesting works generate greater learning and stronger involvement and foster intrinsically motivated behaviours (Das & Long, 2010). Kolb's four-stage experiential learning cycle (1984) emphasizes the importance of emotions for our learning. It starts with a "concrete experience" that serves as the basis for observations and reflections, which are then assimilated into a "theory" from which new actions can evolve (what Kolb calls "active experimentation"). Thus, things we regard as interesting create emotions that strengthen the motivation to explore, learn more as well as adding persistence to our interest over time.

Some aspects of being "interesting"

Time dependency

Similar to the way in which rock bands and artists become popular for a period of time, researchers have a propensity to follow each other in "herds", which means

160   *Hans Landström*

that research tends to cluster around a relatively small set of issues and problems during a certain period. Thus, the works regarded as interesting frequently relate to the "current discourse", implying that over time, topics fall into and out of fashion (Cornelius, Landström, & Persson, 2006, Landström et al., 2012). A novel and interesting problem or theory will attract researchers leading to the emergence of a new cluster. Some research themes will become mainstream while others (and maybe most) will more or less disappear and be replaced by new ones (Barley, 2006). According to Merton (1973) and Price (1986), such clusters occur due to the fact that some invisible colleges decided which issues or problems should be regarded as important for the future progress of the field.

Elaborating more closely on entrepreneurship as a research field (Landström, 2005b; Cornelius et al., 2006) revealed a couple of themes that became regarded as interesting at an early stage, maintained their attractiveness over time and today are considered mainstream in entrepreneurship research. Such research themes include the role of entrepreneurship in the dynamics of society, venture performance and growth, corporate entrepreneurship, research on technology-based entrepreneurship, social networks, and venture capital. However, a main characteristic of entrepreneurship research is its changeable nature (Neck & Greene, 2011; Landström et al., 2012), i.e. new themes emerge all the time and attract new clusters of scholars. In the 1980s research interest was focused on the entrepreneur as an individual with many contributions focusing on his/her traits and characteristics, but also on different categories of entrepreneurs such as ethnic minority, technical and female entrepreneurs. Based on the critique expressed by, among others, William Gartner (1988), entrepreneurship research became more process and behavioural oriented in the 1990s. However, it also became extremely fragmented and many parallel themes emerged. Some of the more important include a strong strategic impetus rooted in the resource-based view, but also progress with regard studies on the influence of regional environments on entrepreneurship and small businesses. At the end of the decade, several influential international comparative studies were initiated (e.g. the Global Entrepreneurship Monitor and the Panel Study of Entrepreneurship Dynamics – projects headed by Paul Reynolds) that over time attracted many scholars within the field. In the 2000s the focus changed to stronger cognitive attention and several themes have emerged such as business opportunity recognition, entrepreneurial orientation, and Sarasvathy's effectuation theory. In addition, there has also been an acceptance of entrepreneurship in a broader sense as opposed to focusing entirely on the creation of economic value, including social aspects of entrepreneurship and societal entrepreneurship.

Contextual dependency

What is regarded as "interesting" is dependent on context. Zahra (2007) as well as Welter and Lasch (2008) demonstrated that entrepreneurship research varies depending on different contexts that make various research topics and methodological approaches more or less interesting. For example, several studies have shown that European and US entrepreneurship research are dissimilar (Huse & Landström, 1997; Aldrich, 2000; Landström, 2005b; Edelman et al., 2009). It was also demonstrated by Bartunek et al. (2006) that what is regarded as interesting varies across the world.

It is difficult to characterize entrepreneurship research in Europe due to the great heterogeneity of the continent, resulting in divergent conditions for entrepreneurship as well as different research traditions. Thus, there are major differences between countries and regions in Europe. Furthermore, entrepreneurship and small business policies in Europe are more controversial and subject to intense public debate than is the case in the US. This has an impact on the research topics chosen, the interest in policy-oriented research and is also reflected in the level of analysis – European researchers tend to focus more strongly than their US counterparts on small businesses and analyses on an aggregated levels. Finally, there is acceptance of a broader range of methodological approaches among European researchers, including qualitative as well as quantitative research, i.e. a greater methodological openness. The European approaches to entrepreneurship research reflect the richness and diversity of European cultures and traditions and the broad heterogeneity that can be found in entrepreneurship research within Europe (Landström, Frank, & Veciana, 1997; Welter & Lasch, 2008).

However, having argued that research and what is regarded as "interesting" are contextually dependent, we must also be aware that scientific activities are becoming increasingly global. For example, Ziman (1994) referred to a shift from "cosmopolitan individualism" to "international collectivism", and Aldrich (2000) described it as an "international isomorphism" – focusing on the mechanisms such as conferences, cross-national working groups, international exchanges, etc. through which scholars from different contexts learn from each other and create homogenizing practices across the US and Europe. It has been demonstrated (Shils, 1975; Scott, 1992) that "intellectual centres", i.e. contexts characterized by a high degree of scientific creativity and regarded as more influential, become role models that attract scholars from other contexts. In this respect, entrepreneurship research has been anchored in a US research tradition and accordingly relies to a large extent on a US research paradigm.

Understanding the balance between novelty and continuity

In my conversation with my daughter on what is considered interesting in music, both Led Zeppelin and The Smiths created a sound that was novel to us and stood out. However, music that is too novel might be regarded as frightening. Thus, a sense of continuity is necessary in order to allow the listener the chance to relate the new sound to his/her previous experience and adapt to it. Thus, what makes a piece of music interesting is not so much the piece itself, but the way that it resonates or clashes with the ideals of the listener. In a similar way, interesting research is characterized by a balance between "novelty"

162   *Hans Landström*

and "continuity", i.e. in order to receive attention and be considered meaningful, a theory or research finding must differ from existing ones but at the same time connect to established knowledge that is already familiar to the audience (McKinley, Mone, & Moon, 1999). Tipping the balance too far on either side will produce rejection or dismissal as an absurdity or, if the continuity is too obvious, as "old hat".

However, a balance between novelty and continuity is not enough to be regarded as "interesting". Silvia (2005) argued that "coping potential", which refers to people's appraisals of whether or not they can understand the novel issue, is a necessary ingredient for something to be regarded as interesting. Thus, the audience needs the ability to understand how the novel sound or new knowledge relates to the familiar ones. For example, earlier studies on curating art have revealed that feeling able to understand art is associated with finding art interesting (Millis, 2001), while in literary studies it has been demonstrated that a sense of being able to understand it will increase the interest in abstract poetry (Silvia, 2005). The conclusion to be drawn is that the ability of the audience to understand the new findings is as important as that of the presenter to break away from old knowledge and assumptions, which is also a strong argument for conducting "good groundwork" in our research. As readers we need to understand the novelty of the work, and as writers, the knowledge base of the audience in order to challenge and position our contributions in relation to it.

Interesting vs. being important and relevant

"Interesting" can also be related to "important". However, important research is not easy to define. Research can be important for an individual researcher in his/her own work, for example, opening up new angles or creating consistency in his/her argumentation, but on a more general level, it can be regarded as important if it addresses the "big" issues in society and tries to solve fundamental problems or raises core issues within the field.

Obviously, the concepts "interesting" and "important" are intertwined – most important studies are interesting and vice versa. However, this is not always the case – being "interesting" does not automatically imply being "important", nor the other way around. In a further analogy to rock music, the 1980s hard-rock band ZZ Top can be regarded as "interesting" in the sense of commercializing hard-rock and using music videos to reach a broader audience – they are probably one of the most commercially successful hard-rock bands in the world – but it is more difficult to consider ZZ Top as "important" in the evolution of rock music as they never created anything really new in the hard-rock genre (at least in my opinion).

Following this line of argumentation, interesting studies do not inevitably become important. For example, studies regarded as interesting due to being well written do not necessarily elaborate on an issue of importance to society or the research field. On the other hand, a study may be important because of the size and representativeness of the dataset, but this does not automatically make it interesting. A state-of-the-art synthesis of a field is often important because it reveals patterns that were not previously apparent and indicates avenues for further research, but these "meta-analyses" are not always regarded as "interesting" (Rynes, 2005).

In addition, we need to relate importance to the concept of "relevance", which concerns the usefulness of the research from the perspective of different audiences (e.g. policymakers, practitioners, other scholars) in various historical contexts (e.g. "research that was particular relevant for policy-makers in western societies during the 1990s"). Thus, relevance is a more specific concept compared to "importance" and relates to the usefulness of the research findings. During the last decade an intensive debate about relevance has taken place in many social sciences, for example, management studies (Rynes, Bartunek, & Daft, 2001; Van de Ven & Johnson, 2006; Daft & Lewin, 2008; Hodgkinson & Rousseau, 2009; Keiser & Leiner, 2009), but also within the field of entrepreneurship research (Frank & Landström, 2013). Important research is usually "relevant" – but not necessarily. In 1945, Kurt Lewin coined the expression that "nothing is as practical as a good theory" (1945: 129), i.e. important and valid theories are also relevant in an applied ("practical") setting. However, Miner (1984) tested some management theories that were deemed important by scholars within the field and found only a weak positive correlation – far from significant – between important theories and their usefulness. Thus, many important theories have not proved to be particularly relevant to "practice".

That will be interesting!

My main argument in this chapter has been that entrepreneurship has been an interesting field of research. However, I see some "clouds on the horizon" in the sense that in order to gain academic legitimacy, the field has become more institutionalized and started to adopt strong "normal science" norms and standards. To ensure that the field remains dynamic and vibrant, individual scholars must continue to formulate interesting research questions and conduct interesting research. Therefore, we should follow in the footsteps of our predecessors and be open-minded and curious and challenge our assumptions, as that will create an interesting research field. I will conclude with some recommendations for the future.

The easiest way for a PhD candidate to write a thesis is to continue what has been done already, based on earlier theoretical frameworks and methodologies that have been in use for a long time. However, we need to encourage young scholars to develop their own research agenda. In order to do so, supervisors must stimulate new thinking in the thesis process, and perhaps even more importantly provide PhD courses that discuss how interesting research can be generated and conducted. In many ways, PhD programmes focus strongly on methodological issues and devote little attention to how interesting research can be accomplished.

164   *Hans Landström*

This is not only the responsibility of supervisors and PhD candidates. Young scholars compete with other researchers to have their articles accepted for publication in scientific journals. Therefore, the role of reviewers and editors is extremely important. Journal reviewers and editors are often overly critical of creative and provocative new ideas in their efforts to emphasize methodological purity, which hinders the publication of interesting ideas in nascent stages of testing (Das & Long, 2010; Landström & Åström, 2011). Thus, in order to maintain an interesting field, entrepreneurship research reviewers need to read the manuscripts submitted in an open minded way and with an eye for development (Smith, 2003).

As shown, many scholars have challenged the *subjects* of entrepreneurship research. A large number of new and challenging subjects are related to changes in society and the economy. Thus, direct communication with members of external audiences could be valuable and I will argue that entrepreneurship researchers should have a closer connection with the real world. Engagement with practice may enable the observation of empirical irregularities or puzzles that challenge existing theories and the explanation may open the way for new concepts and theories (Clark & Wright, 2009).

Looking back on the evolution of entrepreneurship research, our predecessors were often very open-minded when it came to *methodological uses* and were therefore able to challenge the methodological traditions within the field. In order to stimulate methodological openness, PhD entrepreneurship programmes should offer a broad methodological education. In addition, as we have seen from history, many interesting methodological approaches were imported from other disciplines, which highlights the importance of promoting cross-disciplinary collaboration between researchers in entrepreneurship and mainstream disciplines.

Over the past decade we have seen increased interest in theoretical studies in entrepreneurship research (Davidsson, 2008; Landström & Lohrke, 2010). However, most of these studies could be described as "gap-spotting", i.e. spotting gaps in the literature and utilizing them to formulate specific research questions (Sandberg & Alvesson, 2011). However, we need to think differently in order to challenge the underlying assumptions in our existing *concepts/theories*. Challenging assumptions is very demanding and requires considerable time and intellectual effort. "Gap-spotting" is based on the faith in existing studies and their underlying assumptions, with the intention of building positively on them. Challenging assumptions, on the other hand, requires us to be more skeptical in order to determine what is fundamentally "wrong" with the assumptions and try to challenge them (Alvesson & Sandberg, 2011). We need to encourage young scholars and PhD candidates to develop theoretical works within the field and challenge our theoretical assumptions about entrepreneurship.

Acknowledgements

This chapter has been significantly improved by discussions at seminars and workshops. I am indebted to participants at research seminars at Tallinn University of Technology and Lund University. I would especially like to thank

Jonas Gabrielsson at CIRCLE, Lund University, Matthias Fink at the Institute for Small Business Management, Vienna University School of Economic and Business Administration, and an anonymous reviewer for their valuable comments and suggestions.

Note

1 The chapter is based on three research projects that I have been involved in during the last 10–15 years. The first study concerned the Award Winners of the "Global Award for Entrepreneurship Research" (formerly the FSF-NUTEK International Award in Entrepreneurship and Small Business Research) first launched in 1996 by the Swedish Foundation for Small Business Research and the Swedish Agency for Economic and Regional Growth. In the book "Pioneers in Entrepreneurship and Small Business Research" (2005) I portrayed the first nine award winners and summarized their research contributions. The second study focused on the creeds and principles required by entrepreneurship scholars to achieve a better historical "ground work". From this study, two books emerged: Landström and Lohrke (eds.) "Historical Foundations of Entrepreneurship Research" (2010) and Landström and Lohrke (eds.) "Intellectual Roots of Entrepreneurship Research" (2012). The third study, Landström, Harirchi, and Åström "Entrepreneurship: Exploring the Knowledge Base" (2012), built on a unique database of all references in twelve state-of-the-art books on entrepreneurship research. The core knowledge producers within the field and their works as well as the knowledge users of entrepreneurship research were analyzed and discussed by means of bibliometric analysis.

References

Aldrich, H. E. (1999). *Organizations Evolving*. Thousand Oaks, CA: Sage.

Aldrich, H. E. (2000). Learning together: national differences in entrepreneurship research. In D. L. Sexton & H. Landström (eds.), *The Blackwell Handbook of Entrepreneurship* (pp. 5–25). Oxford: Blackwell Publishers.

Aldrich, H. E. (2012). The emergence of entrepreneurship as an academic field: A personal essay on institutional entrepreneurship. *Research Policy*, 41: 1240–1248.

Aldrich, H. E. & Baker, T. (1997). Blinded by the cites. Has there been progress in entrepreneurship research? In D. L. Sexton & R. W. Smilor (eds.), *Entrepreneurship 2000* (pp. 377–400). Chicago: Upstart.

Aldrich, H. E. & Zimmer, C. (1986). Entrepreneurship through social networks. In D. L. Sexton & R. W. Smilor (eds.). *The Art and Science of Entrepreneurship* (pp. 3–23). Cambridge, MA: Ballinger.

Alvesson, M. & Sandberg, J. (2011). Generating research questions through problematization. *Academy of Management Review*, 36(2): 247–271.

Astley, W. G. (1985). Administrative science as social constructed truth. *Administrative Science Quarterly*, 30: 497–513.

Baker, T. & Nelson, R. E. (2005). Creating something from nothing: Resource construction through entrepreneurial bricolage. *Administrative Science Quarterly*, 50: 329–366.

Barley, S. R. (2006). When I write my masterpiece: Thoughts on what makes a paper interesting. *Academy of Management Journal*, 49(1): 16–20.

Bartunek, J. M., Rynes S. L., & Ireland R. D. (2006). What makes management research interesting, and why does it matter. *Academy of Management Journal*, 49(1): 9–15.

Baumol, W. J. (1990). Entrepreneurship: Productive, unproductive and destructive. *Journal of Political Economy*, 98(5): 893–921.

Becattini, G. (1989). From the industrial sector to the industrial district. In E. Goodman and J. Bamford (eds.), *Small Firms and Industrial Districts in Italy*. London: Routledge.

166 *Hans Landström*

Bergendahl, J. (2009). *Entreprenörskapsresan genom beslutsprocesser i team*. PhD Dissertation, Institute of Economic Research, Lund University, Sweden.

Bhidé, A. V. (1992). Bootstrap finance: The art of start-ups. *Harvard Business Review*, Nov-Dec: 109–117.

Bhidé, A. V. (2000). *The Origin and Evolution of New Businesses*. Oxford: Oxford University Press.

Birley, S. (1985). The role of networks in the entrepreneurial process. *Journal of Business Venturing*, 1(1): 107–118.

Bolton, J. E. (1971). *Report of the Committee of Inquiry on Small Firms*. CMND 4811, London: Her Majesty's Stationery Office.

Brush, C. G., Manolova T. S., & Edelman, L. F. (2008). Separated by common language? Entrepreneurship research across the Atlantic. *Entrepreneurship Theory and Practice*, March: 249–266.

Clark, T. & Wright, M. (2009). So, farewell then . . . reflections on editing the journal of management studies. *Journal of Management Studies*, 46(1): 1–9.

Cliff, J. E., Jennings, P. D., & Greenwood, R. (2006). New to the game and questioning the rules: the experiences and beliefs of founders who start imitative versus innovative firms. *Journal of Business Venturing*, 21: 633–663.

Cole, S. (1983). The hierarchy of the sciences? *American Journal of Sociology*, 89: 111–139.

Cooper, A. C. (1971). Spin-offs and technical entrepreneurship. *IEEE Transactions on Engineering Management*, 18(1): 2–6.

Cooper, A. C. (1993). Challenges in predicting new firm formation. *Journal of Business Venturing*, 8: 241–253.

Cooper, A. C. (1973). Technical entrepreneurship: What do we know? *R&D Management*, 3(2): 59–64.

Cooper, A. C. & Komives, J. L. (1972). *Technical Entrepreneurship: A Symposium*. Center for Venture Management, Milwaukee, Wisconsin.

Cooper, A. C., Woo, C. Y., & Dunkelberg, W. C. (1988). Entrepreneurs perceived chances of success. *Journal of Business Venturing*, 3: 97–108.

Cooper, A. C., Folta, T. B., & Woo, C. (1995). Entrepreneurial information search. *Journal of Business Venturing*, 10: 107–120.

Cornelius, B., Landström, H., & Persson, O. (2006). Entrepreneurial studies: The dynamic research front of a developing social science. *Entrepreneurship Theory and Practice*, May: 375–398.

Craig, J. B. (2010). Desk rejection. How to avoid being hit by a returning boomerang. *Family Business Review*, 23: 306–309.

Daft, R. L. & Lewin, A. Y. (2008). Rigor and relevance in organization studies: Idea migration and academic journal evolution. *Organization Science*, 19: 177–183.

Das, H. & Long, B. S. (2010). What makes management research interesting? An exploratory study. *Journal of Managerial Issues*, XXII(1): 127–144.

Davidsson, P. (2008). Looking back at 20 years of entrepreneurship research: What did we learn? In H. Landström, H. Crijns, E. Laveren, & D. Smallbone (eds.), *Entrepreneurship, Sustainable Growth and Performance* (pp. 13–26). Cheltenham, UK: Edward Elgar.

Davidsson, P. (2013). Some reflection on research "schools" and geographies. *Entrepreneurship and Regional Development*, 25(1–2): 100–110.

Davis, M. S. (1971). That is interesting! Towards a phenomenology of sociology and a sociology of phenomenology. *Philosophy of the Social Sciences*, 1: 309–344.

Edelman, L. F., Manolova T. S., & Brush, C. G. (2009). *Still Blinded by the Cites: Has There Been Progress in Entrepreneurship Research?* Paper at the Academy of Management Meeting, Chicago, 9–11 August.

Eisenhardt, K. (1989). Building theories from case study research. *Academy of Management Review*, 14: 532–550.

Frank, H. & Landström, H. (2013). *That's Interesting! An Empirical Study on What Makes Entrepreneurship Research Interesting*. Paper presented at the XXVII RENT Research in Entrepreneurship Conference, Vilnius, Lithuania, 21–22 November.

Garfinkel, H. (1967). *Studies in Ethnomethodology*. Englewood Cliffs, NJ: Prentice-Hall.

Gartner, W. E. (1985). A conceptual framework for describing the phenomenon of new venture creation. *Academy of Management Review*, 10: 696–706.

Gartner, W. E. (1988). Who is an entrepreneur? Is the wrong question. *American Journal of Small Business*, Spring: 11–32.

Ghoshal, S. (2005). Bad management theories are destroying good management practice. *Academy of Management Learning and Education*, 4(1): 75–91.

Gimeno, J., Folta, T. B., Cooper A. C., & Woo, C. Y. (1997). Survival of the fittest? Entrepreneurial human capital and the persistence of underperforming firms. *Administrative Science Quarterly*, 42: 750–783.

Gompers, P. & Lerner, J. (1999). *The Venture Capital Cycle*. Cambridge, MA: MIT Press.

Grant, P. & Perren, L. (2002). Small business and entrepreneurship research: Meta-theories, paradigms and prejudices. *International Small Business Journal*, 20(2): 185–211.

Gratzer, K. (1996). *Småföretagandets villkor. Automatrestauranger under 1990-talet* [Conditions for Small Firms. Automated Restaurants during the Twentieth Century]. Stockholm: Almquist & Wiksell.

Hambrick, D. & Chen, M. (2008). New academic fields as administrative-seeking social movements: The case of strategic management. *Academy of Management Review*, 33: 32–54.

Hodgkinson, G. P. & Rousseau, D. M. (2009). Bridging the rigor-relevance gap in management research: It's already happening! *Journal of Management Studies*, 46: 534–546.

Huse, M. & Landström, H. (1997). European entrepreneurship and small business research: Methodological openness and contextual differences. *International Studies of Management and Organization*, 27(3): 3–12.

Johannisson, B. (1987). Anarchists and organisers: Entrepreneurs in a network perspective. *International Studies of Management and Organisation*, XVII(1): 49–63.

Johnson, M. S. (2003). Designating opponents in empirical research reports: The rhetoric of interestingness in consumer research. *Marketing Theory*, 3(4): 477–501.

Kent, C. A., Sexton, D. L., & Vesper, K. H. (eds.) (1982). *Encyclopedia of Entrepreneurship*. Englewood Cliffs, NJ: Prentice-Hall.

Kieser, A. & Leiner, L. (2009). Why the rigor-relevance gap in management research is unbridgable. *Journal of Management Studies*, 46: 516–533.

Kolb, D. A. (1984). *Experiential learning: Experience as the Source of Learning and Development*. Englewood Cliffs, NJ: Prentice-Hall.

Landström, H. (2005a). Entreprenörer inom entreprenörskapsforskningen (Entrepreneurs in entrepreneurship research). In P. R. Christensen and F. Poulfelt (eds.), *Mod Entrepreneurielle Ledelseformer*. Frederiksberg: Forlaget Samfundslitteratur.

Landström, H. (2005b). *Pioneers in Entrepreneurship and Small Business Research*. New York: Springer.

Landström, H. & Benner, M. (2010). Entrepreneurship research: A history of scholarly migration. In H. Landström & F. Lohrke (eds.), *Historical Foundations of Entrepreneurship Research* (pp. 15–45). Cheltenham: Edward Elgar.

Landström, H. & Lohrke, F. (2010). *Historical Foundations of Entrepreneurship Research*. Cheltenham: Edward Elgar.

168 *Hans Landström*

Landström, H. & Lohrke, F. (2012). *Intellectual Roots of Entrepreneurship Research.* Cheltenham: Edward Elgar.

Landström, H. & Persson, O. (2010). Entrepreneurship research: Research communities and knowledge platforms. In H. Landström & F. Lohrke (eds.), *Historical Foundations of Entrepreneurship Research* (pp. 46–76). Cheltenham: Edward Elgar.

Landström, H. & Åström, F. (2011). Who's asking the right question? Patterns and diversity in the literature of new venture creation. In K. Hindle & K. Kluver (eds.), *Handbook of Research on New Venture Creation* (pp. 34–71). Cheltenham: Edward Elgar.

Landström, H., Frank H., & Veciana, J. M. (1997). *Entrepreneurship and Small Business Research in Europe.* Aldershot: Avebury.

Landström, H., Harirchi G., & Åström, F. (2012). Entrepreneurship: Exploring the knowledge base. *Research Policy*, 42: 1154–1181.

Larson, A. (1992). Network dyads in entrepreneurial settings. *Administrative Science Quarterly*, 37: 76–104.

Lerner, J. (2009). *Boulevard of Broken Dreams.* Princeton, NJ: Princeton University Press.

Lewin, K. (1945). The research center for group dynamics at Massachusetts Institute of Technology. *Sociometry*, 8: 126–136.

Marquis, C. & Tilcsik, A. (2013). Imprinting: Toward a multilevel theory. *Academy of Management Annals*, 7(1): 195–245.

McKinley, W., Mone, M. A., & Moon, G. (1999). Determinants and development of schools on organization theory. *Academy of Management Review*, 24(4): 634–648.

Merton, R. K. (1973). *The Sociology of Science.* Chicago: University of Chicago Press.

Millis, K. (2001). Making meaning brings pleasure: The influence of tides on aesthetic experience. *Emotion*, 1: 320–329.

Miner, J. B. (1984). The validity and usefulness of theories in an emerging organizational science. *Academy of Management Review*, 9(2): 296–306.

Murugesan, P. & Moravcsik, M. J. (1978). Variation of the nature of citation measures with journals and scientific specialties. *Journal of the American Society of Information Science*, 29: 141–147.

Neck, H. M. & Greene, P. G. (2011). Entrepreneurship education: Known worlds and new frontiers. *Journal of Small Business Management*, 49(1): 55–70.

Normann, R. (1976). *Skapande företagsledning.* Lund: Studentlitteratur.

Osterwalder, A., Pigneur Y., & Tucci, C. L. (2005). Clarifying business models: Origins, present and future of the concept. *Communications of the Association for Information Systems*, 15: 1–38.

Pettigrew, A. M. (1987). Context and action in the transformation of the firm. *Journal of Management Studies*, 24(6): 649–670.

Pettigrew, A. M. (1990). Longitudinal field research on change: Theory and practice. *Organizational Science*, 1(3): 267–292.

Pfeffer, J. (1993). Barriers to the advance of organizational science: Paradigm development as a dependent as a dependent variable. *Academy of Management Review*, 18: 599–620.

Politis, D. (2005). *Entrepreneurship, Career Experience and Learning.* Scandinavian Institute for Research in Entrepreneurship (SIRE). Lund University/Halmstad University College, Sweden.

Price, D.J.D.S. (1986). *Little Science, Big Science . . . and Beyond.* New York: Columbia University Press.

Reynolds, P. D. (2000). National panel study of US business startups: Background and methodology. In J. A. Katz (ed.), *Advances in Entrepreneurship, Firm Emergence, and Growth*, Vol. 4 (pp. 153–227). Stanford, CT: JAI Press.

Roberts, E. B. (1968). A basic study of innovation: How to keep and capitalize on their talents. *Research Management*, 4: 18–26.

Roberts, E. B. & Weiner, H. A. (1968). New enterprises on Route 128. *Science Journal*, 12(4): 78–83.

Roberts, E. B. & Weiner, H. A. (1971). Some characteristics of technical entrepreneurs. *IEEE Transactions on Engineering Management*, 3: 100–109.

Rynes, S. L. (2005). From the editors: Taking stock and looking ahead. *Academy of Management Journal*, 48(1): 9–15.

Rynes, S. L. (2007). Academy of Management Journal editors forum on citations – editors foreword. *Academy of Management Journal*, 50(3): 489–490.

Rynes, S. L., Bartunek J. M., & Daft, R. L. (2001). Across the great divide: Knowledge creation and transfer between practitioners and academics. *Academy of Management Journal*, 44: 340–355.

Sahlman, W. A. (1990). The structure and governance of venture-capital organizations. *Journal of Financial Economics*, 27(2): 473–521.

Sandberg, J. & Alvesson, M. (2011). Ways of constructing research questions: Gap-spotting or problematization. *Organization*, 18(1): 23–44.

Sapienza, H. J., Manigart S., & Vermeir, W. (1996). Venture capitalist governance and value added in four countries. *Journal of Business Venturing*, 11(6): 439–469.

Sarasvathy, S. D. (2001). Causation and effectuation: Toward a theoretical shift from economic inevitability to entrepreneurial contingency. *Academy of Management Review*, 26(2): 243–263.

Scott, T. (1992). Scientific research in Sweden: Orientation toward the American centre and embeddedness in Nordic and European environment. *Science Studies*, 5(2): 13–27.

Shane, S. & Venkataraman, S. (2000). The promise of entrepreneurship as a field of research. *Academy of Management Review*, 25(1): 217–226.

Shils, E. (1975). *Center and Periphery. Essays in Macrosociology.* Chicago: University of Chicago Press.

Shugan, S. M. (2003). Defining interesting research problems. *Marketing Science*, 22(1): 1–15.

Silvia, P. J. (2005). What is interesting? exploring the appraisal structure of interest. *Emotion*, 5(1): 89–102.

Smith, D. C. (2003). The importance and challenges of being interesting. *Journal of the Academy of Marketing Science*, 31(3): 319–322.

Spiegel-Rosing, I. (1977). Science studies: Bibliometric and content analysis. *Social Studies of Science*, 7: 97–113.

Stanworth, M. J. & Curran, J. (1976). Growth and the small firm: An alternative view. *Journal of Management Studies*, May: 95–110.

Stevenson, H. H. & Gumpers, D. (985). The heart of entrepreneurship. *Harvard Business Review*, 85(2): 85–94.

Stevenson, H. H. & Jarillo, J. C. (1990). A paradigm of entrepreneurship: Entrepreneurial Management. *Strategic Management Journal*, 11: 17–27.

Steyaert, C. & Hjorth, D. (eds.) (2001). *New Movements in Entrepreneurship.* Cheltenham: Edward Elgar.

Steyaert, C. & Hjorth, D. (eds.) (2004). *Narrative and Discursive Approaches in Entrepreneurship.* Cheltenham: Edward Elgar.

Steyaert, C. & Hjorth, D. (eds.) (2007). *Entrepreneurship and Social Change.* Cheltenham: Edward Elgar.

Steyaert, C. and Hjorth, D. (eds.) (2009). *The Politics and Aesthetics of Entrepreneurship.* Cheltenham: Edward Elgar.

170   *Hans Landström*

Stinchcombe, A. L. (1965). Social structure and organizations. In J. G. March (ed.), *Handbook of Organizations* (pp. 142–193). Chicago: Rand McNally.

Storey, D. J. (1994). *Understanding the Small Business Sector.* Routledge: London.

Utterback, J. M. & Reitberger, G. (1982). *Technology and Industrial Innovation in Sweden: A Study of New Technology-Based Firms.* Center for Policy Alternatives/STU, Stockholm, Sweden.

Van de Ven, A. H. & Johnson, P. E. (2006). Knowledge for theory and practice. *Academy of Management Review,* 31(4): 802–821.

Van de Ven, A. H., Angle H. L., & Poole M. S. (eds.) (1989). *Research in the Management of Innovation.* New York: Harper and Row.

Venkataraman, S. (1997). The distinctive domain of entrepreneurship research. In J. A. Katz (ed.), *Advances in Entrepreneurship, Firm Emergence, and Growth,* Vol. 3 (pp. 119–138). Greenwich, CT: JAI Press.

Welter, F. & Lasch, F. (2008). Entrepreneurship research in Europe: Taking stock and looking forward. *Entrepreneurship Theory and Practice,* March: 241–248.

Zahra, S. A. (2007). Contextualize theory building in entrepreneurship research. *Journal of Business Venturing,* 22: 443–452.

Ziman, J. (1994). *Prometheus Bound: Science in a Dynamic Steady State.* Cambridge: Cambridge University Press.

11 Entrepreneurship research without passion

Let's fall in love again

Matthias Fink, Isabella Hatak, Richard Lang, and Daniela Maresch

Introduction

Entrepreneurship research is not a child of our time (Landström, 1999). Cotrugli (1990 [1458]) already searched for the characteristics of the 'perfect merchant' and Cantillon (1931 [1745]) found similarities among entrepreneurs, beggars, and thieves with regard to their willingness to take risks. The economic impact of entrepreneurs was not first discovered by Schumpeter (1912), even though he laid the foundation for today's entrepreneurship research. However, the objectives, perceptions, and methods of entrepreneurship research as well as the volume of research activities and their presence in specialized journals have seen changes during the last decades. In the course of the last decade the relevant academic structures expanded drastically (Shane & Venkataraman, 2000). Entrepreneurship research seems to have entered a period which asks for a critical reflection of the adopted approaches, which goes beyond the usual critical discussion of published individual findings (Steyaert, 2005; Sarasvathy, 2004).

Hans Landström has put forth a paper investigating what makes entrepreneurship research interesting. While acknowledging individual aspects such as taste, he also identifies more general characteristics of contributions to entrepreneurship research that are interesting. In a nutshell, he concludes that entrepreneurship research is perceived as interesting if it breaks new ground by challenging state of the art subjects, methodology, and/or concepts/theories.

While agreeing with this conclusion and the underlying reasoning, in this discussion paper we will take one step back and argue that entrepreneurship researchers will only engage in challenging state of the art – and thus produce interesting contributions – if they change their attitude towards formulating their own research agenda. Too many of us design our research agendas along what we assume to be the future "hot topics", because we expect papers on these topics to get published more easily in higher standing journals and, thus, to contribute more to our career advancement. The selection of research topics among entrepreneurship researchers has become rather a means to enhance publication records, rather than the initial impetus of research activity. Based on data from a small survey, we will show that this instrumental

172 *Matthias Fink et al.*

approach to research is surprisingly common among entrepreneurship research-ers and that it leads to high levels of frustration. The data show impressively that even the researchers themselves do not find their research interesting.

What's the issue?

Considering the result of considerable efforts in entrepreneurship research within the last two to three decades, it can be noticed that a large number of papers were published in numerous highly specialized entrepreneurship jour-nals each year and that at least an equally high number of presentations were held at international conferences and workshops (Klandt, 2004; Hisrich & Drnovsek, 2002; MacMillan, 1993;). Even for the most hardworking and dili-gent researcher, it has become impossible to follow this information overload (Grichnik, 2006). The offer of products on these bazaars for scientific work is unmanageable. And how many 'customers' ask themselves what happens to these goods? Who is supposed to use them, who will finally benefit from them? Practitioners consider research results as hardly relevant, barely receive them (McKenzie et al., 2002), and implement them even less often (Van de Ven, 2002). It is often sufficient for 'suppliers' to have their goods 'presented' (Zahra, 2007). This does not lead to revenues from the sale to customers, who expect to benefit from these goods, but collects 'bonus points' for the suppliers' careers (Chandler & Lyon, 2001). The content of a paper is less important than the journal where it is published. The choice of the journal is often based on its ranking (Katz, 2003), which quantifies the quality of the journal (Franke & Schreier, 2008) and hence determines the importance and the value of the publication for the career development of the researcher (Suchan, 2008; Rodg-ers et al., 2007).

Thesis 1: Entrepreneurship research produces for itself: the aim of the majority of researchers is the composition of a career-optimal list of presentations at conferences and publications in journals which enjoy the highest possible standing within the relevant scientific community.

Ambitious young researchers are confronted with the frustrating situation that the scientific community only takes them seriously if they specialize their research on a narrow niche (Eden, 2008), which is detached from its surround-ings (Richardson & Zikic, 2007), and if they submit themselves to the thematic ("hot topics") and methodical trends ("accepted approaches") which were set by the respective gatekeepers of the particular field of research (Dowd & Kaplan, 2005). The isolated and narrow fields of research prevent a mutual understanding and integration of the field (Fallgatter, 2004). The dominance of hot topics discourages researchers to select research topics that they personally are interested in.

Thesis 2: The scientific community is highly fragmented in the field of entrepreneur-ship research. Integration occurs at best in the context of small international virtual research groups, which establish around single dominant researchers.

Often the rising pressure to be productive leads to a situation where researchers write more than they read. With this pressure, there is also only limited time to think about the nature of constructs and the meaning of terms in sufficient depth. The meaning of terms such as "born globals" differs from study to study without being reflected and hence potentially distorts the effectiveness as determinant of a certain strategy. Contradictory empirical results may hence arise from imprecise definition and usage of terms (Cesinger et al., 2012).

On the other hand, even more sophisticated quantitative and qualitative analysis methods are available. What can, however, be achieved with a huge dataset on and a perfect analysis of a phenomenon we have not defined yet? Such analyses do most certainly not allow for substantiated and far-reaching conclusions (Hitt et al., 2004; Chandler & Lyon, 2001).

Thesis 3: Methodical requirements are the far more important quality criteria for research papers than content and practical relevance.

That kind of entrepreneurship research is often neither accessible nor attractive enough for entrepreneurs. On the one hand, it remains partly unknown to them or is not understood (Jordan & Roland, 1999). On the other hand, entrepreneurs can hardly translate results of academic entrepreneurship research to their individual situation, namely the current state of their configuration (Vought et al., 2008). For an entrepreneur, mathematic expressions are useless, even if they are irrefutably based on explicit assumptions (Huw, Nutley, & Walter, 2007). Entrepreneurs have subjective theories (without any formulas) on the part of the world which they perceive as relevant (Pollitt, 2006).

Thesis 4: Research results are hardly noticed or applicable outside the relevant scientific community.

Empirical evidence

The sample of this expert survey comprises both members of the Förderkreis Gründungsforschung e.V. (FGF) and members of the Section for Management of Technology and Innovation (TIM) of the German Academic Association for Business Research (VHB). Since these are the by far biggest organizations where entrepreneurship researchers of German speaking countries are members, it can be assumed that the coverage with regard to content and region is very high. The FGF consists of 182 members, and the TIM consists of 176 researchers (status 2008). After eliminating double memberships, the sample adds up to 323. The answers of 105 out of these 323 persons could successfully be obtained in an anonymous and personalized (in order to prevent persons from completing the questionnaire several times) online survey. This gives a return rate of 32.5%.

Out of the 105 persons who completed the questionnaire, 2 were not scientists but consultants or entrepreneurs and were therefore excluded from the evaluation. This leaves 103 cases for the analysis. Thirty-five percent thereof were predoc researchers, 21.4% postdocs or assistant professors, 31.1% university professors (thereof 1 junior professor), and 12.6% professors at universities

174 *Matthias Fink et al.*

of applied science. They were based in Germany (74.8%), Austria (10.7%), Switzerland or Liechtenstein (7.8%), and other countries (6.8%). Sixty-nine percent of the respondents had their academic roots in the field of business administration, 9% in economics and sociology, 3% in psychology, and 2% in computer sciences, engineering and business, and business and human resource education respectively.

The ranking of the critical theses according to the strength of support may be taken as a first picture of the results of the survey:

Table 11.1 Empirical evidence

		Predoc	**Postdoc**	**Prof. (Univ)**	**Prof. (UAS)**	*Average*
Number (%)		*n = 103*	*36 (34.0)*	*21 (21.4)*	*31 (30.1)*	*15 (14.5)*	
Theses						
Entrepreneurship research	Pro	68.0	78.6	78.3	50.0	70.8
produces for itself . . .	contra	32.0	21.4	21.7	50.0	29.2
The scientific community	Pro	55.6	87.5	56.5	40.0	63.2
is highly fragmented . . .	contra	44.4	12.5	43.5	60.0	36.8
Methodical requirements	Pro	51.4	72.2	57.7	66.7	55.6
are the far more important	contra	48.6	27.8	42.3	33.3	44.4
quality criteria for research papers than content and practical relevance.						
Research results are hardly	Pro	65.2	92.9	65.2	9.1	74.6
noticed or applicable	contra	34.8	7.1	34.8	90.9	25.4
respectively outside the relevant scientific community.						

Almost three-quarters of the respondents (74.6%) agree with the statement that the results of entrepreneurship research are hardly noticed and hardly applicable outside the relevant scientific community (thesis 4). A breakdown of the results according to the positions of the respondent in the academic hierarchy shows an interesting picture: almost 93% of the responding postdoc researchers and assistant professors and almost two-third of the postgraduate researchers and university professors share this pessimistic view. In contrast to that, the corresponding share of professors at universities of applied science (UAS) amounts to approximately 9%. It can be shown that the practical research of universities of applied science, which is oriented towards the solution of concrete problems in individual cases, unfolds a higher level of directly experienced benefit than the fundamental research at universities. Also the pressure towards research output is much higher at universities than at universities of applied science.

We find that 70.8% of entrepreneurship researchers share the opinion that the researchers working in this field produce for themselves (thesis 1). This egocentric work ethos is expressed in the fact that the majority of researchers aim at composing a career-optimum list of presentations at conferences and publications in journals which enjoy high reputation among the respective scientific communities. This behaviour is the logical conclusion of the target system demanded by the competitive scientific environment, which reduces career planning to the collection of points for publication achievements based on rankings without taking the published contents and their significance into consideration. The frustration seems to be especially high among postdoc researchers or assistant professors and university professors. Approximately 78% of the respective groups agree with the corresponding thesis. However, only half of the professors at universities of applied science share this opinion. Even if the difference is not significant, the trend suggests a more activity-oriented approach at universities of applied science.

The fragmentation of the scientific community (thesis 2) ranks third in the perception of entrepreneurship researchers, with a consent of 63.2%. This issue is experienced predominantly by postdoc researchers and assistant professors (87.5%) and less by predoc researchers (55.6%), university professors (56.5%), and professors at universities of applied science (40%). A possible explanation for that may be found in the limited professional and personal leeway, where predoc entrepreneurship researchers usually operate. Their research environment is strongly framed by the colleagues at the home scientific community and the supervisor of the doctoral dissertation and hence clearly structured. Postdoc researcher and assistant professors have to develop a new niche of research in order to work their academic way up. Hence, neither the professional nor the personal leeway is clearly delineated or structured. International networks of individual colleagues who work on comparable problems arise. These groups of researchers mostly act in a rather isolated way. Neither other comparable groups of researchers nor the colleagues at the respective home scientific institutions are included in the research activities, since the delineation is the key to the development of the own niche. Once a chair has been obtained, the development of a network in the relevant scientific community seems to have been successful and the fragmentation is experienced less drastically.

The thesis on methodical demands being far more important than relevance with regard to contents still reached a rate of agreement among entrepreneurship researchers of 55.6%. There are statistically significant differences with respect to the preference of the application of more demanding methods to the treatment of demanding questions. Postdoc researchers or assistant professors are more frustrated that the focus is set on methods than postgraduate researchers and university professors. This seems to result from the higher publication pressure on the verge of the Habilitation (postdoctoral qualification). At this stage, in order to qualify for a full professorship, postdoc researchers thrust themselves into high-ranking journals, which are paying more and

176 *Matthias Fink et al.*

more attention to the applied methods in the selection of the manuscripts that shall be published.

The comparison of averages shows that neither the location of the home scientific institution nor the original discipline of the questioned entrepreneurship researcher has significant influence on the results.

Conclusion

The results from the small survey show that entrepreneurship researchers in the German-speaking countries perceive their work as often unconnected, method driven, and largely useless – thus, not very interesting after all. However, they are highly motivated and work hard. Against the backdrop of these results, the remarkable drive of entrepreneurship researchers seems not so much rooted in genuine interest in their own research. Obviously, they are rather driven by their career ambitions, maybe and hopefully with the distant goal of becoming more independent from research evaluation procedures and publication pressure as full professors in the future and then refocusing on the topics they are really interested in. Certainly, the frustration becoming apparent from the data – especially among early- to mid-stage researchers – seems not to be a fertile ground for developing entrepreneurship research that is interesting for others.

We argue that entrepreneurship researchers will only engage in challenging state of the art – and thus produce interesting contributions – if they change their attitude towards formulating their own research agenda.

Thus, we argue that a prerequisite for interesting research are researchers who relax and who are passionate and fascinated by the topics they investigate, rather than by their publication lists, h-indices, and career positions.

Relax, take it easy . . . (by Mika)

However, what can be done to make entrepreneurship research more interesting? If the above argumentation is valid, on the collective level reducing the pressure on researchers especially in the early and middle stages of the academic career might help. On the individual level we should try to escape a situation which we term the "Charlie Brown Syndrome": Just as the famous Peanuts character Charlie Brown spends his life failing to meet the standards set by his nemesis Lucy, to whom he feels increasingly inferior with every failed attempt to be approved, entrepreneurship researchers – in their attempt to satisfy the demands set by admired others, are endangered to lose their ability to develop own interests and passions and to derive personal goals from them. We argue that, for entrepreneurship research to become more interesting, we need to become less Charlie Brownish and more like Snoopy. Snoopy, the relaxed dog, who does not care about Lucy but who does things that are interesting to himself and – looking at the success of the cartoon series – that are obviously also interesting to many others. At the same time, the Lucys in academia need to be unmasked and paid less attention to by the following generations.

Where is the love? . . . (by Black Eyed Peas)

Now that researchers' passion for their own research has been identified as a possible key to interesting entrepreneurship research, we need to clarify where this passion may come from. Intuitively, one might argue that love and passion are genuinely subjective and that there are no intersubjective aspects of entrepreneurship research that make it attract the passion of the researchers and thus interest among the audience. This assumption is also carried in the popular saying "there is no accounting for taste". However, theory of art and especially aesthetics have made strong points that pieces of art have certain properties that make them interesting. It was especially Immanuel Kant who argued that artwork is not *ascribed* but *has* specific properties that makes it interesting. In simple words, Kant defines an artwork as something that involves us intellectually, making us realize the order of things and the balance in this order.

It is not as far a shot to apply the theoretical considerations of what is an interesting artwork to scientific studies and publications. Using different concepts from the theory of art and especially aesthetics for the identification of criteria for interesting entrepreneurship research appears to be a promising approach for future research.

We sum up the argument developed in this discussion paper in a nutshell: there is no interesting entrepreneurship research without relaxed and passionate researchers. Thus, entrepreneurship researchers need to free themselves from their idols and fall in love again with their subject. For this to happen we need less competitive pressure and more cooperation that is based on open communication and trust among researchers.

References

Cantillon, R. (1931 [1745]). *Essai sur la nature de commerce en général*. London.

Cesinger, B., Fink, M., Madsen, T. K., Kraus, S. (2012). Rapidly internationalizing ventures: How definitions can bridge the gap across contexts. *Management Decision*, 50(10): 1816–1842.

Chandler, C. & Lyon, D. (2001). Issues of research design and construct measurement in entrepreneurship research: The past decade. *Entrepreneurship: Theory & Practice*, 25(4): 101–113.

Cotrugli, B. (1990 [1458]). *Il libro dell'arte di mercatura, a cura di Ugo Tucci*. Verona: Arsenale Editrice.

Dowd, K. O. & Kaplan, M. (2005). The career life of academics: Boundaried or boundaryless? *Human Relations*, 58(6): 699–721.

Eden, D. (2008). Thriving in a self-made niche: How to create a successful academic career in organizational behavior. *Journal of Organizational Behavior*, 29(6): 733–742.

Fallgatter, M. J. (2004). Entrepreneurship: Konturen einer jungen Disziplin. *Schmalenbachs. Zeitschrift für betriebswirtschaftliche Forschung* (ZfbF), 56(2): 23–44.

Franke, N. & Schreier, M. (2008). A metha-ranking of technology and innovation management/ entrepreneurship journals. *Die Betriebswirtschaft*, 68(2): 185–216.

McKenzie, C. J., Wright, S., Ball, D. F. & Baron, P. J. (2002). The publications of marketing faculty – who are we really talking to? *European Journal of Marketing*, 36(3): 1196–1208.

178   *Matthias Fink et al.*

Grichnik, D. (2006). Die opportunity map der internationalen Entrepreneurshipforschung. *Zeitschrift für Betriebswirtschaft*, 76(12): 100–125.

Hisrich, R. & Drnovsek, M. (2002). Entrepreneurship and small business research – a European perspective. *Journal of Small Business and Enterprise Development*, 9(2): 172–222.

Hitt, M. A., Ahlstrom, D., Dacin, M. T., Levitas, E., & Svobodina, L. (2004). The institutional effects on strategic alliance partner selection in transition economies: China vs. Russia. *Organization Science*, 15(2): 173–186.

Huw D., Nutley, S., & Walter, I. (2007). Academic advice to practitioners – the role and use of research-based evidence. *Public Money & Management*, 27(4): 232.

Jordan, D. & Roland, M. (1999). An examination of differences between academics and practitioners in frequency of reading research and attitudes toward research. *Journal of Leisure Research*, 31(2): 166–171.

Katz, J. (2003). The chronology and intellectual trajectory of American entrepreneurship education 1876–1999. *Journal of Business Venturing*, 18(2): 283.

Klandt, H. (2004). Entrepreneurship education and research in German-speaking Europe. *Academy of Management Learning & Education*, 3(3): 293–301.

Landström, H. (1999). The roots of entrepreneurship research. *New England Journal of Entrepreneurship*, 2(2): 9–21.

MacMillan, I. C. (1993). The emerging forum for entrepreneurship scholars. *Journal of Business Venturing*, 8(5): 377–382.

Pollitt, C. (2006). Academic advice to practitioners – what is its nature, place and value within academia? *Public Money & Management*, 26(4): 257–264.

Richardson, J. & Zikic, J. (2007). The darker side of an international academic career. *Career Development International*, 12(2): 164–186.

Rogers, P., Campbell, N., Louhiala-Salminen, L., Rentz, K., & Suchan, J. (2007). The impact of perceptions of journal quality on business and management communication academics. *Journal of Business Communication*, 44(4): 403–426.

Sarasvathy, S. D. (2004). The questions we ask and the questions we care about: Reformulating some problems in entrepreneurship research. *Journal of Business Venturing*, 19(5): 707–717.

Schumpeter, J. A. (1912). *Theorie der wirtschaftlichen Entwicklung*. Leipzig.

Shane S. & Venkataraman, S. (2000). The promise of entrepreneurship as a field of research. *Academy of Management Review*, 25(1): 217–226.

Steyaert, C. (2005). Entrepreneurship: In between what? On the frontier as a discourse of entrepreneurship research. *International Journal of Entrepreneurship and Small Business*, 2(1): 2–16.

Suchan, J. (2008). How academic organizational systems and culture undermine scholarship and quality research: A response to Ron Dulek. *Journal of Business Communication*, 45(3): 349–356.

Van de Ven, A. H. (2002). Strategic directions for the Academy of Management: This academy is for you. *Academy of Management Review*, 27(2): 171–184.

Vought, K. L., Baker, L. T., & Smith, G. D. (2008). Practitioner commentary: Moving from theory to practice in family business research. *Entrepreneurship Theory and Practice*, 32(6): 1111–1121.

Zahra, S. (2007). Contextualizing theory building in entrepreneurship research. *Journal of Business Venturing*, 22(3): 443–452.

12 Conclusion

Final thoughts and perspectives

Philippe Riot and Alain Fayolle

In the introduction of this book, Alain Fayolle outlines the questions – we could go as far as saying *preoccupations* – that were raised in June 2013, in the context of a workshop organized at EMLYON Business School in preparation to the Babson College Entrepreneurship Research Conference, in a series of discussions which would eventually lead to the publishing of this book: *Institutionalization of Entrepreneurship: Hopes and Pitfalls for Entrepreneurship Research.*

In a little over ten years, research in entrepreneurship has gone from a "promise" (Shane & Venkataraman, 2000 [2010 Academy of Management Review Decade Award]) to an advanced field of research, thus winning its spurs in the broader domain of Management Science. With this recognition has come an increased institutionalization of entrepreneurship research practices, leading them to converge towards the norms and practices adopted in Management Science, join the same research communities, publish in the same scientific journals, and eventually create dedicated entrepreneurship departments within education and research institutions.

As highlighted by Alain Fayolle, this institutionalization is undeniably a good thing for the members of the research community, as it implies the legitimization of their field and research practices, the emergence of norms for developing and publishing their work, and last but not least, the creation of structures that provide employment opportunities as well as a conducive environment for pursuing their research.

However, is this institutionalization such a good thing when it comes to producing critical and innovative research or when considered from the point of view of non-academic entrepreneurship stakeholders and society in general?

And since we are discussing the possible negative consequences of this evolution, we may here cite Greenwood et al. (2008: 4–5), for whom institutionalization refers to *"more or less taken for granted repetitive social behaviour that is underpinned by normative systems and cognitive understandings that give meaning to social exchange and thus enable self-reproducing social order".* As for Tolbert and Zucker (1983: 25), they suggest three indicators to identify institutionalized practices: *"they are widely followed, without debate, and exhibit permanence".* None of these factors can be considered positive for research!

180 *Philippe Riot and Alain Fayolle*

The time has come to ponder the lessons from the contributions presented here as well as outline some research perspectives for the coming years. The questions we started with and the way they are being raised today may be regrouped under three main themes: 1) the capacity for entrepreneurship research to renew itself; 2) the relationships between entrepreneurship research and the non-academic stakeholders of entrepreneurship; 3) the evolution of research practices with regard to the two aforementioned points. We will then conclude with a few remarks and recommendation.

The ability of entrepreneurship research to renew itself

Has the institutionalization of entrepreneurship research resulted in excessive conformity and an uncritical attitude towards tried-and-tested themes, theories, concepts and methods? These themes, theories, and concepts are initiated and passed on by the prominent figures of the discipline during the training of young researchers and further reinforced by the practices of the major scientific journals and conferences. They are key to scientific legitimacy, professional recognition, and employment, giving them added weight.

We do believe that the institutionalization of research in entrepreneurship can provide much-needed support for young researchers, by showing them the way to a successful career. However, the downside is that it can also produce a "blinkered" – or taken-for-granted – approach to research, isolated from other disciplines, lacking innovativeness and interest (one of the characteristics of interesting research being to challenge taken-for-granted ideas and open new horizons – see Landström, Chapter 10). This "box" was the primary object of the workshop discussions mentioned above, a workshop we had initially entitled "Thinking Entrepreneurship out of the Box".

Yet, can entrepreneurship research be considered as developing in such a box? Are researchers in entrepreneurship really incapable of renewing themselves, of finding new ideas, exploring new territories, using new methods, and mobilizing external disciplines?

A quick overview of this book seems to support exactly the opposite. Indeed, in the various contributions can be found:

- Openings towards new disciplines. In this book, several authors (for example Aldrich, Chapter 2) use insights from other disciplines, especially from the Social Sciences (anthropology, ethnography, history, psychology, sociology, heuristics, etc.) that may provide new research methods (observation over longer periods of time, longitudinal approaches) as well as a better understanding of the various aspects of entrepreneurship. It may be noted that this opening is probably facilitated by the fact that, although entrepreneurship has become a recognized field of academic research, it is not always considered as a discipline in its own right, as pointed by Aldrich (Chapter 2): *"it is not clear that there is a distinct 'discipline' called entrepreneurship studies, rather than a collection of researchers studying similar phenomena from disparate disciplinary origins."* In parallel to this opening, other authors make a critical analysis of the somewhat reductionist nature of entrepreneurship studies contributed by other disciplines, such as economics for instance (Anderson, Chapter 4). This illustrates the ability of researchers to engage in a lively and topical debate regarding the potential contributions and limitations of other disciplines traditionally distant from entrepreneurship.

- Challenging the epistemological postures adopted by the majority of researchers in entrepreneurship. As opposed to the static, distant and descriptive position of the researcher, Hjorth (Chapter 3) suggests a development of studies focusing on processes, movements, the forces at stake and their degree of intensity, as inspired by Foucault, Nietzsche, and Deleuze, in order to make research become an agent of creation and change. As for Coviello et al. (Chapter 6), they are considering the possibility, including the necessary means and processes, to create a new subfield – "International Entrepreneurship" – and give it scientific legitimacy. Fletcher and Selden (Chapter 7) examine the vast heterogeneity of the studies conducted in entrepreneurship as a result of the increasing fragmentation of the field (social entrepreneurship, female entrepreneurship, international entrepreneurship, etc.) and the cross-disciplinary nature of the approaches used. They propose an original and ambitious response to this question.

- A critical reflection on entrepreneurship research and propositions to validate its quality. Among others, Honig (Chapter 8), who is not convinced by attempts to develop a "general theory of entrepreneurship", reminds us that the role of research is also to examine existing theories and to test them empirically. He underlines the small number of replicated empirical studies, even though replication is necessary to assess their validity, especially at a time when cases of data manipulation are no longer uncommon. This leads Honig to question the practices of top-ranking journals, which are reluctant to publish verification and replication studies, as well as the attitude of experienced researchers, who are themselves less than enthusiastic at the prospect of their work being challenged.

- A critical reflection about the founding myths of entrepreneurship and their hidden economic and political dimension. One of the characteristics of the institutionalization of the field is the uncritical adoption of a certain number of beliefs (taken for granted), most of them positive, concerning the field and its practices. It is the case for instance of the vision of entrepreneurship which sees the entrepreneur as a hero of modern times and entrepreneurship as *the* magic solution to support development (emerging countries) or economic growth (developed countries). For researchers in entrepreneurship, it would undeniably be a gratifying and comforting thought – acting as if they believed it would be gratifying and comforting enough. Yet, several chapters in this book set out to debunk this myth. Anderson (Chapter 4) opposes the idea whereby entrepreneurship could be some universal engine of growth *"at personal, firm and national levels"* and refutes the vision according to which entrepreneurship is above all an individual adventure. Honig (Chapter 8) also questions the globalization of the myth of entrepreneurship and reminds us that remarkable entrepreneurial successes are few and far between. He shows how this myth is entertained to foster the illusion of a better future in a world marked by the increasing probability that the next generation will be worse off than the previous one. Honig also remarks on the timidity of the academic world, especially that of major scientific journals, when it comes to collecting specific data concerning the actual benefits and costs of entrepreneurship. Berglund and Skoglund (Chapter 5) offer a critical review of various entrepreneurship-based initiatives whose aim is to support and advise vulnerable populations (such as immigrant women, recently released inmates, and young students with school problems). The authors highlight the ambivalence of these experiences that may, indeed, provide support to the populations concerned, but which also translate the disengagement of the state and the weakening of solidarity in favour of a neoliberal approach whereby each individual is only responsible for him/herself.

Research in relation to non-academic stakeholders of entrepreneurship

Most of the authors in this book, even when it is not the main object of their contribution, question the place and the role of entrepreneurship in society. By the same token, they also question more generally the role of entrepreneurship research.

As mentioned above, the discussions regarding the myths of entrepreneurship show that researchers are capable of adopting a critical viewpoint on the dominant social representation – always highly supportive – of entrepreneurship. Most researchers also agree on the fact that entrepreneurship research should be useful to entrepreneurs and society. As Alain Fayolle puts it in the introduction of this book: *"challenging and debating research orientations is not only an intellectual exercise"*, thus concurring with other authors, such as Zahra and Wright (2011), who consider that the *raison d'être* of research in entrepreneurship is its usefulness.

The problem is that these debates are largely confined to the narrow circle of entrepreneurship scholars and find little echo among entrepreneurs and the institutions that support them. This may have several explanations.

First of all, there is an effect, linked to the institutionalization of entrepreneurship research and education, which leads the community of scholars to close in upon itself and become its own finality, finding interest only in those actors who are already part of the community. The scientific community thus loses its grasp of the real life of entrepreneurs (Sarasvathy, 2001; Baker & Nelson, 2005), their interests, and those of society at large. Drained of its substance, the research produced becomes less relevant due to the lack of knowledge of the realities of the field, and is of little use to entrepreneurs and society. For example, few practical and original recommendations for entrepreneurs can be found among the most recent studies published in major journals. Existing research does little to address the dark face of entrepreneurship (Anderson et al., 2009; Fayolle, 2011), its ideological (Honig, Chapter 8) and political dimensions (Berglund and Skoglund, Chapter 5; Hjorth, Chapter 3). Along with Honig (Chapter 8), one is therefore justified in pondering the real contribution of entrepreneurship to society, as well as the contribution of entrepreneurship research to society, without overlooking the costs generated by such research.

Evolution of research practices

One of the explanations for this situation lies with the evolution of research practices. In the microcosm where research in entrepreneurship has developed over the past 15 years, what matters first and foremost for teacher-researchers is to find their place within their institutions (universities, research centres, reviews, conferences, etc.). But places are limited. It is therefore understandable that they should adopt research practices aimed at maximum efficiency for their career within the narrow circle of entrepreneurship scholars. After all, aren't they encouraged on this path when one looks at the number of seminars and workshops dedicated to the strategies, methods, and tips for publishing in top-ranking journals?

As a consequence, a majority of scholars would adopt an opportunistic behaviour, more especially young researchers, who are more vulnerable. This leads them to focus on the themes, methods, and theories that fit well into mainstream research, even if these subjects are of no real interest to them (Fink, Hatak, Lang, and Maresch, Chapter 11), while rejecting the themes and methods that are more time-consuming (ethnographic approaches, field observation over long periods of time, historical studies – see Aldrich, Chapter 2) or more difficult to publish. Unfortunately, these "unremunerative" academic practices are those which are the most likely to legitimate research (replication of empirical studies/validation of theories) and to bring scholars closer to entrepreneurs and their preoccupations (qualitative studies coupled with observation, participant observation, action-research).

* * * * *

When all is said and done, the various texts in this book show that researchers are not set in their convictions or the taken-for-granted. On the contrary, they are aware that research needs to renew itself in order to move forward and better meet the expectations of the various stakeholders, both academic and non-academic. To this end, they suggest new avenues for research, both at the theoretical and at the methodological level, the latter being foremost among the preoccupations expressed in this book.

However, the various reflections and propositions made remain largely confined to the research community. When it comes to putting them into

184 *Philippe Riot and Alain Fayolle*

practice, the results are not as convincing. *In fine*, although qualified voices are rising to denounce the foibles of institutionalization and its negative consequences, with a view to proposing novel and meaningful approaches that could impact society positively, entrepreneurship research seems increasingly steeped in conformism. It is characterized by a kind of "staying-togetherness", in a microcosm of scholars only communicating with other scholars (the infamous ivory tower), increasingly removed from their economic and social environment.

Researchers are well aware of this problem, and many of them note with regret the distance that has widened between academic research and entrepreneurship, and more especially between research and the various stakeholders of entrepreneurship. Many highlight the difficulties they face when trying to incorporate other disciplines and methods in an attempt to make practices evolve and bridge the distance between the research community and the field. The most frequent reason cited is that this type of research is more time-consuming, with lower acceptance rates in major publications, and is therefore counterproductive in terms of career.

Consequently, many researchers, especially among the younger generation, resign themselves to bring their work into line with mainstream research approaches.

Could this choice – probably rewarding in terms of career – have other positive effects? Can we say that entrepreneurship research is useful to society and entrepreneurs? Can we say that it is interesting, legitimate, and relevant for the stakeholders of entrepreneurship, including the researchers themselves? On reading the chapters in this book, one wouldn't vouch for it.

One of the keys to the problem, maybe *the* key, seems to lie with the evolution of research practices. If research practices evolve in the direction that the authors are calling for in this book, that is to say towards a greater proximity between scholars and entrepreneurs and a closer and more in-depth observation of entrepreneurial dynamics, entrepreneurship research will be scientifically reinforced and will appear more legitimate from a social point of view.

We therefore need to consider seriously what is stalling this evolution. How did researchers succeed in developing a new scientifically legitimate discipline, in advancing the field considerably, and opening jobs for researchers while losing touch with the non-academic world and its stakeholders, more especially real-life entrepreneurs?

This is an important research question, which needs to be addressed. For scholars, it is also an opportunity for action. The institutions that structure the work of researchers today cannot function without them. If researchers know what they want – and on reading their contributions, it looks like they do – what can they do? What should they do to transform their own institutions, universities, research centres and associations, scientific journals, etc.? How can they act – collectively preferably – to make publishing practices evolve, create independent channels for disseminating knowledge, encourage research practices that are currently sidestepped for lack of academic profitability, and eventually change the criteria for the recruitment and career advancement of researchers? Indeed, it is a collective responsibility of the research community to provide answers to these questions and mobilize its efforts to make things change. Nowadays, especially with the internet, numerous channels exist for the dissemination of research and collective action in addition to the more traditional networks: it lies with us to become the entrepreneurs of entrepreneurship research.

This movement concerns the community of entrepreneurship research at large, but it is especially relevant for the younger generation of researchers who are building tomorrow's research in entrepreneurship. Yet this book presents mostly the contributions of experienced researchers. Consequently, we have wished to invite researchers from other generations. To this end, a workshop was organized in August 2014, in Philadelphia, within the scope of the annual *Academy of Management* conference. The contributions of this workshop, which aptly complement the present contributions, will be collected in an upcoming book in the collection *Rethinking Entrepreneurship Research*. This "out-of-the-box" thinking marches on and we hope that the movement will only amplify, for the benefit of all the stakeholders in entrepreneurship.

References

Anderson, A. R., Drakopoulou Dodd, S. & Jack, S. L. (2009). Aggressors; winners; victims and outsiders: European Schools' social construction of the entrepreneur. *International Small Business Journal*, 27(1): 126–136.

Baker, T. and Nelson, R. E. (2005). Creating something from nothing: Resource construction through entrepreneurial bricolage. *Administrative Science Quarterly*, 50(3): 329–366.

Fayolle, A. (2011). Necessity entrepreneurship and job insecurity: The hidden face of entrepreneurship. *International Journal of E-Entrepreneurship and Innovation*, 2(3), 1–10.

Greenwood, R., Oliver, C., Sahlin, K., & Suddaby, R. (2008). Introduction in *The Sage Handbook of Organizational Institutionalism*. London: Sage Publications Ltd.

Sarasvathy, S. (2001). Causation and effectuation: A theoretical shift from economic inevitability to entrepreneurial contingency. *Academy of Management Review*, 28(2): 243–263.

Shane, S. & Venkataraman, S. (2000). The promise of entrepreneurship as a field of research. *Academy of Management Review*, 25(1): 217–226.

Tolbert, P. S. & Zucker, L. G. (1983). Institutional sources of change in the formal structure of organizations: The diffusion of civil service reform, 1880–1935. *Administrative Science Quarterly*, 30: 22–39.

Zahra, S. A. & Wright, M. (2011). Entrepreneurship's next act. *Academy of Management Perspectives*, 25(4): 67–83.

Index

academic chairs 90, 103, 123, 127, 138, 175
academic entrepreneurs 149
academic journals *see* professional journals
Academy of International Business (AIB)
    80, 94
Academy of Management 1, 89, 185
Academy of Management Journal 45, 80, 90,
    95, 96n5, 155
Academy of Management Review 154, 157–8,
    179
action theory 111
action-context relationships 113
action-interaction nexus 112
actor network theory 115
adaptive decision programme 20–1
adaptive tension 112, 115
agency theory 157
Aldrich, Howard 5–7, 12, 14, 15, 18, 19,
    28–35, 41, 51, 52, 150, 157, 161, 180
Alger, Horatio, Jr. 123–4
Alvesson, M. 3, 10n1, 138, 157
Alvey, J.E. 49
American culture 139–40
Anderson, Alistair R. 2, 5, 7, 47, 48, 59, 181
Angle, H.L. 155
Annavarjula, M. 82
anthropology 6, 13–15, 21, 34, 180
Association to Advance Collegiate Schools
    of Business (AACSB) 89
Astley, W.G. 151
Austin, J.L. 46
Austrian school of economics 156
Autio, E. 81
auto-ethnography 143; *see also* ethnography

Babson College Frontiers of Entrepreneurship
    Research Conference 80, 89, 179
Baker, Ted 2, 14, 182
Banks, M. 49
Barley, S.R. 152

Bartunek, J.M. 151, 161
Baumol, William 49, 153
Becattini, Giacomo 155
becoming, entrepreneurial 5, 29, 31–40,
    105, 112
behavioural actions and processes 109, 111;
    theory of 104
Bell, J. 81
Bergendahl, Jacqueline 155
Berglund, Karin 5, 7, 140, 182
Bergson, Henri 29, 34, 35, 38
Bhidé, Amarnath 154
Bianchi, M. 50
biases and heuristics 6, 20, 111
Bijker, W. 115
biopolitics 60
Bird, B.J. 31, 79
Bjerke, B. 47, 104
Bolton Report 153
"Bootstrap Finance: The Art of Start-Ups"
    154
bootstrapping finance 154
born global firms 92, 173
born regional firms 92
Boulevard of Broken Dreams (Lerner) 154
boundary conditions 108
bounded rationality 16, 115
Bradbury, H. 143
Branson, Richard 8, 124
bricolage theory 1, 115, 142, 156
Bruyat, C. 48
Burgel, O. 81
business angels 156
business idea/business model 154
business opportunity *see* opportunity
Bygrave, W.D. 45, 157

Campbell Hunt, C. 81
Cantillon, R. 47, 171
capitalism, neoliberal 153

188 *Index*

capitalist entrepreneurship 62
carriers 103
causality and causation 1, 102, 107–8, 154; relational 107–8; successionist (linear) 107, 117
"Causation and Effectuation: Toward a Theoretical Shift from Economic Inevitability to Entrepreneurial Contingency" (Sarasvathy) 154
Cavusgil, S.T. 80
Chandra, Y. 85
charisma 23
"Charlie Brown Syndrome" 176
Chelekis, J. 85
Chell, E. 46
Chen, M.-J. 78, 83, 88–96, 149
Chetty, S. 81
Chia, R.C.H. 142
Choy, C.L. 79
citation: coercive 131; self- 131, 141
Clark, G.L. 46
Cliff, J.E. 155
coding 130
cognition 1, 20, 94, 110, 128
cognitive neuroscience 21
cognitive psychology 93; *see also* psychology
cognitivism 111
Committee on Publication Ethics (COPE) 133
complexity science 101; research 114; theory 103, 105
connectivity 36
constructivism 19, 103
consumer-as-international-entrepreneur 85
context(s) 34, 45, 47–8, 104, 106–10, 113–14, 155; cultural 139–40, 155; decision 109; and history 17–18; of interesting research 160–1; mediating 109; mental 111; moderating 109; study of 2; of success 111; variables of 109
contextuality, of conceptual frameworks 140; *see also* contextualization
contextualization: embedded 114; self- 113; transactional 113–14; *see also* contextuality
Conway, S. 48
Coombs, J.E. 82
Cooper, Arnold 22, 152, 153, 155
coping potential 162
corporate entrepreneurship 103, 128, 140, 160
Cotrugli, B. 171
Coviello, Nicole 5, 8, 78, 85, 90, 95, 181
creation *see* organizational creation
creative destruction 149

Creative Honest Entrepreneurs (CHE) 57, 63, 66–7
creativity 7, 31, 32, 34–5, 38–41, 68, 104, 112, 114–15, 131, 150, 161
Crick, David 90
crime prevention 68
criminal rehabilitation *see* Criminals Return Into Society (CRIS)
Criminals Return Into Society (CRIS) 57, 62, 65–9, 73
Curran, James 45, 153
Czarniawska-Joerges, B. 23

Dacin, M.T. 85
Davis, Murray S. 151
Dear, M. 46
decision-making 20, 105, 106, 108–12, 127
de Clercq, Dirk 85, 90
Deleuze, Gilles 32, 35, 37, 40, 41n1, 181
Denyer, D. 92
development: interventions for 61–2; sustainable 62, 93; *see also* organizational creation
Dew, N. 39, 40
differentiation 8; of international entrepreneurship, 88
Dimov, D. 101, 104, 113
discovery theory 111
Diversity in Entrepreneurship (DiE) 69, 70, 71
Dostoyevsky, Fyodor 28
Downe, S. 95
Drakopoulou Dodd, S.D. 48
Drucker, Peter 33, 141
drug abuse *see* Criminals Return Into Society (CRIS)
Duberly, J. 82
Dubin, R. 106
Duffield, M. 61–2
duration 35
dynamic creation 112; *see also* organizational creation

Easterbrook, W.T. 59, 72
economic functionalism 116; *see also* functionalism
economics 2, 6, 7, 13, 34, 128, 149; Austrian school of 156; barriers to learning from 16–17; and entrepreneurship 44–5; language of 46; and modelling 15–16; neoclassical 49–50, 116; reductionist view of 51; systems approach to 48; theories of 49–50, 110, 111, 116
economics history 149

Index   189

economics textbooks 45

Edmonson, A.C. 95

effectual logic 112

effectuation 1, 152, 156, 157; theory of 114, 160

Eikenberry, A.M. 59

Ellison, Larry 8, 124

embeddedness, of entrepreneurial action 21, 22–3

emergence, organizational 29, 30, 40; *see also* organizational creation

EMLYON Business School 3, 7, 179

empirical co-variance 111–3

emulation 92, 95

Encyclopedia of Entrepreneurship (Kent, Sexton & Vesper) 153

endowed chairs *see* academic chairs

Engleman, R.M. 108

entrepreneurial action(s): boundary conditions for 108; conditions of possibility of 110; cooperation in 33; and the life course 21–2; role of gender in 47; social relational nature of 33

entrepreneurial becoming 5, 29, 31–40, 105, 112

'entrepreneurial hero' 48, 70, 123–4, 137, 181

entrepreneurial internationalization 79, 81, 85, 95; *see also* international entrepreneurship (IE)

entrepreneurial opportunity (EO) 47, 110, 115, 128; *see also* opportunity

entrepreneurial qualities 109, 110

entrepreneurial security 58–62

entrepreneurship: at the Academy of Management 1; actions of 106–7, 109; across borders 80–1; cognition and 128; as collective 140; diversification of 102; in the dynamics of society 160; economic perspectives on 7, 44–5, 48–9, 110; economic reification of 45–8; fragmentation of 8; functionalist view of 44, 47; institutionalization of 2–3, 5–6, 8, 123–7, 133–5; interdisciplinary dimensions of 127; interesting vs. important/relevant 162–3; language of 46; myth(s) of 2, 8, 48, 123–5, 181–2; outcomes of 106–7, 109–12; and politics 49–50, 153; as a practice 141; as a process or phenomenon 4–5, 102–3, 139, 143, 155, 157; reality shows 123; and self-renewal 180–2; as social achievement 156; socialized conception of 48–51; technology-based 160; theories of 48,

86–8, 104–5, 107–8, 110, 181; venture performance and growth 160; as will to power 37

entrepreneurship by type: academic 149; capitalist 62; corporate 103, 128, 140, 160; immigrant 58, 94; family 103; individual 48; institutional 103; micro-85; nascent 128, 156; societal 150; strategic 103, 128; technological 103; *see also* international entrepreneurship (IE); social entrepreneurship

entrepreneurship education 9, 58, 126–7, 144–5, 164; institutionalization of 126–7; relative to global markets 89; *see also* entrepreneurship students; entrepreneurship studies; Stoned Unquenchable Souls

"Entrepreneurship: Productive, Unproductive and Destructive" (Baumol) 153

entrepreneurship psychology 6; *see also* psychology

entrepreneurship research 9; American 139–40; aspects of inquiry 100, 102, 138; capacity for renewal 10; changeable nature of 160; and coding 130–1; collective 143; and the concept of "interesting" 148–9; context of scholarly work 137; development of 179; ethical considerations in 130–3, 139; European 3, 140, 142, 154, 161; as evolving field 10, 149–51, 183; future of 10, 23–4; "gap-spotting" in 3, 164; in German-speaking countries 173–6; history of 4; individual 5, 12; institutionalization of 138–9, 179; interactive 143; interdisciplinary approach to 7, 24; and non-academic stakeholders 182–3; objectivist 139; on organization and becoming 7; out of the box 2–5, 7, 10, 41, 124, 134, 141, 180; qualitative 3, 5, 11, 19, 86, 95, 104, 116, 130–1, 155, 161, 183; quantitative 5, 104, 130, 139, 154–5, 161, 173; recommendations for improving 129–33; reflexive inquiry 137–8; relationship with entrepreneurial practice 10; relevance of 182–3; replication in 130, 135n2; republication in 128; Scandinavian 143; validation in 129–30; verification in 128–9; *see also* international entrepreneurship (IE) research

entrepreneurship students: education and training of 5, 12, 126–7; empowerment

190 *Index*

of 144; interesting research by 155–6; mentoring of 5, 12; and the shaping of careers 152; stimulation of 151; and thesis selection 163–4, 171
entrepreneurship studies: affirming the entrepreneurial in 38–41; community in 4, 12; and contextual dependency 160–1; creativity in 39; evolutionary perspective 156, 157; history of 47; imagination and storytelling in 39; institutionalization of 150–51, 154; interdisciplinary potential of 28–30; interesting concepts/theories 9, 156–8; interesting methodologies 9, 154–6; "interesting" research contributions 9, 151–4, 156–8; interesting subjects 152–4; movement and intensity in 30–5; multidisciplinary nature of 154; performative approaches to 39; process thinking in 35–8, 41; and time dependency 159–60
entrepreneurship survey 173–6
epistemology 2, 3, 48, 100–1, 105, 114, 116, 142, 155, 181
Equal programme 69
Etemad, Hamid 80, 81
ethical issues 9, 127–33, 139, 143
ethnic minorities *see* Network of Entrepreneurs from Ethnic Minorities (NEEM)
ethnography 13–15, 19, 62–3, 180
European School of Entrepreneurship Research 38
European Social Fund 66
evolutionary perspective 103, 156, 157
evolutionary theory 6, 24, 29, 32, 34
existentialism 28

family businesses 85, 128
family entrepreneurship 103
Farr, William 134
fast and frugal research programme 21
Fayolle, Alain 2, 10, 179, 182
field navigation 8, 100, 101, 104
figshare 130
Fink, Matthias 5, 9, 165
Fletcher, Denise 5, 8, 181
Flyvbjerg, B. 142
force 37–8
Förderkreis Gründungsforschung e.V (FGF) 173
formative teleology 116
Foucault, Michel 32, 33, 37, 40, 60, 181
foundations, role of 5, 12
fraud 139

Frickel, S. 12
functionalism 104, 111–12, 116

Galkina, T. 83, 92, 94
Garfinkel, H. 151
Gartner, William 3, 4, 13–14, 29, 31, 32, 38, 39, 40, 51, 156, 160
Garud, R. 115
Gassmann, O. 82
Gates, Bill 8, 124
Gawell, Malin 62, 66, 67, 68
GEM *see* Global Entrepreneurship Monitor
gender and entrepreneurship 58, 128
generalizability 18, 33, 106
George, Gerry 80, 81, 90
German Academic Association for Business Research (VHB) 173
Giamartino, G.A. 79
Gigerenzer, G. 21
Global Entrepreneurship Monitor (GEM) 86, 125, 139, 160
globalization 5, 12, 124, 182
Goldstein, D.G. 21
Gompers, Paul 157
governance 6, 16, 60, 63
Granovetter, M. 20, 45
Grant, P. 47
Gratzer, Karl 155
Greenwood, R. 155, 179
Gross, N. 12
"Growth and the Small Firm: An Alternative View" (Stanworth & Curran) 153

Hambrick, D.C. 78, 83, 88–96, 128, 129, 149
Harvard Business Review 154
Hatak, Isabella 9
Heidegger, Martin 28, 35
Helin, Jenny 35
Henrekson, M. 50
hermeneutics 36
Hernes, Tor 35
Hesterly 17
heuristics 20–1, 180; and biases 6, 20, 111
The Hiding Hand (Hirschman) 39
Hirschman, A.O. 39
Hirshleifer, J. 45
Hisrich, Robert 90
history 6, 13, 21, 34, 180; barriers to learning from 19; and context 17–18
history of social sciences 19
Hitt, M.A. 80
Hjorth, Daniel 5, 6–7, 45, 104, 140, 142, 153, 155, 181

Index 191

Hofer, C.W. 45
Hofstede, G. 139
Holcombe, R.G. 47
Holt, Robin 35, 142
Honig, Benson 5, 8, 9, 181–3; commentary on 137–44
Houghton, S.M. 109

identity, cultural 139
IDEON science park 153
imagination 7, 31, 32, 39–40, 113
IMF (International Monetary Fund) 86
immigrant entrepreneurship 58, 94; see also Network of Entrepreneurs from Ethnic Minorities (NEEM)
improvisation 1, 142
individual-opportunity nexus 105–6, 110
innovation and innovativeness 22, 45–7, 66, 93–4, 103–4, 111, 134–5, 144, 155
institutional entrepreneurship 103
institutional theory 93, 103
institutionalization 123–7; ethical implications of 127–9; of entrepreneurship education 126–7; of entrepreneurship research 138–9, 179; of entrepreneurship studies 150–51, 154
international business (IB) theory 79, 86–8, 92
International Committee of Medical Journal Editors (ICMJE) 133
international comparisons of entrepreneurial internationalization 85
International Comparisons of Entrepreneurship 79
International Entrepreneurship – Foreign Direct Investment by Small US Based Manufacturing Firms (Kohn) 78
international entrepreneurship (IE) 8, 103, 128, 181; challenges to 81–2; definition of 79; differentiation of 88; emulation in 92; as a field 87–92, 96; future directions 92–3; implications for 94–5; legitimization of 91–2; mobilization of 88–91; professional journals 90, 92, 94, 96n5; university chairs in 90; virtual community of 94–5; see also entrepreneurial internationalization; entrepreneurship
international entrepreneurship (IE) research 78, 161, 172–3; evolution of 79–81; general methodological patterns 86; origins of 78–9; patterns related to parent disciplines 86–7; patterns relating to primary themes 83–5; see also entrepreneurship research

international new ventures (INVs) 78–9
Ireland, R.D. 45, 80, 151

James, William 34
Jarillo, J.C. 47
Jennings, P.D. 155
Jobs, Steve 8, 124
Johannisson, Bengt 4, 5, 9, 38, 140, 142, 143, 153
Johansson, A.W. 140
Johansson, D. 45
Johnson, M.S. 151
Johnson, Peter 80, 82
Jones, C. 2, 34, 38
Jones, Marian 8, 78, 81–3, 88, 90, 93–4
Jones O. 48
journals see professional journals
Julien, P.A. 48

Kahneman, D. 6, 20
Kant, Immanuel 177
Karnøe, P. 115
Karp, T. 45
Katz, Jerry 29, 32, 35
Keupp, M.M. 82
Keynes, J.M. 45
Kierkegaard, Søren 28
Kirzner, I.M. 45, 47, 116
Klein, P.G. 49
Kluver, J.D. 59
Knight, G. 45, 80, 81
Kohn, T.O. 78
Kolb, D.A. 159
Korri, J.S. 82, 92
Kunh, T.S. 80, 82
Kurke, L. 15

Lachmann, L. 113
Landström, Hans 4, 5, 12, 138, 171
Lang, Richard 9
Lasch, F. 160, 180
Latour, Bruno 115
leadership 23, 64
learned helplessness 63
legitimacy building 8, 9, 139, 150
Lerner, Josh 154, 157
Lévesque, Moren 44, 90
Lewin, Kurt 163
life course 21–2
Lindgren, M. 51
linear causality 107
Lipman, B.L. 48
Lippmann, S. 18, 19
Lund Institute of Technology (LTH) 153
Lyotard, Jean-François 33

192 *Index*

MacMillan, I.C. 157
Madsen, Tage Koed 90
Malthus, T.R. 47
management 92, 102, 128, 140, 151;
  innovation 94; journals of 1, 19, 45,
  80–1, 90, 92, 95, 129, 155; organizations
  and 14, 19–20; population 59–60;
  research in 81–2; risk 61; self- 58; social
  performance 72; strategic 93, 95, 100,
  103; theories of 163
management sciences 19–20, 179
management studies 4, 138, 163
Manigart, S. 157
March, James 16, 155
Maresch, Daniela 9
market conditions 109, 111
market-level opportunities 114–15
Martinez, M.A. 14, 51, 52
Massumi, B. 29, 34, 36, 38
McAdam, D. 94
McDonald, S. 45
McDougall-Covin, Patricia 8, 78–81, 83,
  85, 86, 88, 90, 92–4
McGill International Entrepreneurship
  Conference Series 80–1, 89
McManus, S.A. 95
McMullen, J.S. 47, 48, 101, 104
McNaughton, R.B. 81
Mead, George Herbert 35
Mendeley 130
Merton, R.K. 160
meta-analysis 163
meta-theory 105
mētis 142
Meuleman, M. 85
Micro Finance Institute (MFI) 71
microcredit 71, 74
microeconomic theory 50
micro-entrepreneurship 85
Milanov, Hana 90
Miner, J.B. 163
Minnesota Study 155
Minniti, M. 44, 47, 48
Mintzberg, H. 14, 15
mobilization 9; of international
  entrepreneurship 88–91; social 94
modernism 19
Moen, Ø. 81
Morgan, G. 142
Morrow 78
"Movements in Entrepreneurship Series"
  (Steyaert & Hjorth) 153
Mudambi, S. 85
multinational corporations (MNCs) 85
Murray, G.C. 81

music, interesting 147–8, 161–2
Mustar, P. 22

nascent entrepreneurs/entrepreneurship
  128, 156
Nasra, R. 85
National Science Foundation 129
nationalism, psychological 110–11
Neergaard, Helle 5
Nelson, R.E. 2
neoliberalism 59, 68, 124, 153
Network of Entrepreneurs from Ethnic
  Minorities (NEEM) 57, 62, 69–72, 74
networks 4, 52, 57, 66, 68–70, 85, 94–5,
  113–16, 127; actor network theory 115;
  international 175; self- 36; social 5, 6,
  12, 21–2, 46, 109, 114, 150, 156, 160
neuroscience 21
new business formation *see* organization
  creation
Newey, L.R. 94
Nietzsche, Friedrich 29, 32, 33, 36, 37, 41n1,
  181
Nijkamp, P. 48
Nonaka, I. 142
nongovernmental organizations (NGOs)
  57, 61, 62; *see also* Network of
  Entrepreneurs from Ethnic Minorities
  (NEEM)
Normann, Richard 154
Nummela, Niina 90

OECD (Organisation for Economic
  Co-operation and Development) 86
ontogenesis 34, 38
ontology 8, 52, 78, 82, 93, 100–1, 105,
  114–16, 155
openness 36–7
opportunism 16
opportunity 36, 38, 40, 62–3, 65, 81, 89,
  93, 100, 108, 156, 184; creation of 112,
  115; development of 113; discovery
  of 110; emergence of 114; enactment
  of 115; identification of 8, 107, 109;
  individual-opportunity nexus 105–6,
  110; political 89; recognition of 20, 156,
  160; *see also* entrepreneurial opportunity
opportunity tension 112, 115
organizational creation ("organization-in-
  creation") 3–4, 7, 29, 30, 32–3, 35–6, 38,
  40–1, 48, 103; *see also* dynamic creation
organizational entrepreneurship 103;
  see also corporate entrepreneurship
organizational imprinting 18
Organization Evolving (Aldrich) 157

organizations and management 14, 19–20
organization studies 17–19
outcomes, firm-level 111
Oviatt, Ben 78–81, 83, 88, 92–3
owner-managed business 104

Packendorff, J. 51
Panel Study of Entrepreneurship Dynamics 160
"Peanuts" analogy 176
Perren, L. 47
Pettigrew, Andrew 155
phenomenology 103
philosophy 4; process 7, 28–9
phronesis 142
Pittaway, L. 48
plagiarism 129, 139
PLoS ONE 130
Politis, Diamanto 156
Poole, M.S. 155
population ecology 103
population management 59–60
positivism 104, 112
post-positivism 101, 105
potentiality 7, 35, 38
power relations 61
Price, D.J.D.S. 160
proactiveness 111
process emergence 112
process philosophy 7, 28–9
process theory 35, 108
process thinking 7, 35–8; on force 37–8; on openness 36–7; on potentiality 38; rational view 157; on temporality 35; on wholeness 36
professional journals 80, 127–31, 140–1, 172–3; ethics in 130–3; international entrepreneurship 90, 92, 94, 96n5; retractions in 129; transparency in 133, 135
"The Promise of Entrepreneurship as a Field of Research" (Shane & Venkataraman) 1
psychological nationalism 110–11
psychological rationalism 111, 115
psychology 4, 6, 13, 20–1, 34, 102, 128, 149, 180; cognitive 93; entrepreneurship 6; social 102
publication, opportunities for 5, 12; see also professional journals

qualitative research 3, 5, 11, 19, 86, 95, 104, 116, 130–1, 155, 161, 183
quantitative research 5, 104, 130, 139, 154–5, 161, 173

rationalist teleology 116
rationality, bounded 16, 115
Reason, P. 143
Redlich, F. 47
Rehn, A. 140
Reid, J. 61, 73
Reitberger, Göran 153
relationality 34, 36
relationship marketing 46
replication 128–9, 130, 134, 138, 140–1, 181, 183
Reproducibility Initiative 130
research: biases and heuristics 111; cognitivist 110; firm-level 112; medical 134; opportunity development 113; psychological rationalist 111; theory-driven 1, 4; see also entrepreneurship research; international entrepreneurship research
resilience 61, 73–4
resource mobilization 150
resource-based theory 103
responsibility 9, 61, 65–6, 68, 73, 131, 132, 143–4, 164, 185
Reynolds, Paul 160
Ricardo, David 47
Ricks, D.A. 79
Riot, Philippe 10
risk society 68
risk-taking and risk-seeking 71, 80, 93, 109, 111, 115, 125, 171
Roberts, Ed 153
Rose, M. 48
Rugman, A.M. 92
Rynes, S.L. 155

Sadrieh, F. 82
Sahlman, William 157
Samuels, W.J. 48
Sandberg, J. 3, 10n1, 157
Sapienza, H.J. 157
Sarason, Y. 113
Sarasvathy, Saras 2, 32, 39, 46, 104, 142, 152, 154, 156, 157, 160
Sartre, Jean-Paul 28
Så tänds eldsjälar (Westlund & Westlund) 63
Say, Jean-Baptiste 47
Schatzki, T.R. 142
scholarly publications see professional journals
Schumpeter, Joseph A. 4, 30–1, 33, 45, 47, 93, 140, 171
Science Exchange 130
science of imagination 32
science of the artificial 32

194 *Index*

scientific/intellectual movements 12–13
Section for Management of Technology and Innovation (TIM) 173
security, entrepreneurial *see* entrepreneurial security
Selden, Paul 8, 181
self-citation 131, 141
self-government 60–1
self-reliance 58, 62, 64, 68
Selten, R. 21
Semmelweis, Ignaz 134
Serapio, Manuel 89
Servais, P. 81
Sewel, W.H., Jr. 18
Sexton, Donald 153
Shane, S. 1, 2, 116, 156
Shepherd, D.A. 47, 48
Shotter, J. 112
Silvia, P.J. 162
Simon, M. 109
Simons, Henry C. 16, 59
Skapande företagsledning (Creative Management; Normann) 154
Skoglund, Annika 7, 182
Sköldberg, K. 138
small and medium-sized enterprises (SMEs) 48, 82, 94
small business 46, 104, 153–4, 160–1
Smart, P. 92
Smith, Adam 47, 49
social capital 52
social constructionism 101, 155
social entrepreneurship 46, 57–9, 72–4, 103, 128, 150; and entrepreneurial security 59–62; *see also* Creative Honest Entrepreneurs (CHF); Criminals Return Into Society (CRIS); Network of Entrepreneurs from Ethnic Minorities (NEEM); Stoned Unquenchable Souls
social issues, entrepreneurial approach to 59; *see also* social entrepreneurship
social sciences 163, 180; history of 19; research in 142
Social Sciences and Humanities Research Council (Canada) 81
social theory 103
social value 153
societal entrepreneurship 150
sociology 2, 4, 6, 13, 34, 128, 130, 180; barriers to learning from 23; contributions from 21; and embeddedness 22–3; field-based research in 14; of science 149; theory of 102
Söderlund, Peter 67

Solow, R.M. 49
Spicer, A. 2
Spinosa, C. 139
Spinoza, Bernard (Baruch) 29, 32, 36, 37, 38
Stanworth, John 45, 153
Stapel, Diederik 129
Starr, J.A. 31
Stephan, U. 85
Stevenson, Howard 47, 156
Stewart, Alex 15
Steyaert, Chris 38, 39, 139, 140, 142, 153, 155, 158
Stinchcombe, A.L. 18
Stoned Unquenchable Souls 57, 62–5, 73–4
Storey, David 154
storytelling 39
strategic entrepreneurship 103, 128
strategic management 93, 95
Strategic Management Society 94
Sweden: entrepreneurship in 7, 182; social entrepreneurship in 57; *see also* Creative Honest Entrepreneurs (CHF); Criminals Return Into Society (CRIS); Network of Entrepreneurs from Ethnic Minorities (NEEM); Stoned Unquenchable Souls
Swedish Agency for Economic and Regional Growth 63

Taalaas, S. 140
Takeuchi, H. 142
Tang, Y.K. 78
Taylor, Frederick Winslow 31
TCE *see* transaction cost economics (TCE)
technological entrepreneurship 103
technology, and bricolage theory 115
technology-based firms 157
Teach, R.D. 22
teleology 116
temporality 35
textbooks 2, 45, 124–6, 157, 159
theory/ies: action 111; actor network 115; agency 157; of art and aesthetics 177; behavioural process 104; bricolage 115; complexity 103, 105; construction of 45; creative and performative nature of 39; discovery 111; driving research 1–4; economic 49–50, 110, 111, 116; effectuation 114, 160; entrepreneurship 48, 86–8, 107–8, 110, 181; evolutionary 6, 24, 29, 32, 34, 105; generation of 128; generative 107; grounded 19; institutional 93, 100, 103; interesting 151, 156–7, 163; international business 79, 86–8, 92; international marketing 81; meta- 105;

post-positivist 105; practice 142; process 35, 108; psychological 102; relationship with art and practice 5; resource-based 103; social 103; social psychological 102; sociological 102; structuration 113; trait 104; variance 108, 111; *see also* theory development

theory building *see* theory development

theory development 8, 19, 83, 85, 100–1, 108; contemporaneous mode of 102; modes of 101–2, 105–8; multivariable (variance) 111; relational mode of 112–16; successionist mode of 102, 107–9, 111–12, 115–17

Theory of Economical Development (Schumpeter) 140

Thurik, R. 49

Tolbert, P.S. 179

trait theory 104

Tranfield, D. 92

transaction cost economics (TCE) 15–17

Tversky, A. 6, 20

Uhlaner, L.M. 85

Understanding the Small Business Sector (Storey) 154

unique phenomena 18

universities of applied science (UAS) 174

University of Colorado Denver 89

Utterback, James 153

Vaihinger, H. 31

Van de Ven, A.H. 108, 155

Van Praag, C.M. 44

variance theory 108, 111

Vaughan, D. 14

Venkataraman, S. 1, 2, 104, 116, 156

venture capital 128, 160

venture capital firms 85

venture capitalists 157

Vermeir, W. 157

Versloot, P.H. 44

violence, domestic 72

Walsh, D. 95

Watson, T.J. 14

Weick, K.E. 40, 139

Welter, F. 108, 160

Wennekers, S. 49

Whitehead, Alfred North 35

WHO (World Health Organisation) 86

wholeness 7, 35–6

Williamson, Oliver 15

Wohl, R.R. 48

women as entrepreneurs 58; *see also* Network of Entrepreneurs from Ethnic Minorities (NEEM)

World Bank 86

Wright, Mike 2, 85, 90, 182

Wright, Richard W. 79, 80

Yang, T. 14, 31

YouTube 63, 66, 65

Yu, J. 82, 92

Zafirovski, M. 50

Zahra, Shaker 2, 48, 79, 80, 81, 82, 90, 92, 94, 160, 182

Ziman, J. 161

Zucker, L.G. 179